GORDON KUHN

PREDATOR
THE MAN WHO DIDN'T EXIST

A NONFICTION TRUE CRIME SERIES

BOOK ONE OF TWO

"DO YOU KNOW HOW TO FLY?"

By

Gordon Kuhn

GORDON KUHN

DO YOU KNOW HOW TO FLY?

Copyright 2016 by Gordon Kuhn. All rights reserved. Printed in the United States of America. No part of this book may be used or reproduced in any manner whatsoever without written permission except in the case of brief quotations embodied in critical articles or reviews. For information contact Poet in the Rain Productions and the author himself, Gordon Kuhn at GKUHNWRITES@AOL.COM

This is a book of non-fiction. The material within has been compiled from research done over a period of six years. It contains direct quotations from courtroom documents as well as from interviews. Local newspapers were also reviewed along with postings on social media by interested persons.

There are quotations taken from other writer's works that are very brief in nature and identified, noted, with source location.

The cover was designed by the author.

ISBN-13: 978-0-692-77405-2
ISBN-10: 069277405X

First Edition

Poet in the Rain Productions

Printed by Create Space, Inc.

OTHER BOOKS BY THE AUTHOR

FICTION
The Pelman Murders

REVIEWS

"What an interesting plot. I was constantly guessing who and how these characters were connected. Very detailed and clever. Loved it! Can't wait for the next book. This was not a mindless read. Pay attention or you'll miss something!!"

"Twelve murders, ten suspects. Confusion over identities. Embezzlement. Fraud. Incest. Blackmail. Insanity. Intrigue at its best.

Simply captivating. A solid, poignant tale of violence and innocence . . . cool, brisk and polished. . Kuhn's unique imagination has made him a past master of fast and witty dialogue, and architect of memorable characters. The Pelman Murders follows that tradition with a meticulously plotted storyline. Gripping and full of genuine page-turning surprises. I really enjoyed this story. There were so many twists and turns that I had to keep reading to see how the story ends. Fantastic plot interwoven with strong characters. Gordon Kuhn has created a beautiful world full of character to root for and against.

Rich and compelling...It takes a master like Kuhn to juggle a character study with shocking thriller elements and put readers on a vast emotional roller coaster ride. ."

"Mystery readers will find "The Pelman Murders" an intriguing novel. I'm sure, Gordon Kuhn, a newly published author, will soon be recognized as a writer of much talent."

"LIKE A GIANT JIGSAW PUZZLE! As the fascinating story unravels the reader meets a host of characters, some of whom you'll love to hate. Even for a dedicated mystery fan, there always seems to be a piece missing until in a surprising ending the whole picture is revealed. This mystery will keep you turning pages wondering if what you just learned is the clue that explains the complex situations. It won't be. Don't start this before bedtime unless you want to be up all night. Even if you don't, it will probably keep you awake till the early hours."

POETRY
The Widow's Cliff

REVIEWS

"As with any collection there is something for everyone between the covers. For me - I found several gems. Absolutely amazing poems full of life and emotion. Beautiful and soft, yet powerful.
.

There is a remarkable freshness to the poetry and I hope that he will soon publish another collection. I enjoyed reading the poetry in this book because the emotions are raw and explicit. You know right off the bat what this writer is thinking and feeling. This book contains some tear-jerking poems that expose a myriad of emotions, the writer emotions as well as your own. This is a definite must read!"

"If you enjoy reading words that evoke emotion and feeling, then The Widows Cliff and other Poems is the book for you.

With his words, this writer is able to draw out feelings of loneliness, sadness and even fear. Often the title of the poem belies the emotion hidden in the poem. I had read a few (I love poetry) but decided it was time for something a little lighter. I hopped over to the poem entitled, The Owl and the Rabbit. To both my surprise, this poem evoked fear. I remember so well as a little girl, looking at some old person and being afraid of them...and I'd forgotten that long lost feeling until I read those words.

The words of Poet Gordon Kuhn are a welcome addition to my poetry collection."

"Gordon Kuhn has a gift with words. He can create beauty very simply, or with a complex twist arouse horror. He uses metaphor creatively. In the poem '4th of July', for instance, he describes the heavy grey clouds as whales, and then pursues this idea throughout the poem, building up a living picture; and again in 'Flakes of White' he compares snowflakes to kites, an image which pulls us into the reality of the flying flakes. The poem after which the collection is named, 'Widow's Cliff', begins with a few beautiful lines describing the dead woman's body seen floating in the sea, '...to fetch her quiet back / from where her body rested / so casually afloat...' and then plunges into the details of the story, leaving us thunder stricken and aghast.

'Dark Hallways' was one I particularly liked for its descriptive power, and the opening lines of 'I love a simple sleepy city street', 'I love a simple sleepy city street / one tree lined / sidewalk framed.'

Right at the start of the book I was impressed by the imagery in 'The empty glass', 'and each muttered empty word strikes like a heavy stone.'

Kuhn can also be very amusing. 'Have you ever seen a naked otter' is a more light hearted poem, and 'I'm Tarzan' has an ironic twist at the end, where the former wrestler has descended to selling meat, 'He is polite to everyone / and from a mobile freezer / sells boxes of/ his grade A frozen meat.'

This is a fascinating collection, and if you enjoy the skillful use of words, I would strongly recommend you to buy it."

If poems were paintings, Gordon Kuhn would be a master in several schools, most notably classical and impressionistic. These poems are finely spun of gossamer thread, as simple and as profound as a drop of water falling into a still pool at the bottom of a deep well. There is so much to linger upon in this book; it deserves to be read over and over again."

"I have not been much into reading poem, however, this book caught and kept my attention and is highly recommended with a great price."

"This book was one of the best books of Poems I've had in months. I would recommend this book to everyone who needs an awesome read at a nice price."

"I recently received this book of poetry from the author in exchange for a fair review. In all honesty I have to say that I have enjoyed this man's work, and this collection very much. In fact it's been one of the most enjoyable experiences with a book of poetry I have encountered in quite some time. Admittedly, I am not a fan at all of modern poetry that tends to be very dark, and, doesn't rhyme or conclude as classic poetry does. As a poet and editor myself, I have loved and composed my own poetry since boyhood and I am quite set in my ways. This collection is the perfect cross over in my opinion as to the modern touch, while still keeping the classic style alive and thriving. Author Gordon Kuhn augments his subject matter with great depth as to reciting a real story, as well as delving into much heartfelt emotion. Emotion that gathers the reins of both matters of the heart, as well as being poignant and reminiscent. In many ways Kuhn's excellent style reminds me of Elizabeth Barrett Browning. Both in its structure, and in its imagery. And I am also very impressed with Kuhn's versatility of subjects. There is such a wide range of subject matter put to verse here. it's almost as if the author writes opposite of so many others. That is, instead of thinking about something and writing it down, he instead just writes what he is thinking. The end result being a very versatile style of wonderful poems that I feel will delight many, and be well worth your time. I enjoyed this book very much and feel you will be both entertained and inspired by it as well... Highly recommended... :)

Rabbit in a Box

REVIEWS

"This gentleman can write!!!! What an exceptionally fine poet we find in Mr. Gordon Kuhn. A benchmark that, I feel, distinguishes at true master is if you are not only hooked on the first read, but you them find yourself constantly being drawn back too the book, time after time, and then discovering a totally different facet of the work. These moments make you feel like a kid opening a Christmas present. Rabbit in a Box is just such a book. I did not "read" this book, I "felt" it very strongly. In my opinion, only an exceptionally fine writer is able effectively communicate such strong emotions. Anyone who may write poetry needs to read this book and see how a master approaches his work. Don't miss out on Mr. Kuhn's other book of poetry on Amazon Kindle titled 'The Widow's Cliff and other Poems".

"You will find many of your own feelings and experiences reflected in this marvelous collection. These poems beg to be read aloud. Poetry is his way of expressing his emotions. Good, bad, love, or hate, for the reader. These specially selected words will comfort and console, encourage and support, through the days of despair to a future of hope.

"Very well written, brings out all your emotions and when a book can do that you know it is an excellent read. I love the title Rabbit in a Box. I have found this little book to be quite a gem. I would definitely recommend it for anyone."

"Especially good is "On Love" which touches the heart, and "On Music" that uplifts the soul. Many of the titles evoked my interest and attention, especially "Don't Mess with My Coffee" and "Lays". Well done!"

"There are some powerful sentiments here. Strong words softly spoken and raw emotions laid bare. I will return to these poems time and time again, they are thought-provoking and inspiring. I have MY favorites, now read it for yourself and choose yours."

"Powerful poetry - free verse that may set you as free as it does the author. I have his WIDOWS CLIFF as well and recommend both of these books without reservation except that the thought, words and poetry are so powerful much of it will leave you stunned. I recommend that you read both aloud - to yourself or others, but don't be surprised at the tears or laughter you will not be able to hold back. These are not just books - they are life and death in words."

NON FICTION, TRUE CRIME
Predator, Book Two, The Woman in a Pink Top

This is a new book and has not been reviewed.

AUTHOR'S NOTE

This is a book of nonfiction. All the people, places, events and details described in the book are real. There are no characters made from composites. However, there is one alias at the request of the person themselves. There are no invented quotes, no invented or imagined conversations, except that where errors in transcripts occurred I have corrected them instead of using [sic] where those errors occurred.

The story contained within has been compiled over a period of six years from the inception of this project to present day of writing, in which I have collected over 6,000 pages of documents, conducted numerous interviews, visited locations where crimes occurred, and attended court proceedings. The events outlined are taken from records and, in some cases, interviews with victims, friends of victims, family members, attorneys, and law enforcement. The quotes in this book are taken directly from official court documents and interviews. In some cases events are based on people's recollections.

In writing this book, I have tried to show the emotional trauma of the events without dramatizing such for the purpose of shocking the reader or for their amusement. The events and actions of those in this book are easily researched and can be confirmed. Granted, in some cases I have had to piece together events where the information was sketchy. In such cases, the recollections of those present at the time or having learned from those who were there are used as bridges to fill in the hollows of the story, but at no time to bring false to pretend to be true.

That being so, I have done my best to maintain the story to be as factual as I can. I have written it in narrative nonfiction format. That is to say that it is a combination of truth blended with storyline to produce a true tale that reads like a novel.

ACKNOWLEDGEMENTS

A tremendous "thank you" goes out to all the people involved in these cases who took time to visit with me. Most notably among these are the victims who survived the brutal attacks, their friends and, in one case, a widower and his sister-in-law. How incredible that I was allowed to visit with them and learn of their pain and suffering in one on one interviews that took place in coffee shops, a jail house visit, and once in a medical office.

In addition to victims, their relatives and friends, I also interviewed sheriff's deputies, attorneys, the former fiancé of the killer, and the killer himself.

Being a fiction writer, it was an odd place I found myself in when researching this book. I wrote it out of the desire to pay homage to those whose lives were touched by the incredible cruelty of a man who could have done so much more in his life than to create pain, terror, and cause horrifically torturous deaths.

A special thank you to retired attorney Ms. Marilyn Kline for her patience with me while correcting writing errors and providing me with detail on how court rooms function. Then there is Doctor Terry Clekis, a local veterinarian, who took time to read through a substantial amount of the content of both books giving me a clear view into a reader's perspective of what they expected and how the horrors in this book would impact them.

Michele Quinones was a major help in writing this book. Her support for this project was greatly appreciated as were the help from Law Enforcement personnel, State Attorney Scanlan, and others close to the case were invaluable in putting this book and the following book together. Without so much assistance and involvement by others, I would never have been capable of producing this book.

Then there are those who listened to me patiently as I aired my insecurities about writing this book, the number of pages written, the number of pages yet to go, word count, chapter locations, problems finding agents, editors, publishers, software problems, and two computer crashes. First and foremost, among those is my wife, Jan. For over a period of six years she has watched me wrestle with and agonize over this book. The others whom I have assaulted in my quest for understanding of what I was attempting to accomplish include trees, dogs, waitresses at Bob Evans, and pretty much anybody who came too near and doubtlessly came to regret having done so.

I also need to acknowledge Ms. Gina Maniaci, LCSW who is a Team Leader at the VA Vet Center in St. Petersburg, FL for her support over the years on this project. Additionally, the following persons also need to be acknowledged: Mr. Tom Stout, a retired State of Florida Law Enforcement Officer for his conversations with me about DNA, courtroom etiquette, and finger print analysis. Others include dog trainer Mr. Ted Kraft. Fellow writers, Ms. Julieanna Blackwell for her advice and support along with Mr. Dick Harrison for his fantastic reviews on my other works and his advice on writing. I wish also to thank Ms. Sherry Roberts for taking time to read, review, and comment on this work.

FORWARD

"How is it that *you* didn't know? How could *you* not see these things about him?" Michele Quinones leaned her head slightly to the side as she repeated the same questions that had been put to her by those she thought she knew and whom she thought knew her.

Her face was expressionless; however, her head and right hand responded with a slight rise and then dip as she placed emphasis on each "you" echoing the questions put to her repeatedly in disbelief by family members and friends.

It was a pleasant Sunday afternoon, April 14th, 2013, and the one-time girlfriend of Delmer Smith, an attractive, intelligent, forty-two-year-old woman, sat with me at a small table outside the Panera Bread Company in the Coco Plum Plaza in North Port, Florida, drinking iced coffee. We had just finished lunch at the sandwich shop where we met to discuss her relationship with a man who terrorized women living alone in Sarasota and Manatee Counties in 2009.

She paused in her thoughts, her unblinking, dark-eyes held mine in their grasp. I could see in her gaze that she was hurting deep within.

"That is what they asked me. You know? Over and over again." She looked away and down, and then added, "It wasn't so much a question," she said, "but more of a demand."

A short-lived smile touched her lips. Her voice lowered, softened. She lit a cigarette, busying her fingers, took a deep draw on it, then blew the first exhale up and away from my direction. "My friends," she inhaled again. "My family," she said quietly, more to herself than to me.

Her eyes were still looking down and with the palm of her free hand she absentmindedly smoothed her dress. "It was like, you know, I was at fault for some reason. I was the guilty one. That is what they wanted to know." She took a sip of her drink and looked around at the other lunch customers seated at tables near ours who were, like she and I, enjoying a soft Florida breeze. "Every one of them." She paused, then added, "'He was your boyfriend,' they said to me," her voice climbed with passion. "Like that gave me some kind of magical insight into the man. It's all bullshit." Her eyes dropped to the pavement, then up, fierce, black.

"'You lived together. And, you are telling me, telling us you didn't know?'" She thumped her chest with a thumb and turned her head quizzically to look at me. Our eyes met and once more I could not look away. Her chin was high and her eyes, moments before warm and friendly, had grown suddenly cold, hard, flinty.

I could see, could feel the emotional intensity that burned inside her. She felt wronged by the very people she thought would have been there for support. She wanted to say to each of them, *"What about me? All these questions are about why I didn't know. What about me? Don't any one of you who are aware of the relationship that I had with Delmer recognize that I had feelings in this? Don't you recognize my fear? My bewilderment? My sense of betrayal? Is it only that you want to know why I didn't know? Well, better yet, if you were around him, why didn't* ***you*** *know?"*

She didn't need to say those words. I felt them emanating from her heart and soul. I saw them in her eyes, the way she held her head, the silence that surrounded her as she sat and stared with a distant look into her coffee while slowly stirring the iced drink with her straw.

This was our first meeting, Michele and mine. However, it would not be the last.

"How is it," she began again, voice drifting, slowly turning reflections of past events over in her mind, seeking answers, freedom from sins she had no control over. Then she turned to me and I could see that the anger was draining.

The sun was behind her, and its light filtered through the profusion of auburn curls that framed her face. They were dancing and bouncing in the gentle wind that swirled around us.

Her face had grown soft. It was almost hidden within what appeared to be a hundred curls that moved as though alive. And, in the midst of the entire wild tumble were her eyes. Deep, dark, mysterious, and profoundly sad.

"How is it that you didn't know?" she repeated, echoing the accusing tone used against her.

"I'll tell you," she leaned towards me, a spark suddenly backlit her eyes. "I just now realized why. Have a guess?" She tilted her head waiting for an answer.

"Well, I would think it was because he portrayed himself in such a manner that you couldn't see who or what he was," I said, feeling the need to say something, anything, even if it was wrong. I felt that I needed to contribute, to help her deal with what I felt was an incredible "aloneness" that had befallen her through no fault of her own other than falling in love with him.

"No," she replied softly. "No." A light smile drifted across her lips, but the sadness remained in her eyes. "No. Wrong."

"Then what? Why didn't you know, or could tell?" I asked.

"The answer is simply this: I once met a man who didn't exist."

GORDON KUHN

The Criminal Mind

Doctor Samenow in his book, *Inside the Criminal Mind*, exhorts us to remember that "… we must begin with the clear understanding that the criminal chooses crime. He chooses his associates, his way of life, the kinds of crime he commits. He rejects society long before society rejects him; he is victimizer, not victim. The criminal values people to the extent that they can be manipulated; he believes he is *entitled* to whatever he desires; he does not justify his actions to himself."[1]

---

[1] Stanton E. Samenow, *Inside the Criminal Mind,* ISBN 0-8129-1082-6, Copyright © 1984 by Stanton E. Samenow, Times Books.

PART ONE

WHO IS DELMER SMITH?

GORDON KUHN

CHAPTER ONE

Birth of an Evil Seed

Delmer Smith III was born July 19, 1971 in Detroit, Michigan to a couple who are now both deceased. He is one of multiple children from this mixed-race union. His mother, Velma Shelton, was white and his father was black. Delmer is light skinned, light enough to pass for being white in many circumstances. The mixed bloodlines will provoke identification confusion in the future when, as an adult, he is the suspect in several crimes.

He is given his father's name and the family happily pronounces him to be Delmer the 3rd. His name, and that of his father, is a variant of Delmar (also used within the family) and comes from Spanish and "Old" French. It means "of the sea." The choice is, perhaps prophetic in an eerie way.

The sea is a mercurial place. It can be calm, inviting, sublime, and soft at one point in time and then, with little if any warning, it will become treacherous, evil, violent, destructive, a merciless killer. And, so it was to be with Delmer the 3rd. As it is for the sea, he also will be a mystery to those he meets in life. Michele Quinones, his onetime fiancé, told me as she was trying to make sense of their relationship, "He was the man who didn't exist."

She went on to say to me, "I recall one day we were fishing and he was standing off behind me and I looked up at him. He didn't know I was watching him. What I saw was a man stripped for a moment of what or who he was. He was so soft standing there, a little boy. So strange," she smiled as she thought back. "He was so at peace. And yet, there is this other Delmer that I did not know or even suspect might exist. I saw him for what he might have been, what he could have been, not as he was."

He was a burglar. He had a weird sexual appetite. He preyed on women who were elderly, or close to being so. Moreover, he was a brutal killer without compassion for his victims, or sense of guilt for what he did to them.

This is a man who is an enigma to many—perhaps even to himself. In his wake will be both terror and love as well as questions—questions that no one will ever be able to fully answer.

The newborn entered the world as all children do, coated in a wet blanket of blood and body fluids from his mother, which left his small wrinkled body coated in a shining slime that needed to be hurriedly washed off. But first, so his mother could touch him, the doctor laid him up high on her stomach. The newborn wriggled about and let go a torrent of crying while the doctor clamped and cut the umbilical cord. Then, nurses carefully lifted him and took him over to a table and water to clean him up.

He was quite a sight, all slick and slimy from the birth, his lungs sucking in huge gulps of air to expel in great rips of crying in protest for having been taken from a warm place and thrust into cool air beneath blinding lights, assaulted by monstrous noises, and unknown things touching him while his arms and legs swatted here and there and at everyone around him as he let his anger be known. Soon, they brought him back to Velma, wrapped tightly in a soft blue blanket and laid him down so she could hold him close. It was only a short while later that Velma and the baby were transported to her room where she could spend more time examining and loving on her baby. And then a small flood of waiting relatives and friends arrived to greet her and the newborn.

Exhausted, he had closed his eyes and drifted into a deep sleep ignoring the trip down the hall on the stretcher to where they lifted he and his mother onto her hospital bed. It was much later that he felt someone tugging on his blanket and holding his tiny hands.

He opened his eyes to the harsh glare of ceiling lights and a cloud of faces peering down at him all with smiles beaming well wishes. But he didn't understand all that and he didn't understand why they were holding his hands and marveling at how strong he was. "What a grip," someone said. "Just look at how he holds on." Little could the friends and relatives surrounding him then imagine that those tiny hands would grow and one day beat, sexually assault, drag, and even kill women not much older than his own mother was then.

Then he was surrounded in safety and comfort by his parents, brothers, sisters, other family members, and a handful of family friends. They most assuredly were like others when addressing a new born for the first time. They would have remarked at how tiny his fingers and toes were in comparison to theirs. Perhaps they marveled about how strong the tiny hands were as his fingers curled about theirs and tightened, never suspecting that those fingers one day would be suspected of curling around a baseball bat and beating a woman to death in Sarasota, Florida.

They would have laughed as they tried to get his attention by making odd sounds and tickling him. And he, like all newborns, probably just yawned and looked this way and that, not focusing on any one person or thing. They would have wondered about his future. They surely laughed and were excited about his prospects and, like many parents and well-wishers do, probably even imagined him becoming some famous and wealthy person, maybe even the President of the United States. However, it was not to be. A bad seed is hard to recognize when so tiny. He would become famous, in a sense, as he terrorized parts of Sarasota and Manatee Counties because of the brutality of his crimes.

It is doubtful that anyone present in Delmer Smith's life then would have dared to predict, or could have imagined, that thirty-eight years later this then tiny bundle of life would be under arrest and accused of being a violent serial rapist, home invader, burglar, murderer, and suspected drug trafficker. All they would have seen before them then, wrapped in a soft blue hospital blanket, was a baby reaching up, sleepy eyed, with curling fingers and toes, stretching, a wonder of life.

No one could have anticipated his troubled youth or his struggle with education. This child would repeat the second grade, and then the third, the fourth, and the fifth. At age fourteen, and in the fifth grade, he was surrounded by nine and ten year olds. Then, suddenly, he was promoted to the ninth grade skipping all the years between, and placed into a special needs class. Testing would determine his verbal IQ to be seventy, one point above what they deemed as being "retarded."

Not one of his then admirers saw the monster he would become. However, as he grew older, there were several neighborhood events, referred to anonymously by those who knew him as a child, which surfaced in and before his teenage years, that were indicative of a troubled future. No one then recognized his lack of impulse control that would plague him. It would not be identified until he was much older and then on trial for his life.

Nevertheless, Delmer Smith has another side to him that was noted by Michele Quinones, softer and protective of those he cared for. It was also discussed in open court during the presentencing stage of his Manatee County murder trial for the death of Kathleen Briles when the defense introduced two of his family members who, as young girls, had their lives significantly influenced by his interactions with them over the years.

CHAPTER TWO

He's my Uncle

It is August 14th, 2012 and Mr. Brunvand, Delmer Smith's Manatee County defense attorney, will introduce two young women to the Court. They have traveled to Bradenton, Florida from Detroit, Michigan out of love for the defendant. Brunvand plans to show a different side of Delmer to the Court. It is an attempt to obtain some leniency for his client to avoid the death penalty[2]. "Good morning," he said to the first woman. She had just taken a seat on the stand and been sworn in, "Please tell the Jury your full name."

"Alicia Phillips."

"And Alicia, how old are you?" He smiled gently at her.

"Twenty-nine."

Brunvand continues with questions regarding Ms. Phillips residence and employment. She has come from her home in Bradford, Michigan where she lives with her 3-year-old daughter. She has come to Bradenton to speak in open court on behalf of a man being held on first-degree murder charges.

"How do you know Delmer Smith?"

"He's my uncle."

Brunvand asks her if she can point out Delmer in the courtroom "and tell the Jury what he's wearing?"

She does so, indicating a man seated at the defense table wearing "a striped blue shirt, collared shirt."

---

[2] The murder trial is covered in book two: *The Woman in a Pink Top.*

"And is he someone that you consider yourself close to?" Brunvand gently asks.

"Yes, I love him very much."

"Do you recall an instance as a child where Delmer came to your aid?"

"Yes," Ms. Phillips went on to tell about an instance where she had "been bad" and was being punished for it by getting "a spanking." She explained that her grandmother, Velma Shelton Smith, Delmer Smith's mother, had picked up a switch, her apparent singular choice for dealing with such issues, and was spanking her when her nose began to bleed. Delmer, she told the Court, stepped in between his mother and his niece protecting her from being struck anymore by his mother.

"And he calmed me down, and—you know, he always came to my aid."

The same hands that will protect his niece from being beaten by a switch held tightly by his mother so many years before will one day gently wash a girlfriend's hair and then make hot cups of tea for her mother. Yet, for almost six months in 2009, those very same hands, so seemingly comforting and protective for a few, will brutally terrorize a number of women and several men—needlessly.

The acts of those hands will send out a shock wave of fear in two counties. They attack and maim. In one case, those reportedly defensive and shielding hands will kill. In another they are suspected of having killed. And, in yet another, they will hang a naked woman out over a 12-story-high balcony while the victim is asked, "Can you fly?"

"He was my favorite uncle," Ms. Phillips went on to say. "He gave me birthday presents, Christmas presents, he would take me out. He would guide me, you know, try to guide me in the right direction. He made us promise to finish school … refrain from having babies. He just tried to make sure that we were on the right path. He was always someone I could talk to."

Yet for his victims there was little discussion, only inflicted pain. One, hit from behind while working in her yard, stunned, bleeding, kicked and bruised will be dragged into her house, tied with electrical cord and left on her bed wondering if she will be raped—fearing she will be.

She manages to release herself from her bindings when she believes he is no longer in her home. Freed, but afraid her attacker might still be close, she runs, staggers toward an intersection with US 41 hoping she won't pass out on the way there. Attaining her goal, she collapses and, thankfully, is spotted by someone driving past who recognizes her.

Ms. Phillips went on to explain how much Delmer had meant to her as a child. "He would always be on me about doing the right thing … I did always have his voice in the back of my head saying, 'Do right, do right.'"

"Do you love your uncle?"

"Yes."

"And despite the other part of him … heard about through the news media, you still love your uncle?"

"Yes, I do. He's family… we don't have much left. He's still in my prayers, you know. Yes, I do love him very much."

There is no discussion about the two women who were the first known to have been assaulted by a man who meets Delmer Smith's description. The defense attorney does not speak about the older one, aged 83, being vaginally and rectally attacked or that she, and her 53-year-old daughter, needed medical attention following the break-in, robbery, and sadistic sexual molestation. That is not part of the current case, so the prosecutor will not speak of it either.

Also not part of the current case will be the baseball bat slaying of a woman not much older than the two witnesses. Delmer Smith is considered as the prime suspect in that lady's death, but there are problems with the County being able to prove it without any doubt. "There was blood everywhere," a source will tell me. "Absolutely everywhere." There was so much blood, I was told by law enforcement, that finding any trace of Delmer's DNA in the mix is, at this moment in time, scientifically difficult if not impossible.

"They found male DNA," a local private detective told me angrily. "But, they claim they cannot pull enough profile in from the DNA they found to identify that bastard [Delmer Smith]. They claim," he hissed. "I don't buy it."

Brunvand would next bring Phillips' 23-year-old cousin, Christiana Smith, to the stand as a witness. "There's some tissue there if you need it," he told her and then introduced her to the Jury. After a moment allowing her to collect herself, he questioned her about her childhood and Delmer's interaction with her.

As it was, being much younger than her cousin, Alicia, Christiana's relationship began while Delmer was in prison for bank robbery. "I was too young to know exactly that he was gone to prison," she said, going on to explain that when she became older she learned and understood.

"I remember talking to him on the phone a lot through my teenage years."

"Did you feel that he provided guidance to you?"

"Yes."

Brunvand explained that Delmer stood the chance of receiving either a life sentence or a death sentence based on his conviction for murdering Kathy Briles. He asked if she understood that. "Yes," Christiana said.

"And you still love him very much?"

"Yes, I love him a whole lot."

The prosecution saw no need in asking any questions and both witnesses were released.

The tragedy of this one man's life was clearly evident in his nieces' remarks and in the trial itself. Smith's nieces loved him. And, unlike his victim, he was able to sit in the courtroom and listen to them speak of their love for him.

Kathy Briles also had people who loved her. Those people testified too. However, they were unable to speak directly to her and tell her of the love they felt for her. Smith had ripped that right from his victim's family and friends. The judge would have to take all that into consideration, as would the Jury.

But the Court would also have to take into consideration events in Delmer Smith's earlier life that may have caused his abject cruelty in the first place. A look into his formative years and at his mental state prior to sentencing would be necessary to avoid an appeal for lack of having failed to consider those issues.

There are many studies about criminals where research traces such behavior back to their childhood. One prominent researcher in this field is Dr. Samenow. He penned that while it is true that children, all children, test their boundaries ever pressing outward, there is a difference between the normal child (is there truly such) and the troubled child. "The criminal child's departure from parental and societal expectations involves more than isolated acts," he wrote. "Beginning as early as during the preschool years, *patterns* evolve that become part of a criminal lifestyle. As a child, the criminal is a dynamo of energy, a being with an iron will, insistent upon taking charge, expecting others to indulge his every whim. His appetite for adventure is voracious. He takes risks, becomes embroiled in difficulties, and then demands to be bailed out and forgiven."[3]

There are indications that Delmer Smith was such a young teen. A variety of reports from various sources all seem to support his having problems at an early stage. The question is: why? What factor was present in his life that pushed him down the path toward being a criminal? It is possible that Dr. Samenow's research can offer a clue toward perhaps not fully understanding but at least being able to spot hints that, in hindsight, were clearly there.

In his book, Dr. Samenow writes of such similar activities in a variety of children stating his belief that the sociopathic child is:

> ... unlike most other children.... While the others were seeking recognition through schoolwork, sports, or social activities, this child thumbs his nose at it all. He establishes himself by doing what is forbidden.

---

[3] IBID.

CHAPTER THREE

Rape in a Car Wash

The date was June 28, 1986 when Officer John Rock of the Warren, Michigan, Police Department was dispatched at 11 A.M. to investigate an unarmed robbery outside a local carwash. He was advised the complainant would meet him at Raseem's Market, a neighborhood grocery located on Dequindre Street. It was where she had fled for help. When Officer Rock arrived, he was hurriedly approached by a woman who identified herself as Ms. Elizabeth Sabbagh, one of the co-owners of Raseem's Market.

Ms. Sabbagh explained that there was a woman inside the store who had asked her to call the police. She went on to say that the woman, who appeared to be in her mid-twenties, told her she had been at the car wash across the street when attacked by an unknown male who was working there. Ms. Sabbagh said the woman claimed to have been robbed, raped, and almost murdered and had asked the store owners to call the police for her.

Officer Rock approached and quietly introduced himself to the woman. His well-practiced lawman's eye swept over her quickly. She was obviously distraught. Tear trails spoiled her makeup. She was trembling. Her arms were clutched across her chest and stomach in a protective mode. Her jeans were streaked with oil and dirt from a fall in the car wash's parking lot and her legs were clamped together as she leaned slightly from her waist giving the impression that she was in pain.

"I ... I was raped," her eyes, wide with shock and alarm, shifted down and then back up with a mixture of anger and terror lighting them, "and ... and robbed, and he

... he tried to kill me," she sobbed, her voice rising with anxiety.

"Where did this happen?" the officer said softly, attentive to her condition, "Ms.—uh—Ms.?"

"Kathy—Kathryn Johnson."

"Alright, Ms. Johnson, where did the attack take place?"

"Over—over there," Kathryn pointed shakily across the street at the car wash known as J.R's. "It happened over there." Her face muscles went tight. "I was having my car washed and this guy," she sobbed, "this guy pushed me into the bathroom and raped me."

"Did you say anything to the management? Was the guy a customer?"

"No, he works there. The guy who did it works there. He's all alone over there. The owner went off on an errand. He's wearing jeans and—and a yellow t-shirt."

Rock looked over his shoulder to the car wash just as another Warren City Police Officer pulled his car up in front of Raseem's. The officer noted that the door was open to the car wash's office; however, he later reported that he could not see anyone on the property.

Ms. Johnson went on to explain that she had been the only customer at the business when the attack occurred. She said she turned her keys over to an individual, whom she believed was an employee, and went to wait in the office while he ran her car through the wash.

Once out of the wash, he drove it into an area where detailing and wax jobs were performed to finish cleaning the interior. Thinking he was almost finished with her car, she approached him and gave him a six dollar tip. He took the money, stuffed the bills into his pants pockets, and told her he had some more work to do on the car and that she should wait for him in the office while he finished. She returned to the office and was standing looking out the front windows at Raseem's Market across the street thinking about items she needed to buy when he approached from behind and grabbed her in a neck lock. He immediately dragged her into the woman's darkened restroom, her arms flailing the air.

Once inside, he kept the light off and pushed her up against the wall with one arm. "Don't say nothin', bitch," he said. "Don't scream because I got a gun."

At the mention of a gun, Officer Rock visibly stiffened a bit and immediately put out a call for assistance just as Officer Kulesa joined him inside Raseem's.

Kathryn told the officers that her attacker made her sit on the toilet seat as he unzipped his pants. "Suck my dick, suck my dick, bitch," she said he ordered.

He held his penis in one hand, she recalled, and tried to grab her head and force her toward him. She said she twisted away from him refusing to service him.

He tried once more and once more she refused, this time pushing him back. "No. Get off me. Get away." Her voice must have seemed small, strange, squeaky, not hers. Her throat surely was constricting in fear, tightening.

Her attacker's next move was to violently force her onto the floor where he jerked her pants down and assaulted her.

"Did he make penetration?" one of the responding cops would later ask while writing a supplemental report.

"Yes. Yes," she said. "I felt him."

"Did he climax?"

"I don't know."

Following the sexual assault, her rapist then rifled through her jeans and found $110 that he shoved into his pockets. But it was not enough, she told them. He wanted more. "Where's the rest of your money?" she said he shouted at her.

"That's all I have," Ms. Johnson replied.

He opened the bathroom door and told her that he'd be "right back."

But then, as he closed the door behind him, she heard him say softly, "I gotta figure out what to do with you."

The thought of attempting an escape came to her, but, then, perhaps not. Maybe, she thought, she should wait hoping the owner of the car wash would return. Besides, if she could get outside, where would she go? He had the keys to her car. But then she recalled his parting ominous remark ominous, "I gotta figure out what to do with you." Perhaps everything was beginning to move too quickly for him.

A sudden sense of desperation surely had come over him. He must have realized that he had not thought this out. This was an impulsive act, done for the excitement of it. But now, it left him with a serious problem: her! With that thought echoing through her mind, she began to panic and looked around the filthy room for something she could use to defend herself with, but found nothing. And then she heard her car start up.

Adrenaline surged. She clambered painfully to a standing position and hurriedly put her clothes in order readying for an attempt at freedom knowing her life was an issue now.

Then it happened, just as Ms. Johnson reached out with a trembling, timorous, searching hand for the doorknob, the door suddenly swung open. Daylight burst in, sweeping from behind and around the rapist, blinding his victim momentarily.

"Come here, bitch," he growled and, jerking her by her right arm, pulled her out of the small room and toward himself.

An inner voice told her she would have to fight if she wanted to live. She would have to fight and she would have to remember what he looked like to be able to identify him.

She pushed away, trying to jerk herself free from his grip. But, his strength overpowered her. He quickly managed to drag her out of the bathroom, through the office, and outside, shoving her up against the building wall while forcing her to walk in front of him. She quickly glanced around looking for help, but found no one in sight. What she did see spiked her fear.

He was pushing her towards where her brown Pontiac sat with its engine running near the building with the trunk open. Sensing he planned to put her in the trunk and that her life was clearly in danger, she reached for the wall in an attempt to find something to grab onto to stay the movement to the car and painfully broke off a fingernail as he jerked her forward. "Get in the trunk," he shouted at her. "I'll leave it open, just get in!"

Fearing he was going to kill her, she began to scream hysterically. "No—please, no," she begged, spinning on him. "Please leave me alone." She clutched at anything close to slow their progression toward the rear of her car. She was desperate to prevent him from placing her in the car's open trunk. "No," she screamed once more, pushing back at him and urgently working at trying to pry his hands free from her arm. Glancing at his face she saw confusion in his eyes. She sensed the early stages of panic in her attacker. Taking advantage of it, she struggled harder, her wrists and arms were growing slippery with sweat as was his hands and she felt his grip on her loosen and slip. Her legs, shaking with the terror she felt, lost the strength to hold her upright and she collapsed, falling backwards in a sprawling heap on the pavement near the front of her car.

CHAPTER FOUR

Get Back!

The suddenness of her fall jerked Kathryn completely free from her attacker's grasp. As she lay on the ground, she looked up through tears and pain and saw puzzlement on her rapist's face. To her the look pathetically screamed out, "I don't know what to do. I don't know what to do." She was certain his mind was searching for answers and it was then she realized she was completely free of his grip.

She was sprawled out on a mixture of oil-stained asphalt and gravel. She rolled over and was then facing away from him. The rocks had cut into her hands. But fear covered the pain and she was unaware of the bleeding wounds. She noted her car was just off to her side with the engine running. The driver's door was open, waiting, as was the trunk.

Then, a rage took hold of her that she had never before felt.

It started small, kindling-wood small, then flared, reaching up. The flames were climbing into a bonfire of emotion. Every muscle in her body tensed and readied for a fight. She began struggling to stand. She knew she needed to do so quickly, while he was confused and not hanging onto her.

Now!—she told herself, while he was stunned! And, she recalled her earlier thought about the need to be able to identify him later.

She suddenly spun around coming up on all fours, now facing him, staring, memorizing. *Blue jeans, yellow t-shirt, gym shoes, in his twenties—maybe older, maybe white or just light skinned black, with an afro, short brown hair.* She finished her thoughts with one word—*asshole.*

The nerves in her face were noticeably twitching, contorting her features into a vicious, anger-filled statement that warned him not to get too close. Kathryn brought a knee up to balance herself. One bloodied hand went palm down on the pavement. Her eyes blazed with hatred, focused on her attacker. Then she was up—standing—not fully, but both feet were under her. Balanced in a crouch, her hands held forward, her fingers curled claw like. The fighter was emerging from the depths.

"Get away from me," she said, at first almost in a whisper. Then—louder, "Get away from me."

Suddenly she exploded with anger. "Get away from me!" she roared and spat at him, almost in a snarl, still half crouched, half erect. Her saliva flew through the air at him, spattering him. "Get away!" Her face had taken on a sinister look. The terror was still there but now—now the fighter was beginning to fully emerge. "Get away from me! Now!" she screamed with an explosive rush of air. Her lungs were bursting with fury.

Every fiber in her body felt on fire. Never in her life had she felt such rage. Never before had she conceived of the possibility of having to kill someone over her personal safety. But, this was life and death. Her family's faces flashed in her mind.

No, she was not going to get into the trunk. No! She would no longer allow him to abuse her.

She would kick, scream, and tear at his face with her nails if he even touched her now. She was no longer the fearful, startled victimized woman in the bathroom. No. She was now a desperate female whose sole mission was to stay alive even if it meant killing her attacker.

Kathryn sensed an immediate chance opportunity to get away that needed to be taken advantage of instantly. Strange sounds came from her throat, gurgling, growling noises, half-spoken words, high pitched, threatening, and animal like. Her legs, trembling, suddenly felt a rush of strength. She backed slowly, fearful, angrily screaming at him, her left arm reaching out, feeling for the car with her fingertips. Finding it, she turned suddenly and dashed for her car's open driver's door circling the vehicle while the attacker stood open mouthed at the spot where she had broken free of his grasp.

He watched as she raced for the open door seemingly unable to move. In his confusion, he hesitated moving toward her. He sensed dangerous change in his prey's attitude. It brought more confusion and then—suddenly—fear.

A chasm of panic had opened up inside of him and it was growing.

He was almost frozen in the disbelief that the tables had been turned. She was getting away! He could not allow that. There was no choice in this matter. He knew when he left her alone, going to get her car, that he had committed himself to killing her the minute he dragged her into the bathroom. He could not allow her to live. She knows, he thought. She knows! His brain screamed at him.

"Stop," he shouted, springing after her, but his move was far too late, in a stumbling, loosely jointed attempt to prevent her from getting away. Just as he placed his hands on the side of her car, she slammed the driver's door closed.

Total panic now set in. He had given her the opportunity to make a rush for freedom, and now he stood helplessly outside the car and watched as she slammed the lock button down.

She placed the vehicle in drive, glanced up at him, and then stepped on the gas.

CHAPTER FIVE

An Arrest

Officer Rock and his partner, Officer Kulesa, slowly drove their patrol cars across Dequindre Road to J.R.'s Car Wash. As they went, their eyes scanned the area searching for anyone in or near the buildings. Both men focused on the office. They pulled their cars to a stop alongside the business. Their overhead lights were flashing. It was a warning to anyone who might drive onto the property that just then might not be a wise decision.

Rock looked up as a third patrol car raced toward them on Dequindre with its siren screaming. He could see Officer Schade at the wheel and waved for the newcomer to go behind the building.

He and Kulesa carefully un-holstered their weapons and began their search of the structure paying close attention to the interior rooms as well as the surrounding parking lot. "He said he had a gun," Ms. Johnson had told them, and they were not going to take any chances.

Officer Schade soon radioed that he had made contact with a man behind the building. He had taken him into temporary custody, not knowing if he was the one they were looking for. The man offered no resistance and claimed ignorance of having any knowledge of any disturbance at the car wash.

Ms. Johnson had told the police her assailant had been wearing a yellow t-shirt, and that he was possibly in his twenties. The person standing in front of the patrolman was clearly a large male that could pass for an adult—but he was wearing a red T-Shirt.

"What's your name?"

"Delmer," the youth wet his lip with his tongue and shifted his feet as he glanced nervously around at the surrounding area, "…Delmer Smith."

"How old are you," Schade asked.

"Fourteen," was the soft reply.

Schade looked him up and down and noted that the boy was avoiding eye contact. Delmer began kicking at a rock sticking up in the pavement.

"Fourteen, and you didn't see anything going on here."

"No." He continued kicking the rock, not looking up at the officer.

"Did you change t-shirts? Where is it the one you took off?"

"What?" Delmer looked up startled.

"The one you took off, where is it?"

"I don't know what you're talking about. I only have this shirt. I don't own a yellow t-shirt." The reply shot out angrily.

Schade smiled. "I didn't say what color it was."

The boy went silent.

In a matter of only a few minutes, the discarded shirt was located in a trash can and shown to Delmer. He denied having worn it. But the cops instinctively knew better. They were certain he switched shirts. Rock stood in front of the boy and waved the discarded shirt slowly thru the air before the teen. "Looks like your size," he said slowly.

"Never saw it before," Delmer said, rubbing the back of his neck and looking down and away from Rock's eyes.

Then, smiling a cop's smile, the one that sends the message, "I know better and I have the power and you don't" smile, he said, "And it is still warm, how do you figure that?" He tilted his head slightly to one side waiting for an answer that never came.

Delmer was thinking fast, but nothing was developing except a lot of—ums, ohs, and uhs—and that was all that would surface. The officers continued to question him. Delmer at first denied having any contact with Ms. Johnson and then, memory suddenly refreshed, began telling a wild tale about having seen another man assaulting her.

"I didn't do nothin'." His face tightened in anger and fear as he watched the officers around him. He could tell by their comments and body language that they were sure they had the correct suspect in custody. "What? You don't believe me?" he fussed. "Why aren't you lookin' for that guy I told you about? Look, I didn't do nothing. I came here 'cause my mother sent me. She and the guy who owns this place are friends. I don't know nothin' about some woman being attacked except I seen somethin' strange goin' on in a car that went through the car wash. That's all."

The officers cuffed him.

By the time Mr. Momtaz, the owner of the car wash, and Delmer's mother, arrived on the scene, Delmer was under arrest and had ready an elaborate story about watching a car pass through the car wash with "a black woman" in it when, suddenly, a black male appeared in the car with her. "I don't know what was goin' on, but they were struggling and this guy was all over this lady. All I could do was watch."

"What happened then?" Rock asked while watching the boy's dancing eyes.

"The car went through the machines," he said excitedly, nodding his head in the direction of the car wash. "Then this black guy jumps out of the car and runs off." Delmer began shifting his weight from one leg to another.

"And the woman? What about the woman?"

Delmer cleared his throat. "When the guy jumped from the car she was alone then and she just drove across the street to Raseem's. I don't know what happened in the car. I don't know what happened to her. She didn't say anything to me. I was just standin' over there watchin'," he nodded toward where the car wash office was. "I don't know anything else. I didn't do anything." He was speaking rapidly and the pitch of his voice was rising quickly. "Why do I have these things on?" he referred to the cuffs.

"Because you're under arrest," the officer said dryly, as he led the youth over to his patrol car.

Much to Delmer's surprise, Velma Shelton gave approval for her son to be given a lie detector test, trusting in his tale of innocence. After all, she pointed to the fact that he said he saw this other man in the car with the victim and the victim was obviously distraught and most likely confused. And, according to Velma, Delmer was simply "not that kind of boy."

Delmer took the lie detector test.
He failed.
Velma's son was tried in juvenile court and found to be guilty of the violent attack on Kathryn Johnson. He was sentenced to 18 months at The Boys' Training School in Michigan.

The hope of everyone he knew then was that while he was at the youthful offender prison, for that was what the "school" unabashedly truly was, that Delmer will adjust and become a responsible citizen because of the "training" he will be given. Instead, while there he learned from others in his age range how to be more proficient as a criminal.

It is a curious thing, in our society, how we wish for circumstances to not be as they are revealed to us. It is in the failure of what we perceive to be reality. We argue our positions in an attempt to force reality to comply with how we believe it to be. We do this even when it is obvious to everyone that the falsity of the notion we subscribe to and which we refuse to abandon in hopes of being proven "right" in the end, results in the occurrence of the exact opposite reaction.

    Citing an example for the above, Dr. Samenow wrote of a family who saw a different reality than what was the truth. The family, as so many families do in such situations, refused to accept the fact that anything was wrong with their child. He wrote regarding parents of such a youth, "… his mother and father did not perceive a pattern unfolding but assume that his waywardness is merely a stage of development. This 'stage,' however, never ends." While parents, friends, and others are victimized the "… criminal child remains unmoved and unaffected." Instead, Samenow writes, "he establishes himself by doing what is forbidden."[4]

    So, based on the understanding that within a complex issue such as this that many around the criminal cannot see the person as they truly are based on what they want or perceive reality to be. It is completely logical then that, even in the 2012 murder trial, in which Delmer Smith was found guilty of the horrific beating death of a local Bradenton, Florida, doctor's wife, his nieces could speak of a different Delmer Smith, a different reality for them than what was presented in the trial. In essence, they refused, in a personal way, to accept the criminal nature of their uncle based on their own perception of reality that accepted but discounted the criminal acts.

---

[4] IBID.

They reportedly knew Delmer to be a wise and loving uncle who, they claimed, was one who always cautioned them to "do the right thing" in their lives. He was a man that Alicia claimed came to her defense once when she was being "spanked" with a switch by her grandmother, Delmer's mother.

It was unbelievable to them that this protector, this friend, this loving uncle, who in reality had not been around for most of their lives because he was in prison for bank robbery for fifteen years, could do such a horrible thing. But he did.

The simple fact remains that Delmer Smith chose this life, much as Dr. Samenow reported was the usual case of someone like Delmer. He chose his victims. He chose to rape, terrorize, maim, and murder. He, for many, is an enigma. However, he will now spend the rest of his life behind bars branded as the monster that he chose to be. The question is: why?

He preferentially attacked women fifty years old and up. He would threaten them, abuse them, and, on occasion, sexually violate them sadistically, violently.

The question remains as to why? What was the cause of the extreme violence extended toward older women? Delmer isn't talking. His family isn't. His mother and father are dead. Any reason for his acts is all speculation.

But, he is now a convicted killer living in a small cell cut off from the world for the most part.

He is a predator and can never again be allowed freedom.

He is a creature without a conscience.

He truly is the man who didn't exist.

CHAPTER SIX

Home Invasion

Three years later, on December 27th, 1990, then 18-year-old Delmer was arrested for the crime of arson at a residence on Sunset Street in Detroit. He was suspected of having set a fire at the residence on October 31st, 1990.

A witness claimed having seen Delmer enter and leave the house and that a glow could be seen through the front room window. The witness also claimed Delmer bragged to several of his friends about setting the fire. However, the case was dropped when the complaining witness did not show up in court to testify.

On January 8th, 1991, records 19 years old, indicate that Delmer was arrested for suspicion of having been involved in a murder, but the case was dropped and no further comment was made concerning the issue. The officers involved have long since retired and moved away or died. No other information was available.

On April 10th, 1991, Delmer was arrested after burglarizing a residence around 1 A.M.. Once inside, and moving as quietly as a cat, he came across a 73-year-old lady sleeping in the first floor bedroom of her residence.

The woman later told officers that she woke at the sound of a male voice speaking nearby and was startled to find a man hovering over her wearing white gloves and holding something shiny in his hands. She said he advised her to remain quiet and covered her head with a bed sheet to prevent her from observing him. "I don't want to hurt you," he said quietly, "I'm only interested in your money and your jewelry."

"My purse is over there. Just there, by the door. It's hanging from the doorknob," the victim stammered, pointing with an outstretched hand from underneath the sheet. "It's all I have, please take it, just take it and leave," she said, her voice shaking with fear. "Please don't hurt me."

The man, who was later identified as Delmer Smith, quickly located her wallet within the purse and took out approximately $100 that he shoved into the pockets of his trousers. He then spotted a second purse sitting atop a table in the kitchen. It belonged to another woman who was asleep in a room on the second floor. From that purse, Delmer took four $100 bills, a set of car keys, and a garage door opener. It was time then to leave. Delmer, with his pant pockets stuffed with the cash he had taken, the garage door opener and a victim's car keys held tightly in his hand, ran into the night toward the detached garage.

However, luckily for the victims, and not so for Delmer, an unmarked police car with Detroit police officers in plain dress was slowly passing by just as Delmer exited the house in an unusual and suspicious hurry leaving the garage doors wide open as he drove away.

Sensing something wrong, the officers moved to a position behind an unsuspecting Delmer. They followed him for a bit to determine where he might be going and to run the tag in order to establish to whom the car belonged. However, the victim had immediately called the police once she was sure that Delmer had left her home, and a radio call alerted the officers behind Delmer who then attempted a traffic stop. But, Delmer decided to make a run for it with the unmarked car following close behind until the pursuit ended at his mother's house where he unsuccessfully attempted to hide.

The noise of his arrival, and that of the siren, woke up the household and soon his mother was on the doorsteps talking with the officers who demanded to be let inside to arrest Delmer, which she did.

CHAPTER SEVEN

Bank Robbery

On May 22nd 1991, Delmer Smith was sentenced to two and a half years to be served at Jackson State prison. While incarcerated there, he met Jerry Gonyea who was a "tough guy" according to Delmer. The two would soon become close friends and Delmer's education would now be at the criminal level of graduate study.

Jerry saw potential in Smith for being a career criminal and began to groom the younger man for such a role. Smith saw Gonyea as a mentor and drank in the lessons and wisdom that poured forth not only from Gonyea but also from Gonyea's jailhouse buddies. As it worked out, Gonyea was released from prison before Smith was and was waiting for Delmer when he got out and needed money.

Gonyea, sensing an opportunity to take control of the younger man, immediately loaned Smith $2,000. However, Smith was only allowed two weeks to repay the money with $500 in interest to be included. The two weeks passed and, as Gonyea had expected, Delmer was unable to pay back the loan. Jerry waited calmly for Delmer to admit to the inability to return the funds and then advised him of the penalty for such a failure.

Delmer would become an assistant, an employee of Jerry Gonyea. He was to accompany Jerry on his criminal activities and aid the older man in the completion of those acts, which included armed bank robbery. Delmer fell right into place happy to be forgiven the debt while working with the older criminal and was, as Gonyea believed would be the case, a natural.

On February 18th, and then again on March 16th, 1994, Gonyea, with Delmer's help, held up the Comerica Bank in Taylor, Michigan. In each case, they used several stolen cars taken from Thompson Chrysler Plymouth in Southgate, Michigan, where Gonyea had worked for a short while as a car salesman. It was there he constructed the idea of robbing banks and using several stolen cars for the getaway. Having access to the keys, he simply took them and made duplicates.

The idea was that moving from one car to another would prevent detection of where they were going and cause confusion among anyone attempting to follow their trail. As soon as they had a bag filled with as much cash as they could collect from the tellers, the ecstatic pair charged happily out of the bank waving their pistols in a threatening manner at anyone in their path. They left the bank on the run and jumped into the first car that they had left waiting for them in the parking lot. It didn't matter if someone saw them get into a car and recorded the license plate because the plates on the cars were all stolen as well.

Jumping into the first car, adrenaline rushing through their veins, they let out whoops of happiness in celebration for having accomplished a successful robbery and get away. They then sped away toward where the second car was parked, rolling the windows down to let fresh air rush over them as the masks they wore to conceal their identities while in the bank were hot and caused them both to sweat excessively.

Arriving at the second location, they sobered a bit and quickly looked around and, in particular, behind them down the road they had just traveled making sure no one was following. They then exited the first, resumed their merriment chattering happily about their conquest, and then transferred into the second car for the drive to where the third car was parked.

By the time they reached the next car, the pair was beginning to come down from the adrenaline high and they were much calmer. They were confident then that they had just made off with a sizeable amount of cash and that their method of escape would definitely prevent anyone from following them. They believed that the string of cars would just appear as though the vehicles had been stolen by several people and that there was no relationship between the bank theft and the car thefts.

At that point in their wave of crime, as they strode confidently to the next car, they were absolutely certain that no one could possibly connect the dots between the cars and the bank robbery. And so, they walked calmly, heads up, broad smiles on their faces, from the third car to the waiting fourth.

The final vehicle would then be used to get them into the neighborhood where they lived. They would then walk home from that car complementing each other on an outstanding robbery and get away.

Neither man thought law enforcement would be able to determine their escape path by using this elaborate and time-consuming technique. Neither would later explain how they had come to that conclusion. "We just did," Gonyea said at one point in response to an officer's question.

The very fact that they were using cars from the same auto dealer should have been a cause for their having some concern. After all, Gonyea had worked for the dealer. One would think that it would have been logical that the dealership might have turned over information on current and prior employees to law enforcement thinking that the thief or thieves might have been among that group. But the pair remained highly confident that there was no way to trace the thefts to them. They were wrong.

The second bank robbery at the same bank in less than a month actually brought about the pair's undoing. Flush with success from the first robbery, they went back thinking how easy it was. Who would suspect? No one, they believed, would ever expect that bank to be hit again so soon and it had been so easy on the first try.

Adrenaline racing, their nerves flooded with waves of energy and excitement, the pair entered the bank shouting at everyone to get on the floor. They waved firearms in the air threatening to kill anyone who made trouble. Children cowered behind their mothers. One wept. A woman appeared close to fainting and grabbed a desk to steady herself as she slipped to the floor.

In the meantime, outdoors in the parking lot, a customer had just driven in not knowing what was taking place inside the bank. He was getting out of his car and was preparing to go inside when Gonyea and Smith ran out drawing his attention.

The bank-robbery team raced outside carrying several bags of money. In their haste, and awash with a triumphant feeling, neither Gonyea nor Smith spotted the man who was close by and could clearly see them. As the men ran, the bank client noted that one of them was clawing at the mask covering his face.

It was Gonyea.

His mask was irritating his skin. It was hot. His face was covered with sweat and the itching was extremely discomforting. Without thinking of the danger of exposing himself, Gonyea pulled off his mask as the pair ran for their getaway car. He was just thankful for the cool air that rushed over his face drying the sweat and relieving the itching. But he was unaware that the bank customer had gotten a sufficient look at his features and that he would later sit with a police sketch artist who would put together a drawing of the bank robber. Following a hunch, the police then took the drawing to the car dealer. Gonyea was immediately identified.

With Gonyea identified, the next step was to identify his associate. This was done with the help of a "confidential informant" who supplied enough information about the pair that surveillance was set up on both men. Fifteen days after the second bank robbery, the FBI visited

Delmer Smith at the small apartment he was renting. Realizing he had one chance to protect himself, he agreed to cooperate and quickly confessed. He then told the officers that he was only the getaway car's driver and that he was innocent of any other misdeed. The trial would prove otherwise. Witnesses testified that Delmer had been inside the bank with Gonyea and that both men had been armed.

For his part in the holdups, Delmer was sentenced on July 20th, 1995 for bank robbery and aiding and abetting as well as carrying a firearm during a crime of violence. He was awarded 120 months for the robbery and 78 months for the firearm possession. The sentences were to run consecutively for a total of 198 months. Delmer was off to federal prison for 16 1/2 years. Gonyea, having been recognized as the leader and organizer between the two, was sentenced to 29 years and 3 months. They were sent to separate facilities.

Delmer assimilated easily into the prison scene. He was around others like him. He knew his limitations. There was a structure to his day that was greatly needed and had been missing all of his life. He learned how to use the system and the system learned how to use him. He worked out at the gym and became stronger. He played on the sports teams and built friendships and learned from those who had been there longer and who would most likely never become free men again.

As with many men who are incarcerated, Delmer was approached online and in the mail by several women. Many would send him photos of themselves in sexual poses. Some offered liaisons with him following his release from prison. Some sent money. One such acquaintanceship resulted in a marriage after ten years of communicating by phone and mail.

GORDON KUHN

PART TWO

Terror Arrives in Florida

CHAPTER EIGHT

Marriage, Parole, a New Life

Donna D. Taylor was 23 years older than Delmer. She was a compassionate woman who wanted to reach out and make a difference in other people's lives. Aware of the harshness of prison life, and feeling that many confined were not responsible for their actions but were jailed solely because of the evils of a society that surrounded them. Believing it was a combination of circumstances, and not a personal internal evil that forced them to take the actions that they had, she felt an overwhelming desire to reach out and connect with one of these men, offering friendship and hope for a better tomorrow. And she found and connected with Delmer Smith.

She remarked that what drew her to him were his comments to her about what he wanted out of life: a home, family, and a good job. And so, based on those statements over a prison phone, Donna married Delmer while he was in prison, sight unseen and became Donna D. Taylor-Smith.

During the time Delmer was incarcerated, Donna never visited him at his request. She provided financial and legal assistance and worked at trying to get his release from prison. When he was paroled, she provided him with airfare to Tampa, Florida where she picked him up at the airport in September of 2008. "His luggage was one small bag," Donna recalled. He stayed with Donna for about two months and then left her for a younger woman: Michele Quinones.

He met Michele at a Home Depot store in Bradenton. They flirted and he returned the following day to flirt some more.

"He had these dogs, Chihuahuas, and they were so cute," she told me. "It was like everything I was interested in so was he." It wasn't long until the two quickly formed a bond of friendship which soon became a romantic relationship. Then, shortly before Thanksgiving in 2008, Delmer left Donna and moved in with Michele with whom he would later become engaged while still married to Donna.

For Michele, a young woman in her prime, filled with the excitement of being alive and the hope of having a family, life seemed to be moving in the right direction. However, in January of 2009, they both became unemployed. A financial struggle began with both searching for means to create income. It was not long until the strain caused their connection to each other to falter and an unexpected chill came into their relationship.

By April of 2009, their love for each other had mostly fizzled out. A heated exchange took place in which Michele bluntly accused Delmer of being neglectful of her. She also recognized the growing lack of desire for any intimacy between the pair. It would come to light later, that during this time, Delmer had other relationships. One of them with a neighbor that supposedly had resulted in a pregnancy that was later either terminated by abortion, miscarriage, or simply was never in existence. The details were never confirmed; however, the pregnancy was later alluded to in a jail house recording of a phone call between Delmer and his then mistress.

In 2013, as Michele and I sat drinking coffee at a small restaurant in North Port, the issue of the pregnancy came up and she grew visibly tense. She crushed one cigarette out, lit another, and, just after taking a deep drag and exhaling a blanketing cloud of smoke, then said to me, "It was all bullshit, pure bullshit."

I found overtime that Michele had no problem with being absolutely blunt.

She turned to me with eyes blazing anger. "All bullshit," she repeated. "Ha!" she began. "It's called a pussy trap." She leaned towards me, her face tight. "Get a man you want, get knocked up, or at least convince him that you are, then that's it! What's he gonna do? Huh? What's he gonna do?" Her brown curls bounced with every word.

    Michele and Delmer stayed together until August of 2009.

CHAPTER NINE

6 Months and 12 Attacks

The following list of cases in 2009 was established by a task force of police and sheriff detectives in the adjoining counties of Sarasota and Manatee because of similarities. Delmer Smith was regarded as a "person of interest" in all of these cases. However, it must be kept in mind that even though Delmer is suspected to be the assailant in all these cases there is automatically a prevailing belief that he is innocent unless found guilty of the crimes in a court of law. And, only two of these cases were brought to trial. Both resulted in convictions.

February 16TH, 2009 BPD[5] C# 09-1952

It is early morning and a solitary jogger finds herself suddenly pursued by a male who catches her near the intersection of 26th and Riverview in Bradenton. Before she can do anything to defend herself, or maneuver to escape, he is on her.

He hits her, stunning her, and forces her down behind a section of seawall where they become invisible to any passing traffic. There he beats her with rocks and pushes her to the ground. "Don't scream," he snarls, "or I'll shoot you." He waves a black handgun in front of her for emphasis.

He strips her jewelry from her and angrily asks, "Is that all you got?" Then he's gone, almost as quickly as he appeared. There was no clear evidence to support either an arrest or a conviction in this case.

---

[5] BPD = Bradenton Police Department.

February 22nd, 2009 SSO[6] C# 09-13624

A private residence on Osage Terrace in Sarasota is invaded at approximately 8:30 P.M.. The thief will remain within the dwelling for approximately ½ hour. It is believed the attacker gained access from an unlocked front door. He confronts an elderly woman and discovers her middle-aged daughter resides there as well. There is sexual violence that takes place in this case as well as a battery which has eerie foreshadows of the Briles' murder in less than six months' time. DNA links Delmer to this case but it remains untried. The victims no longer live in the area.

March 7th, 2009 SPD[7] C#09-12283

Midafternoon on Bougainvillea Street, in a residential area of Sarasota, a woman is attacked in her yard. She is caught from behind, beaten, and severely injured. She is told to, "Shut the fuck up." Her house will be ransacked and jewelry stolen. The attacker snarls, "I have a gun and will use it." Delmer is considered the attacker, but the case was not prosecuted in Sarasota because of the focus on SSO C# 09-19146.

March 11th, 2009 SPD C# 09-12974

Just prior to midnight there is an attempt to break into a home on Goldenrod Street in Sarasota. The female victim fights back until her husband joins in and together they drive the invader out from their residence. The attacker disappears into the night. No evidence to link Delmer to this crime, only comments that were made by the attacker and the attacker's method of quickly and violently establishing control.

March 13th, 2009 MSO C# 09-12659

---

[6] SSO = Sarasota Sheriff's Office
[7] SPD = Sarasota Police Department

A morning attack in Manatee County takes place on 19th Ave. NW just before 11 A.M.. The assailant entered the house through the open garage. He strikes the victim in the head with a handgun. The thief is in the house for approximately 25 minutes and takes cash and jewelry with him when he leaves. The victim is left unbound lying on the kitchen floor. No evidence to support an arrest or trial for Delmer but, again, there are similarities in the attack and comments made by the attacker.

March 14th, 2009 SSO C# 09-19146

Shortly after 10 P.M., the master bedroom window is forced and entry is gained into a home on Carmilfra Drive in Sarasota. This was prosecuted and earned Delmer Smith a life sentence. It also paved the way for the death sentence in murder case MSO C# 09-39137.

March 27th, 2009 MSO C# 09-15291

The attack takes place at approximately 12:30 noon in the 9700 block of Oak Run in Bradenton. The attacker gains entrance through the open garage. The thief displays a silver handgun with which he threatens the victim. His actions are interrupted by being surprised by the presence of another person in the house. He abruptly leaves having taken nothing.

March 31st, 2009 MSO C# 09-15975

At 2:30 P.M. an attack occurred in the 4300 block of 53rd Ave. (SR 70) in Bradenton. The victim opened the front door and she was immediately attacked. She sustained an injury to the back of the head. "Don't look at me or I'll kill you," the man said. "Is there anyone else here?" The man demanded money and jewelry and left in about 5 minutes with the cordless phone. The case had some similarities with others but not enough to bring about an arrest.

April 5th, 2009 SSO C# 09-25815

Murder! At 7:46 P.M. (the reported time) on Jo-Ann Drive in Sarasota a woman, Georgann Smith, is found beaten to death with a baseball bat. Delmer Smith is high on the list of suspects but for reasons revealed later, he was not prosecuted.

April 20th, 2009 BPD[8] C# 09-4938

It was just before noon when a man wearing a mask entered a home in a quiet residential area on 32nd Street NW in Bradenton. There will be two victims: a retired attorney and his wife. He will leave them horribly beaten. Injuries to the woman include face and head injuries, a broken nose, inner thigh and vaginal bruising. The husband's teeth will be knocked out along with head and facial injuries. The thief will take cell phones, cash, the woman's purse, wedding ring, earrings, a Kodak camera along with other items. The victims will be left lying on the floor hogtied. The case could have been tried, but the victims told the prosecutors it would be better for them to focus on the Briles' murder case.

May 25th, 2009 SSO C# 09-39374

Slightly before midnight the lady in a 12th floor condominium unit at Whispering Sands Drive in Sarasota was awakened to find an unknown male in her apartment. He beat her and dragged her naked through the condo from room to room while he looked for articles to steal. Twice he forced her out onto her 12th floor balcony where he angrily asked her, "Do you know how to fly?"

August 3rd, 2009 MSO C#09-39137

Kathy Briles returns midafternoon from shopping to the semi-secluded home that she and her husband have lived in, loved in, and raised their children in and meets a man unknown to her in the backyard. Months later, Delmer

---

[8] BPD = Bradenton Police Department

Smith was convicted of her brutal slaying and awarded the death penalty. This case is covered completely in Book Two: *The Woman in a Pink Top.*

CHAPTER TEN

Osage Terrace

On February 22, 2009 at approximately 2100 hours, the Sarasota County Sheriff's Department received a desperate call for assistance from a residence on Osage Terrace. Officers were immediately dispatched. Upon arrival, they found two adult female victims who had been robbed and assaulted: a mother and daughter.

The mother was eighty-two years of age and the daughter was fifty-three.

This would be the department's first contact with an unknown and violent predator that preferred to attack middle-aged and elderly females living by themselves. Cases such as this are always examined for the possibility that they may be linked to other crimes. Similarities are considered and profiles developed, and, except for the unusual sexual attack, Osage Terrace appeared not unlike any other such home invasion investigation. However, the violation of the victims sexually made this case standout from other unsolved home invasions.

Detective M. Lefebvre was originally dispatched to the scene. Detectives Mike Dumer and D. Tuck, known by their colleagues as the Duckmer team, were sent to the scene by Detective Sergeant Walsh the following day.

The detectives learned that the daughter, Carol D'Ambrosio, had been in her bedroom at the rear of the house and that her mother, Eileen McGrath, had been in the front room seated on the couch immediately prior to the attack. Carol said she heard her mother scream and the sound of her falling, and that she raced down the hall to find out what had happened.

Stepping into the front room, she found an unknown man standing over her mother holding the older woman by the hair on the back of her head. She said he was close to six feet tall and appeared to weigh over two hundred pounds. His elderly victim weighed only one hundred twenty-five pounds and was barely five foot five inches tall.

"He had a black wool ski mask over his face and head," the women both said simultaneously.

"He wore dark clothes," Carol added, turning to look at her mother who was being checked on by a nurse.

"Rubber gloves ... don't forget he had on rubber gloves," her mother joined in.

"And," they both said together with widened eyes, "he had a gun."

"It was aimed at me," Eileen said with a "huh" and a shake of her head. "Can you imagine that?" She looked up at the nurse who was hovering over her. "Why would he do such a thing?"

The nurse smiled reassuringly and shook his head as he gently placed a blood pressure cuff on the elderly woman's arm.

"He told me that he had a gun," Eileen said, "Well, it was right in my face for God's sake. He didn't need to tell me that. I could plainly see it. What did he think that I was blind or something?"

"I heard him tell mother that he had a gun and that she had better not scream or he'd shoot her," Carol told Lefebvre. "That was when he spotted me as I just came into the room."

"Who are you?" Carol demanded of the intruder as she quickly closed the distance between her and the attacker in an attempt to defend her elderly parent. "Leave my mother alone!"

The invader immediately reacted by letting go of McGrath and violently grabbing the younger woman. He forced his pistol into her mouth and ordered her to be silent and threatening to kill her if she did not comply. When he was satisfied he had them securely under his control, he began dragging them toward the closest bedroom, that of Ms. McGrath. Once there he forced the mother to lay on the bed and the daughter on the floor.

While keeping an eye on his victims, the thief, later identified as Delmer Smith, proceeded to turn his attention to the dresser drawers and closets in the room. Digging through them, he tossed unwanted contents onto the floor. Not finding much worth stealing in that room, he then expanded his search to the rest of the residence, collecting items as he went. At one point Smith returned to the bedroom to force Carol D'Ambrosio to accompany him to the residence's laundry room. "I need a screwdriver, bitch," he demanded. "Get me one. Now!"

Carol located the tool for him to force open the several small metal boxes that he previously had discovered. Taking from them what he desired, he began again searching the rest of the house while dragging Ms. D'Ambrosio by her hair along with him.

While ransacking the house he continued to threaten both women and demanded they turn over any medications to him. "I want your crack," he would say, "I need your crack. Where's your crack?" This was wording he used in several other attacks. However, when the women told him they had no such drugs, he then demanded they turn over any money they had so he could go buy drugs for himself. He also demanded access to any pepper the women might have, but D'Ambrosio did not know why he wanted it.

Finally, satisfied there was nothing else to steal, Delmer, still holding D'Ambrosio by the hair, dragged her into the front room where he roughly forced her to lie down on the floor. Looking for a means of binding her, he spotted a space heater nearby that had an extension cord running behind a chair. He grabbed the line and tied her with it. Once she was secured he needlessly began striking her with his fist and kicking her in the side. He then returned to the bedroom where he had left Carol's mother.

Standing in front of her, he pointed at her breasts and commented on them, "Not bad for an old lady." He then flipped the elderly woman onto her stomach, tied her with electrical cords, jerked down her panties, and then, while laughing; he repeatedly shoved the handle of the screwdriver Carol had given him to open the metal boxes with into the elderly woman's anus. After a moment, and without a word, he dropped the screwdriver onto the bed next to his victim and moved back to the front room where he again attacked Carol D'Ambrosio as she lay tied on the floor. He looked around for something to hit her with besides his hands and feet and seeing the space heater nearby grabbed it and swung striking her in the head. This scene of sudden and unexpected cruelty would foreshadow the violent death of Kathy Briles in August of 2009 in Manatee County.

D'Ambrosio, like Briles, was tied. Both women were unable to defend themselves. Both women were then beaten by being hit repeatedly with an object the attacker found nearby. D'Ambrosio is lucky she was not killed.

Her mother was sexually attacked with a foreign object inserted into her. This act will be repeated with other women.

Kent A. Wiehl, PhD., states in his book *The Psychopath Whisperer*[9] that the majority of serial killers are driven to murder "usually in association with sexual dominance or sadism." He states that they have a "paraphilia (a sexual-based disorder), like sexual sadism." He believes the urge to kill comes from that disorder. Their having a "lack of emotion, empathy, or guilt over their actions is derived from psychopathy." "I thought I was gonna die," Carol D'Ambrosio told the investigators. Her voice was soft and shaky. She looked to the floor and then back at the two men standing before her. "I—I thought this

---

[9] Kent A. Wiehl, PhD., *The Psychopath Whisperer,* Crown Publishers, Copyright © Kent A. Wiehl, PhD., ISBN 978-0-7704-3584-4, e-Book ISBN 978-0-7704-3585-1

man is going to kill me and my mother ... and why ... why?" Her voice rose as she recalled the terror and turned questioning, plaintive eyes up at the officers who shook their heads. There was no answer they could provide.

Apparently satisfied with the beating he had given Ms. D'Ambrosio, Delmer left the house, but not before spreading the pepper he had earlier asked for all around the floor with large concentrations at the front door both inside and outside. He then disappeared into the night taking with him their jewelry, cash, personal cell phones, and other items for a total theft of approximately $5,000. Several of these items would later be discovered in his possession.

As quiet descended on the residence, Carol realized the attacker had left and she began working on her bindings. Once relieved of the ties holding her, she ran to a neighbor's house and called 911 for help.

Both women were transported by ambulance to Sarasota Memorial Hospital where they were treated for injuries. Ms. McGrath was found to have suffered from bleeding on the brain, had a lower back injury, and then the sexual trauma. D'Ambrosio suffered a severe concussion, received ten stitches in her mouth, four broken ribs, bruising on her arms, chest and legs, and two black eyes.

In August 2009, items allegedly stolen from them were discovered left at the residence of a girlfriend of Delmer Smith's in Venice, Florida and were returned to them. Subsequent to that finding, other articles were located at another female friend's home in North Port, Florida and also returned to the victims once identified by them or the victim's relatives. Sadly, no one came forward to identify any items that belonged to Georgann Lee Smith of Jo An Drive. So that case remains open and unsolved.

CHAPTER ELEVEN

The Hunt Begins

As Detectives Dumer and Tuck returned from the hospital to the residence on Osage Terrace, no one, at that point, realized that this single occurrence in Sarasota County was the beginning of a broader based and more violent trail of crime. Twelve cases would be examined as being related based on certain criteria: statements, actions taken, threats made, items taken. It would eventually involve seven different law enforcement agencies and bring to light the failure of a highly regarded DNA recording system run by the FBI.

Back at Osage Terrace, the detectives split up and began their normal follow-ups with the officers first canvassing the surrounding neighborhood. Following this, Detective Dumer visited local pawn shops on both February 22nd and 23rd. He supplied them with descriptions of items taken from McGrath and D'Ambrosio. None of the pawnshops visited had any of the stolen articles, but said they would keep an eye out for them. Then, on the 23rd, Detectives Dumer and Tuck went to the Sarasota County Court House where they submitted a GPS precision location request for the stolen cell phones to the Hon. Rochelle Curly, a Twelfth Judicial Circuit Court Judge. It was granted and Detective Dumer scheduled a long-term "ping" on each unit, but all attempts were unsuccessful in making contact.

The detectives also immediately began contacting individuals in the area known by law enforcement for a variety of reasons. The hope was such contacts would aid in locating the person or persons responsible for the Osage

Terrace attack. In many cases, contacts with known criminals would result in profitable leads. But not in this case.

Whoever the thief was, clearly it was someone new. If not, then one of the existing members of the criminal element had learned how to make themselves invisible, not only to law enforcement, but to their contemporaries as well, or generated significant fear within that group to keep them quiet.

By the time the investigation closed, with Delmer Smith in custody, over 100 "persons of interest" would be contacted and interviewed. An unexpected byproduct of the investigation was the exposure of other crimes in the area resulting in multiple arrests. It also helped broaden the field database of contacts and events that might not have happened had it sadly not been for these cases.

On February 24th, Detective Dumer began researching the list of credit cards believed stolen from both of the Osage Terrace victims. He contacted the banks involved to see if any activity had occurred. The response was negative. He was then notified by Detective Tuck that one of the cards had been found by the owner, Eilene McGrath.

On the 25th of February, Dumer spent the day visiting the pawn brokers in Sarasota and also in Venice. Reports had come in that some of the items brought into the various stores were similar to items reportedly stolen from McGrath and D'Ambrosio. Dumer went to the stores and photographed the items to show to the mother and daughter. Neither woman identified any of the jewelry.

On March 7th a phone call to the Sarasota Police Department sent officers racing towards a home in an affluent area south of downtown Sarasota near Sarasota Memorial Hospital.

They arrived on Bougainvillea Street and found the fire department had also responded with EMTs who were inside the home treating the victim: Barbara Branning. Ms. Branning, a gentle schoolteacher, sustained injuries that were not only physical but psychological as well.

When I last spoke with her in 2012 she had still not fully recovered from the incident. I was stunned by the fact that she was still horribly haunted by what Delmer Smith had done to her that wonderfully warm day in February of 2009 when she was happily working in her yard, oblivious to the fact that she was being stalked by a predator, and would soon find herself to be violently attacked in broad daylight.

CHAPTER TWELVE
Bougainvillea Street

On March 7th, 2009, at approximately 1542 hours, the Sarasota Police Department (SPD) was alerted that an attack had taken place at a single-family residence located on Bougainvillea Street in a quiet neighborhood within the City limits not far from busy U. S. 41. A fifty-nine-year-old petite divorcee with graying hair who lived alone reported that she had been struck on the head by an unknown assailant while in her backyard near her Jacuzzi; and she had the lacerations to prove it. The woman, Barbara Branning, told the Officers who responded that she had been attacked from behind while doing some gardening and power washing at the rear of her home.

Detective Linda DeNiro's report stated that Branning required sutures to close the lacerations on her head and that she also sustained a broken nose. DeNiro added bluntly, "She was beaten brutally."

It was December of 2012 when Ms. Branning agreed to my interviewing her. Sensitive to her fears, I picked a local coffee shop in a book store near where she lived.

I arrived first and went straight to the sales counter ordering a large coffee. Then I turned my attention to finding a table that was slightly secluded but still in an open area so she would not feel confined. No sooner had I started to sit when I noticed a petite woman standing near the entrance to the coffee shop area. She had a hopeful look of anticipation on her face aimed directly at me. I was certain it was Ms. Branning, and so I smiled at her. She acknowledged the smile with a nod and walked quickly to where I stood saying, "Gordon? Are you Gordon?"

"Yes, and you must be Ms. Branning."

"Yes." She smiled warmly. "Call me Barbara." With that she extended a slender hand in greeting which I clasped in mine. I was amazed at how small and delicate it felt and knew that my hand swallowed hers. I sensed that I needed to be careful in order to not squeeze because I feared I would crush her fingers. I also noted that she was bending forward ever so slightly as if she was protecting herself in some way.

I found Barbara to be a striking woman. She was petite with lightly dusted grey hair that framed her delicately boned features. It was the type of cut, being neither too long nor too short, that a busy woman would choose. The style was simple. She could hop in the shower, hop out, towel off, and her hair would be mostly dry. A quick blast with a blow dryer, add some light makeup and out the door she could go without a lot of fuss.

Our hands separated and Barbara politely excused herself. "I'll be right back," she said, and pointed at the sales counter where a young woman stood, hands on her hips, waiting for the next customer.

In a few moments, the kindergarten teacher returned to our table with her drink and a warm smile that spoke directly from the gentleness of her soul. However, I could clearly see that the soft grin also held a hint of sadness. When I looked closely at her eyes, I found looking back at me a frightened human who I sensed was desperately seeking someone or something to fully trust again. My hope became that I could be gentle and wise enough to provide some immediate sense of security for her as we talked. I knew that such a sense would be fleeting and fragile. Nevertheless, I wanted her to feel safe and to be open to me.

"I'm very glad you decided to meet with me."

She smiled in return.

"I know going over this is not the most fun thing for you to do. My hope is that it will help you get rid of some of the pain left in its wake by simply talking about it."

"Let's hope." Again, she smiled, but it was somewhat weak, elusive in a odd way.

It was clear to me from our discussion on the phone, and then my meeting her in person, that trust and the ability to offer instant friendship had once been factors in her life. But Delmer Smith's attack had ripped those special qualities of her personality away. The violence he visited upon her had left her badly damaged.

Barbara leaned forward in her chair and took a drink of coffee, and then began. "I was in my house setting up my computer and had come outside to do some more work in the yard. It was a beautiful day, gorgeous, and too nice to be inside," she remembered, both hands wrapped around the coffee cup holding her latte.

"I'd been doing some gardening and had started power washing. You know," she laughed quietly while looking down at the floor, "if you start power washing it oddly becomes difficult to stop, and that was my case." Her eyes came up to meet mine. "So, I finished what I was doing with the computer and headed outdoors again. I was listening to my iPod and believed myself to be alone in the yard.

I don't think I had gotten very far outside when I was suddenly hit by something from behind. God, it hurt and I was —it was like I was blinded. Everything was dark yet there was—it is hard to explain." Her eyes asked for understanding and I nodded that I did.

She continued, "It was just a shattered experience of vision, light and dark. I could see light but couldn't discern items around me. I know I must have screamed," she said, "because he continued to hit me and yell, 'shut up. Shut up or I'll kill you.'"

She paused for a second, "I think it was fortunate that I had a hat on too when it happened. It was a like a straw hat with a broad brim and it softened the blow, fortunately.

Even so they later found glass in the wound which then became infected."

"The police report says you were hit and then you fell to the ground. Is that when you fell to the ground, right after you were hit?"

"No, no I didn't. Not right away. A bit later, not just then, it was later when I fell. But I was stunned. I didn't know what hit me. I thought something had fallen off the roof. And, I was having a difficult time seeing. Then he started to beat me. He hit me with his fist on the side of my face. I would learn later he fractured my jaw. And I think I must have moved somehow from where I had been hit to where I fell which was onto gravel. I recall the gravel and it hurt when I landed on it. And then he kicked me and struck me again as I lay there. I had a pair of glasses on and they came off and were destroyed most likely by having been stepped on."

The man, later identified as Delmer Smith through forensics, stripped the jewelry from her fingers and arms. One particular bracelet proved to be a problem and she helped him get it off, as she feared he would grow more violent if it persisted in not sliding off her arm. He also removed an iPod from her shirt pocket, and when he did his hand brushed over her breast causing her to recoil fearing a sexual assault. Sensing her thoughts, he told her with a snarl, "I'm not interested in any of that shit." However, he continued roughly pushing her around and shouting at her to be quiet as she lay on the ground in front of him.

"Shut the fuck up, bitch," he yelled at her. "Shut up!"

Delmer then got the stunned Branning to her feet and forced her to walk toward her residence. He was close behind her and he kept tight hold of her clothing to avoid her getting away.

Upon entering her home, pushed and shoved from behind, twisting, turning, staggering, she was horrified to find that it had been ransacked, evidently by the same attacker who was forcing her forward while threatening her with death if she caused him any trouble. She suddenly realized that he must have been in the house at the same time she had been. A chill ran through her to think that she had not been alone there in the quiet of her home, feeling secure, and yet—.

He led into her bedroom where he demanded that she turn over any jewelry she might have there. Additionally, he demanded that she surrender any narcotics she might have while shouting at her, "Give me the crack. Where is the crack?"

Branning described as best she could the clothes he was wearing: green pants, black canvas slip on sneakers with dark soles, including the fact that he was wearing blue gloves, and she believed he was carrying a gun. However, at no time was she able to see his face. In fact, she said, "I purposely kept my eyes lowered. I was afraid of a reprisal if I made eye contact with him."

He pushed her down on the bed and the fear of being raped once more entered her thoughts. However, his intent was to tie her up and he did so with remarkable speed using a dog leash that he had found within the residence. He then tied a scarf across her mouth as a gag and tied that to the leash. As soon as he was finished and satisfied she would not get free easily, he left her.

"I knew by the quickness and his ability in tying me that he must have done so many times before," she remarked.

She took another drink of coffee. "He left me lying tied up on the bed and went off to search through the house, I guess. I could hear him moving around for a bit and then silence. I don't know how long I laid there. I was really afraid he might come back. I didn't know where he was or what he was doing, but I didn't hear him anymore and after a while I began to wonder if he was still in the house."

As she had begun to suspect, Delmer had quietly slipped out of the house leaving her alone. When he left, he took with him items he could easily carry. She would later discover that her jewelry, several pieces of handcrafted silver, and an Apple Macintosh notebook computer where missing.

When she believed Delmer was no longer in the house, she went to work on her bindings, loosening them, sensing how they were tied, twisting and prying at them with her fingertips, finally setting herself free.

Once her bindings were removed, she attempted to stand, but dizziness caused everything to shift this way and then that. Her balance was suddenly difficult to maintain as she struggled to her feet.

She wanted to go outside, to get out of the house, she told me. But she was afraid that by leaving, by going outside, she would run into him and that he, discovering her being intent on escaping, would beat her even more seriously than he already had. She recounted having staggered through the house, pain from her injuries growing more severe.

Was he still there? She told me she wondered and feared he might be playing a game with her. The hallway outside the bedroom had become a tunnel of doom that she must pass through knowing that at any moment he might jump out of the shadows and beat on her again.

The sound of her movements, to her, was akin to that of a parade of elephants on the move. Every step was filled with its own terrors. Passing down the hall, moving through the residence, which seemed somehow to have become transformed into an alien, forbidding place, she made her way through the silent house searching for a safe way out. And then, she told me, "I saw daylight!"

A door was open. She didn't know if it was the back or the front she was so disoriented at that point. But, it didn't matter. It was open and she rushed for it stumbling, falling, staggering into the open air. The sunlight burst around her, blinding her momentarily. She placed her hands above her eyes shielding them and looked around frantic that he might be there waiting for her.

She was outside!

She spun, looking for her assailant through blurred vision, tears running down her cheeks. He was nowhere to be seen.

The first thought that came to her then, she said, was that of running to her neighbor's house; but she quickly chose not to because the woman next door was elderly. "I didn't want to involve her. I was afraid that if he was still around he might hurt her. So, instead, I began walking, stumbling, I guess, down the sidewalk toward the Tamiami Trail."

The pain from her injuries and the shock of being assaulted wore on her at every wavering step. She wanted to run but found she couldn't and knew she was lucky to be walking. "If you could call it walking," she said, "as it was more a stagger than a walk like I was drunk."

She was in agony, her face wet with tears. He body shook with fear that she would encounter him before she managed to find help. She knew she would not survive another vicious beating.

One house, then another, another, she stumbled over a crack in the sidewalk and cried from a sudden onslaught of pain that ripped through her. Another house passed. And then another. She could see the traffic through blurred vision; feel the vehicles moving past on the highway. Darkness swirled. A fog seemed to be wrapping itself about her. She feared she would pass out.

She stared through hazy vision at the traffic flying past at the intersection half a block from her. Then it was a quarter block—and then thirty feet—then twenty! She could see the drivers, but they didn't seem to see her, to notice her. It was like she wasn't there. "Why won't they look at me?" her mind screamed. "Someone ... someone, please see me." She tripped—a bad break in the sidewalk. She stared at it not really comprehending.

She nearly twisted her ankle. There was gravel and pieces of loose cement lying at her feet. Pain raced through her shoulders and neck as she turned her head looking back to make sure he was not pursing her. Her face, by now, was a raging fire of agony. The back of her head felt as if her skull had been laid bare and cracked open. She was certain she was bleeding.

She forced herself to walk on. Ten feet remained to the corner. She was feeling weak and was afraid she would fall before she got to the sidewalk's end—and then five feet remained. She envisioned that she would collapse and that he would then find her in a fetal position and that no one would see them struggling as he pulled her back to the house that she now feared being anywhere near. Then, almost surprisingly, she was there—a foot—less, from the curb.

A flash of color shot past close before her, dizzying, assaulting her sense of balance. Then another and another passed in a blur. Wind from passing cars tugging at her clothing in bursts. Her hair swept one way and then the other. Dirt swirling in the air choked her as sand particles peppering her skin and clothing. Exhaust fumes eddying about her, clinging to her skin, her hair, being sucked into her lungs in as she gasped for air.

The Tamiami Trail surged with traffic inches away from where she stood reeling back and forth and side to side facing the six lane thoroughfare. She sensed she was slipping further into shock and near the moment she would black out. "Look at me," she told me her mind begged, trying to nonverbally reach out to the passing drivers, to communicate her need for help, mentally imploring them to stop. "Please stop! Please look! Please see me!"

All the while wondering why they continued to pass her by. It was as though she was a ghost and not visible to them or even there. "Look at me! Please, someone look at me." She gazed out through her blurred vision. She felt desperate, alone. Her arm was weakly raised in the air trying to wave at those driving past. She was not aware that she had managed to bring attention to herself. She staggered around in shock and pain nearly falling off the curb and into the path of oncoming traffic.

But, almost immediately, several of the passing drivers clamped down on their brakes and were pulling over to the curb, then making their way back to assist her. She recalled through the fog that was enveloping her of hearing the voice of one woman asking, "Is she drunk?" Other voices quickly responded that she was not. Her physical injuries were quite evident. Then she was startled to hear her name being spoken.

"Ms. Branning? Is that you?" The familiar voice of a young woman reached through the babble of voices and drew Barbara's attention to the source.

She looked up through the haze that was clouding her vision and recognized one of her former students. "Yes," she said weakly. "I've been attacked. I need help."

She paused, recalling the incident, and then continued, "So my student and the others helped me. Someone called the police." She smiled.

After a moment, I continued with my questions. "And so you then landed in the hospital for treatment for your injuries."

"Yes."

"I believe you said he hit you on the back of the head with a bottle, is that correct?"

"Yes. He struck me with a bottle. It was a beer bottle. He must've been drinking from it."

"So, it must have been empty, or at least mostly so, when he hit you."

"Yes, thank God. I'm sure if it had been full the blow would have been fatal. When they treated me at the hospital they were surprised to find that I had glass embedded in my scalp. They had to take it out with tweezers. And then the wound became infected and I had to have treatment for that."

"But you sustained other injuries, am I correct?"

She looked at me with a slight sad smile and sighed. "Yes. I had a fractured jaw. I had numerous bruises and scrapes. The infection in my scalp was not easy to get rid of. And, I am now a diabetic."

"You believe your diabetes is a result of having been attacked?"

"Yes! I'm sure of it. Plus I suffer from PTSD."

"PTSD, by that you mean…"

"Post-traumatic Stress Disorder," she explained. "Delmer Smith altered my life. I'm still trying to get it back. I don't think that most people realize the horror a person feels when being so attacked."

"No, you're right, they don't."

"Your entire life is torn apart. Everything is changed. Now everything is questioned. You no longer feel safe. You no longer feel secure in your own residence. All that has been stolen from you. It is not just the material things that have been taken. Oh yes, those things matter. They're part of your history, who you are, and they matter. However, everything else in your life is suddenly distorted."

"I'm sure. That was a very traumatic event you lived through. It had to affect you. I'm curious about your house … where you lived ... do you still live there? … I would think it would be very hard to have suffered such a harrowing event, to have had the sanctity and security of your home violated to be able to remain there."

She sat back in her seat, her eyes growing sad, "I've moved. I can't live there. I've tried to erase the event from my mind but I can't. I've moved in with a friend and I feel safer. I don't think I can ever live alone again."

"Did you take anything with you left? I believe you took your Jacuzzi is that right?"

"Yes, I took the Jacuzzi. But, I had to paint the exterior as I did not want it or anything that I brought with me to remind me of what happened that day."

We sat and talked for well over an hour that evening about her life as it was then. She spoke of her job as a teacher, her love of children. She told me she now has a need for silence and protection from the daily stresses of life she once faced easily prior to her having been attacked. Ms. Branning told me she is afraid most of the time and that she hates it when someone will tell her that she should, "get over it." Those of us who know trauma know it does not work that way.

Delmer Smith left a permanent mark on her life, both physically and psychologically.

We parted friends and pledged to stay in touch. I would next see her in Bradenton, Florida, in 2013 in court when Delmer was sentenced to die for having murdered Kathy Briles.

CHAPTER THIRTEEN

Goldenrod Street

On March 11th, 2009, just three days after the Bougainvillea attack, at about 2341 hours a call came into the Sarasota Police Department (SPD) from a residence on Goldenrod Street. Goldenrod is two streets away from Bougainvillea. It is also just a short distance from U.S. 41.

The residents reported an intruder wearing a mask and dark clothing and possibly carrying a pistol, suddenly appeared through unlocked French doors and attacked the fifty-year old woman who lived there.

Turning to face the masked trespasser who suddenly appeared near her, the woman was staggered momentarily by a blow to her head. She later reported to Sarasota Police Detectives that what struck her "looked like a small handgun."

"Are you alone?" The intruder demanded coldly as he made to grab her.

"Yes," she lied, mildly staggered by the glancing strike, but still in command of her thoughts.

She knew her husband was down the hall in a bedroom. By lying she hoped to protect him and give him the opportunity to go for help; and then she made the decision to fight. Her elbow came up and she swung a karate-like strike at the intruder's face that startled him but did little else to cause him any harm. He cursed at her and made a grab for her threatening to hurt her if she continued to resist. Nevertheless, she continued to fight fearlessly, wrestling against his strength, trying to break free of his grip.

As they struggled, the sound of their fight was loud enough that the woman's husband heard the commotion and called out asking if his wife was okay. That startled the intruder who then turned and ran from the house, leaving through the same French doors through which he had entered the house. The couple immediately phoned the Police Department.

A K-9 was brought to the home and it began to search going out the French doors the assailant had entered and left. The dog traveled several blocks trailing the individual believed to have broken into the Goldenrod Street home; however, it finally lost the scent at a point most likely where the man entered a vehicle used to leave the area.

On March 12th, Detectives L. DeNiro and Grant of the SPD met with Detectives Dumer and Tuck. Similarities had been discovered between the Bougainvillea attack and the Osage Terrace home invasion that needed to be discussed. Also, another recent case in Manatee County was found to have similarities to the two in Sarasota County. This placed both counties on alert to the possibility that law enforcement was dealing with one perpetrator who was traveling from county to county.

CHAPTER FOURTEEN

Carmilfra Drive

On the night of March 14th, an attack occurred at a residence on Carmilfra Drive. The home, located within a stone's toss to U.S. 41, with Phillippi Creek running behind it. The victim, Nicole Marshall[10], was female, white, petite, and over fifty. The attacker demanded "crack," money, and jewelry. He showed that he was armed and threatened to kill her. When he left, she was tied with electrical cords and left lying in the middle of the front room floor. She was fearful that she might strangle herself in trying to escape.

Even small movements seemed to tighten the cords, particularly the ones that ran from her neck, down across her back, to where her legs were tied. She lay on her stomach and prayed someone would find her or that she would be able to get the electrical cords to slip. Slippage of the plastic on plastic would allow her the opportunity to, perhaps, get free. It was worth a chance, but dangerous. In either event, wait for help or take the gamble and try to free herself, death was a possibility. She chose to risk freeing herself and set about to get the electrical cords to loosen their hold by getting the plastic to slip, thereby creating a loose fitting that she could then capitalize on by expanding the opening.

This home invasion became the most important of all the Sarasota cases as it yielded a sample of Delmer Smith's DNA found in a drop of sweat. That evidence, along with identification of property stolen from the victim that night, led to the trial that resulted in Delmer being sentenced to

---

[10] Marshall is an alias at the request of the victim.

life in prison for the break-in and is covered in the next part of the book.

It was almost midnight when the phone rang at the home of Sarasota Sheriff's Detective Michael Dumer. He was notified by Sergeant Tutko that a home invasion had occurred at 5240 Carmilfra Drive. His presence was requested at the scene. He was informed that both forensic services and the victim's assistance departments were in route. Sergeant Tutko told him that the victim had reported an unknown male suspect had attacked her at approximately 2210 hours while she sat watching TV on her couch. The suspect had made off with a variety of objects leaving the victim tied up with electrical television cables. She had managed to work herself free and had escaped to a neighbor's house. Dumer immediately drove to the crime scene.

Once there, he learned the victim was being transported to Sarasota Memorial Hospital with a possible heart attack. Unable to speak with her, he then spoke to Tutko who informed him that the scene had been cleared and secured.

Officer Thomas approached Dumer and told him that he had been one of the first officers to arrive. He and an officer named Swinney had secured the area and placed crime scene tape around the residence. While they stood talking, Dumer made note of the tape's presence, a fact he would later testify about. Even with all the security and the compliance with the rules of evidence protection in place, an unforeseen problem would occur.

Unknown to anyone at that time, and completely unexpected, Officers Thomas and Swinney would later refuse to supply samples of their DNA. Those samples were requested to eliminate any DNA found for which there was no known donor. To have an unknown donor present would allow a sharp defense attorney the opportunity to say to a Jury that perhaps the unknown donor was the criminal and not the defendant. Their refusal was an act that sent shock waves through not only the Sheriff's Office, the State Attorney's Office, but also brought about national attention to the case.

While the men stood and talked, Sergeant Rhonda DiFranco of the forensics department arrived and set up to enter the crime scene. Dumer had been told he could enter by Sergeant Tutko, but he declined wanting to wait for DiFranco to arrive.

DiFranco began with examining the area surrounding the home and then entered with Dumer close behind, but he stopped before going too far into the house fearing he might accidentally cause contamination and left DiFranco to process the scene.

On March 15th, at 2 A.M., Dumer was finally able to meet with the victim, Nicole Marshall., and with her neighbor, Carrie Mackey, who was present in the hospital room with her. Nicole Marshall told Dumer that she had been alone in the house when an unknown male suddenly attacked her. The detective listened carefully to Marshall as she told him the details of the attack. Certain comments began to sound to the detective like he had heard them before. The size of the attacker, remarks made by the suspect, and his actions all seemed to point to this being one individual. But who?

He was unaware of anyone in the criminal element in Sarasota that fit the profile being developed. Dumer and Walsh both concluded that this might be someone new to the scene and extremely dangerous. They began talking with the people who might know of this new person, street people, convicted people, people in general who had their ears open, but nothing. This person was hidden. They hoped he would surface before the violence increased and someone was killed.

Detective Dumer launched into an investigation fully committed to solving the crime. He began checking with pawnshops for items that could belong to Marshall. He and other officers canvassed the neighborhood looking for answers. He reviewed the notes on Osage Terrace, noting similarities. Then there were more interviews with the victim and her husband. He spent time on the phone to internet services about the stolen computer, searching for Skype communications to or from the machine. Other contacts were made with the City Police, meetings with other detectives, and activities that shook the criminal trees in Sarasota shaking out those individuals who needed to be in jail.

Even so, connecting with the other departments was a slow process. On April 2nd, Dumer and Sergeant Walsh began reviewing and comparing case reports from the other three local law enforcement agencies: The Sarasota Police Department, the Bradenton Police Department, and the Manatee County Sheriff's Office.

On April 9nth, Walsh assigned Dumer to participate in a multi-jurisdictional effort to review those cases that appeared to be similar. It was time the local jurisdictions came together in a joint effort to bring this person to justice.

CHAPTER FIFTEEN
Terror Roams a Neighborhood

The attack on Barbara Branning in the upscale residential area near Sarasota Memorial Hospital ignited a wave of terror that did not abate until after Delmer Smith had been arrested and convicted of the home invasion on Carmilfra Drive. According to Lisa Evans, a nurse who lived in the neighborhood, "The citizens who lived in the area received neighborhood watch notices of what the attacker may have looked like. Everyone was alert," she said.

Janna, a home health care physical therapist, told me that during her rounds visiting patients in the area she found the fear to be "almost palpable." She had always phoned before visiting any client to let them know she was on the way. "Even after he was caught, people still were very cautious about making sure their homes were locked," she told me.

Lisa Evans, a Registered Nurse said, "All of the neighbors were kept aware by both the media news organizations and the neighborhood watch system." Neighborhood watch provided the neighbors with descriptions of the attacker. "Several of my neighbors," she said, "took to walking their dogs at the same time. We truly feared strangers in the neighborhood and were nervous when alone." That held particularly true for those aged 50 and up and living alone, as they were apparently the preferred target.

CHAPTER SIXTEEN

Jo-An Drive

On April 6th Detective Dumer was notified that a homicide had been committed sometime between April 5th and April 6th at a single family residence on Jo An Drive. Detective C. Dusseau led the investigation concerning the brutal death of Georgann Lee Smith. What she and other investigators found when they entered the home stunned them.

It was a horrific scene that investigators were called to view and process in a quiet neighborhood unknown for such scenes of incredible violence. It was obvious to anyone who observed the scene that the victim, a martial artist with two black belts, had put up a valiant, desperate, but losing fight for her life. The woman's friends said she kept a baseball bat near the front door for protection. Law enforcement personnel determined that Georgann's attacker had managed to get the bat away from her and had then used it on her.

According to a friend of Georgann, who viewed the interior of the house, the struggle to survive had moved room to room leaving blood splattered walls, furniture, and floors. Georgann was found naked in a pool of her own blood. Her battered, tortured body was found lying half on a soiled mattress that she had been using to sleep on in the front room of her home, as her bedroom was too hot.

Word slipped out that during the attack, she had been sexually assaulted with a plastic sailboat. Her attacker had inserted it into her vagina while she was alive, and then once again when dead. The assault was so violent that her bladder had been perforated.

The Assistant State Attorney's office, faced with the problem of tying Delmer Smith to the actual murder, declined to prosecute him. This case remains open in the hope of finding the proof needed to arrest, charge, and try Smith successfully for the crime. According to a variety of sources, the problem is twofold.

First, there is a lack of identifiable male DNA. There was so much of Georgann's blood present that whatever male DNA there was blended with hers to the extent that a complete profile could not be established for her attacker. They found male DNA, but not enough of it.

The second part is the lack of identification by family, friends, and neighbors of articles taken from Georgann's home and found in Smith's storage locker in Venice, FL. Not one person has come forward and positively identified any of her belongings, so the case remains open.

CHAPTER SEVENTEEN

Do You Know How to Fly?

On the 26th of May, at approximately 0056 hours, a frantic 911 call for help sent several sheriff deputies racing to 20 Whispering Sands Drive on Siesta Key. They were directed to unit 1206 where they discovered a battered 62-year old divorcee, Beth Brady.

Beth Brady reported having been robbed, beaten, threatened with a horrifying death, and sexually assaulted by an unknown male. Realizing her need for medical attention, the responding officers called for an ambulance and the 62-year-old-woman was transported to Sarasota Memorial Hospital where Detective Rhonda DiFranco met her at 0800 to photograph her injuries and collect the rape kit that had been performed on her by an attendant nurse. In the meantime, Crime Scene Technician Jarecki was processing the scene taking photographs and looking for prints or other evidence.

Brady was also interviewed at Sarasota Memorial by Detective M. LeFebvre and Detective Kaspar who filed reports with Sergeant Walsh and copied Detective Dumer. Detective Tuck joined in the investigation along with Detective McGath. They conducted interviews with neighbors and others and chased down tips. Tuck was assigned to help a US Marshall with surveillance on a possible suspect who was known to Brady but who was later determined to not be the assailant. Dumer was kept updated by everyone working the case because of the belief that the assailant was the same man that had committed the prior attacks.

When Kaspar arrived at the hospital at approximately 0500, she met with Brady in the Emergency Room where she was being kept for observation. Finding Brady able to talk, Kaspar then conducted a recorded interview during which Brady sobbingly detailed the events of the prior day and evening leading up to and including the attack.

Reviewing the interview, Dumer, Walsh, and others noted striking similarities in what Brady said had happened to her to that which had taken place in several other attacks in Sarasota and, they had recently learned, also in Manatee County.

The attacker repeatedly demanded that the victims turn over their "coke" and any money they might have. They were also constantly threatened with death if they did not do exactly as told. When the thief had come to believe there was nothing left of value to take, he then would deliver a senseless and brutal beating to the victim who was securely tied and unable to defend themselves. In more than one case the victims had to endure depraved sexual acts. It was beginning to become clear to law enforcement that they were after someone who was fairly intelligent but extremely violent. Yet, nothing they had so far was pointing the way to an identifiable person.

Whoever it was they were looking for had shown they were experienced in covering their tracks. None of the street informants were helpful. It was, for the detectives, as if they were chasing someone who did not exist. But, they had his sweat. And, because of that, they had his DNA. So, he was real. He wasn't a ghost. He wasn't someone who didn't exist. They just needed another mistake on his part to happen; and then, hopefully, before he could attack again, they would have him in the flesh as well.

Like the other victims, Beth was a white female. She was in the right age group at 62. She was short at 5'3", but slightly heavy at 162 pounds. And, most importantly, she lived alone and likely would put up little defense. The only thing that set her apart from the others was her penchant for visiting local bars where she played pool and picked up men.

So it was that on May 25th, 2009, at just past 2330 hours, the attractive 62-year-old Beth Marie Brady had been asleep when something woke her. It was an odd noise, "a thump or a bump," as she described it, not recalling exactly as she was sleepy at the time.

At first, she thought the wind had blown a window curtain into a lamp. But then, as she peered down the semi-dark hallway, she thought she saw movement "right near the dining room table." Something large moved and slipped into the shadows.

"Okay and did this person say anything to you? Or did you speak first?" Kaspar asked.

Her sleepiness was now erased, replaced by a cold chill. She yelled out, "Who's there?"

"Police!" came the sharp, loud reply.

Confusion.

What?

Police?

What would police be doing in her apartment, unannounced, in the dark, at close to midnight? It didn't make sense to her.

She shook her head in disbelief. A cold feeling immediately swept over her. She stepped slightly backwards, attempting to retreat further into her bedroom even though there was no place there where she could hide.

Then, suddenly, before Beth could respond or make any sound, someone wearing black charged out of the shadows directly at her. "He attacked me like a bull."

The attacker was upon her immediately and he threw her first up against a wall, stunning her. A neighbor reported hearing a loud "thud" but thought it was nothing to be concerned about and fell back asleep.

He then twisted her violently about and forced her face down onto her bed. There the barrel of a handgun was placed against her temple.

"I'm going to blow your brains out if you don't do exactly what I say," a man's voice snarled, his face close to her ear. "No screaming, no crying, I want your money. I want your jewelry. I know who you are, a rich bitch."

The assailant held her face down on the bed for a few moments longer, then struck her in the ribs with his gun as she struggled to be free. Suddenly he pulled her legs apart and bending her knees backwards, thrust himself up against her as if he were having sex with her while he was fully clothed and she was in her nightgown.

He then asked her about a safe. "Where is it," he snapped at her. She told him and then he dragged her by her hair to that location where she opened it to reveal an empty space. Furious, he pushed and pulled her outside the front door and pushed her up against and slightly over the balcony while asking with a hiss, "Do you know how to fly?" Sobbing, she begged him to not drop her for she would surely die.

He pulled her back off the railing and roughly dragged her back inside her apartment where, just inside the door, he ordered her to remove her nightie at the doorway. Beth was then taken into the dining room where she surrendered what cash she had. It still wasn't enough to appease him.

He next demanded her rings, and when she couldn't get them off, he went to the kitchen and came back with soap and a knife and said, "If I can't get the rings off with soap, I'll cut your fingers off. I want those rings."

The soap helped. He was able to pull off three of her rings, but the fourth would not move and so, frightened that he would cut her, she used her teeth to grab it and pull until it slid off while he stood over her. As soon as he had the rings in his possession, he produced a small decorative blue bottle he had found in the kitchen. He forced her to sit and then pushed the bottle inside her mouth.

"Suck it like a dick," he demanded, but he pushed it too far into her mouth and she gagged and pushed his hand away. In retaliation, he forced her down on the floor and rammed the bottle into her vagina while saying to her, "I hear you like it in the ass too."

"Please don't do that," she begged, crying out. "You're gonna kill me. You're gonna rip me open." Ignoring her pleas, he continued forcing the bottle into her until she began bleeding.

He then grabbed a handful of her hair and dragged her back to the balcony where he again threatened to drop her over the railing. "Are you ready to meet your maker?" he snarled at her.

She broke into sobbing, clinging to him as best she could. He told her to stop crying while dragging her back off the railing. He then forced her back into her bedroom where he hit her knocking her out. She came to later to find he had tied her up before he left the apartment taking with him her cash, rings, and several other items he thought were of value and could be sold.

CHAPTER EIGHTEEN
Terra Ceia

She lay face down.
At least, that is how *they* found her body—face down.

They being her husband and the hastily-established Manatee County team of sheriff's deputies, forensic personnel, fire department paramedics, and the county coroner's office staff that had been called into service on August 3rd, 2009, in the middle of the night. It was their job to descend on the horrifying scene at a residence in a quiet neighborhood in response to her husband's frantic 911 call.

Manatee County 911, what is the nature of your emergency? [11]

The operator's voice was calm, well-practiced, having responded thousands of times in the same cool manner during stressful telephone calls as this would soon become.

Caller: (Unintelligible) I just got home, my wife is on the floor!

The voice was breathless, filled with shock and terror.

It was slightly past 3 P.M. when Kathy Briles drove off U.S. 19 on Terra Ceia Island onto Bayshore Drive. Her car was loaded with groceries and other items that she had been putting together during the day for a special dinner with her husband; Dr. James "Jim" Briles, a local physician who she knew was seeing patients at his office in Palmetto and, most likely, would not get home until late as it was his

---

[11] The 911 call posted here and in subsequent pages was taken directly from the court transcript.

custom to spend as much time with his patients at the office and at the hospital as he possibly could.

Their home was not far from the intersection of 19 and Bayshore. It was an old wood frame home that sat back off the road and overlooked Terra Ceia Bay. It was a refuge from the world not only for the Briles but for a large collection of stray cats and one stray dog. Kathy was an animal lover and would find and bring home feral cats in need of love and attention. The dog had just showed up one day and stood in the road blocking Jim's pickup truck. Finally, after several days of the same routine, Kathy took food and blankets out to the dog who soon, like the cats, became a permanent family member watched over closely and lovingly by Kathy and Jim.

As she approached their home, she noted a car she was not familiar with parked in front of the house in the spot she always used. Not overly concerned about who the owner might be, because they were having work done on the house, she parked and went to find the other car's driver.

Calling out "hello," she went behind the house and came into contact with Delmer in the backyard. She would have approached him without any fear and asked him why was he there, what he was doing. Could she help him in some way? Weeks later her husband would locate her missing set of house and car keys in the grass not far from the storage shed that had been broken into and, from which, the very duct tape used by her assailant to tie her up had been stolen from. They soon realized that at that exact spot, where the glint of the metal keys had caught their eyes, hidden, as they were in a confusion of blades of grass, that Kathy had been initially attacked and that her desperate fight to remain alive had begun.

Three years after the Manatee County 911 system recorded the emotion-filled phone call from a distraught

James Briles, the prosecution introduced the tape as evidence in Case No. 2010-CF-000479, The State of Florida vs. Delmer Smith, a murder case.

The Court, Jury, and gallery would sit and listen completely absorbed by the conversation being played back for them. While the horror of the night slowly became indelibly evident for everyone else in the room, the defendant appeared indifferent. He spent most of his time looking at the highly-polished wooden conference table-top where he sat, or at his handcuffed hands which were kept low behind the table so the Jury could not see them.

He focused on them, turning them over, then right side up. He twisted them one way, then another, carefully examining each hand like a person would checking to see if they might need to wash them. Perhaps, in this case, to remove the invisible stain and erase the scent of his victim's blood that only he was conscious of.

The 911 operator immediately obtained the caller's name, address, and phone number. He then went on to ask questions of Briles concerning the nature of his call and then:

Briles: (unintelligible) she's tied up. It looks like someone hit her on the head with something here. I don't know. It's just....

His voice stumbled, falling away, trailing off. His breathing was haggard, short gasps for air recorded and now played for the courtroom.

911: Are you with her now?

Briles: Yeah (unintelligible)—I think she's already dead!

911: How old is she?

Briles: Kathy is in her — 40s. She was — born in — 1960. Holy — shit. Please (unintelligible)....

The painful distress in the caller's voice was clearly palpable as it tumbled into a stumbling pile of meaningless garble.

All who sat in the relative safety and comfort of oak-paneled courtroom 5-A of Florida's Twelfth Circuit that day in Manatee County and listened to the replay of the taped telephone call made that alarming night would never forget what was said; nor would they ever be able to erase from their memories the emotions they felt individually as a result of hearing the heartbreaking descriptions of the scene as addressed in that tragic recording.

The autopsy of Kathy would reveal that there were two periods of intense physical abuse. The first caused internal tissue tears that, in order for her to have survived, needed immediate medical care. The second violent attack was designed to bring about death.

It is August 6th, 2012 and Dr. Wilson Broussard is on the stand being questioned by Mr. Iten. The prosecutor refers to a photograph of one of Kathy's organs. It had been taken during the autopsy of Mrs. Briles. Iten asked Broussard to explain what the photo depicted.

"This is a laceration or tear of the liver in the abdomen," the doctor testified. He went on to say that it was "moderate to large, approximately five, six centimeters of laceration between the two liver lobes." He added that there was blood in the abdomen found in a liquid state as opposed to being "clotted." The presence of the blood in the abdominal cavity told him that at the time of the inJury "... she was still living, you know, her heart beating."

The question that the prosecution wanted answered then was what caused the inJury, and what was the survivability of such an inJury.

"Now, did you see any corresponding external injury on the body that related to this internal injury?" Iten asked pointing to the picture on display.

"No, I did not."

"So, what does that tell you?"

"Either something very, you know, blunt hit that area, the clothing probably masked any changes that might have abraded the skin. So something sharp didn't hit that area."

At the time of the investigation, an antique sewing machine had been found on the floor near Kathy's body. It had a significant amount of Kathy's blood on it.

"How about the sewing machine," Iten wondered aloud. Was the absence of an external injury with the related internal injury sufficient for Broussard to determine if the sewing machine would have caused it?

"It seems like it, to me, if the sewing machine would have caused this, it would have left an external mark, either from the backside or from the front."

"So, what would cause an injury like this?" Iten asked slowly.

"Again, something blunt, a kick, a knee to the abdomen." Broussard replied calmly.

Iten was silent for several seconds. He looked down at the floor and then back up at the doctor. He wanted to establish, needed to establish, that the violence suffered by the abdomen would have proved to be fatal without any other injuries. "By itself," he then asked, "would have this injury been survivable?"

The doctor leaned forward in his chair. "Not without medical attention."

"So with quick medical attention, could it have been survivable?"

The doctor cleared his throat, hesitating with his answer. Then quietly and carefully he replied while slowly nodding his head. "Yes, like very quick."

The murder trial started August 8th, 2012 and is reviewed in *Book Two, Predator: The Man Who Didn't Exist, The Woman in a Pink Top*

CHAPTER NINETEEN

Tavern on the Island

The Venice Police Department received a call about 0130 hours on August 14th, 2009 concerning a fight at the TOTI (Tavern on The Island), a combination gay, straight, and bisexual bar. The caller, struggling to be heard over angry shouts coming from the patrons inside the crowded bar, reported that there had been an altercation between three men and that two were injured with one of them needing immediate medical attention. The third male had left the bar and his location was unknown.

Officers Guinart and Long were dispatched at 0147 and found 30-year-old Jason Byrne along with 28-year-old Joshua Hoogerhyde waiting for them. Both men had injuries. Jason had blood trickling from his nose. His face was puffy with swelling and reddish in color. Joshua also had swelling on his face that was reddish as well. He claimed that he had been struck just the once in the face while Jason had been struck multiple times.

According to Byrne, Hoogerhyde, and multiple witnesses, the fight started when Bryne's girlfriend (Erin Tripp, age 30) had been dancing with Hoogerhyde's girlfriend. Byrne noticed that Delmer Smith was filming them from the stage where a deejay (Michele Quinones) was playing music.

Byrne approached Delmer asking that he stop taking unsolicited pictures of his girlfriend. Angry words were exchanged and Delmer suddenly grabbed Byrne by the throat and began pummeling him with repeated blows to the head and face. Other bar patrons, including Hoogerhyde and Byrne's girlfriend, rushed to the defense of Byrne who appeared stunned and unable to defend himself.

Hoogerhyde pressed his way through the growing crowd on the dance floor. He quickly approached the raised platform where the melee was boiling over hoping to intervene and help his friend Byrne. Delmer, sensing Hoogerhyde's movement in his direction, quickly released Byrne who immediately slumped into the arms of those around him.

Among those attempting to protect the stunned Byrne was his girlfriend Erin. She had been screaming for the men to stop fighting and, in desperation, fearlessly pushed herself in-between them in an attempt to use her body to shield Byrne from the savage beating he was receiving.

Delmer immediately retaliated against her striking her several times in an attempt to make her back away. The blows stunned her, but not enough to cause her to stop shouting at her attacker or from trying to drag Byrne away from Delmer's hammering, flying fists.

Dropping Byrne, Delmer stood his ground mid-stage in a well-practiced fighting stance, feet planted, his body balanced, fingers tightly curled into fists, head lowered slightly, his jaw tight with anger, eyes dark with hostility. He surveyed the crowd that had filled in the dance floor surging, mob like, in his direction with angry comments being hurled at him. In their midst, Joshua Hoogerhyde was pressing his way through the swarm of shouting people. Hoogerhyde finally had gotten one foot up on the stage and was stepping forward with the other when Delmer hit him with a solid blow to the face. Hoogerhyde staggered backwards from the lightening attack falling off the stage but was caught by those behind him.

With the help of the crowd who pushed him forward, Hoogerhyde managed to regain his footing on the raised platform. But just as he started to stand, he was immediately met with another huge blow by Delmer that drove him backwards again.

Realizing he needed to leave, Delmer glanced at Quinones and then stepped down from the stage. The crowd awkwardly made a narrow path for him to move through while some shouted obscenities. No one attempted to stop him.

CHAPTER TWENTY
Arrest and Discovery

By the time Officers Guinart and Long arrived, Delmer had already left the tavern. However, he was summoned back by Quinones at the request of the police who wanted his explanation of what had taken place. Delmer admitted filming the woman and striking the first man, Byrne. He told the investigating officers that he had been forced to defend himself and Quinones when Byrne rushed the stage. However, the Tavern had video surveillance equipment running and once the police reviewed that evidence they arrested Delmer. He was charged with aggravated battery and was incarcerated in the Sarasota County Jail, but was released four days later on August 18th having posted a $15,000 bond. However, authorities would soon discover an error in his release.

At the time he bonded out, the judicial system in Sarasota County was not aware that he was on federal parole from his conviction for bank robbery. The Aggravated Battery charge violated that probation and a warrant for his arrest was issued by the United States Marshall's office in Tampa. The Venice Police Department rearrested Delmer on September 10th, and transferred him to the Pinellas County Jail pending processing of the federal parole violation.

The federal arrest afforded law enforcement the opportunity to make inquiry about his belongings. At the time he was arrested for the parole violation, he was no longer living with Quinones but had moved in with a woman named Shannon Barrett in Venice. She turned

Delmer's property over to the Venice Police Department as soon as she knew of the arrest.

On September 15th, Captain T. McNutty of the Venice PD phoned Mike Dumer. The captain was aware that Dumer was looking for several items taken in home invasions in the Sarasota area. He contacted the detective telling him that they had obtained an Apple Macintosh notebook and other items that Dumer might wish to look at.

Dumer quickly responded by contacting SPD detective Linda DeNiro, and the two drove together to the Venice PD where they met with McNutty who instructed Venice Lt. R. Solanes to bring out from the department's storage two computers that had been dropped off by Barrett. DeNiro immediately recognized one, a silver 13-inch Apple Macintosh notebook. Looking up from the machine, DeNiro nodded her head and smiled when Dumer asked her if the Macintosh was an item she was looking for. "Yes," she said. "I believe this one belongs to Barbara Branning. "How about that one?" She pointed to the laptop in front of Dumer.

Dumer smiled and turned on the Hewlett-Packard Pavilion. In a matter of moments, the detective knew that the HP had been stolen from Nicole Marshall. Both officers looked down at the retrieved stolen articles before them and realized at the same moment that all the months of investigation suddenly had brought them to this point. The man searched for was no longer a ghost. He no longer appeared to be nonexistent. He was flesh and blood; and, he was sitting in the Pinellas County Jail.

GORDON KUHN

PART 3

Florida vs Smith

Sarasota County

CHAPTER TWENTY ONE

Key Issues of the Sarasota Trial

A criminal's worst nightmare is, of course, being identified.

Such was the case with Delmer Smith, and he went to extraordinary lengths to avoid leaving behind DNA, fingerprints, or any other item that might lead law enforcement to his door. But, in the end, it was his over abundance of caution in how to prevent such an event that led to his downfall.

During Delmer Smith's 18 years behind bars, he had been surrounded by some of Michigan's most notorious criminals; and, it was a society that accepted him as he was, a violent offender in the early stages of his education. These men, many far older than he, talked, and he listened.

For the first time in his life, he related to those around him and them to him. He would never again fear being beaten by his mother with a switch from one of scrawny bushes in the family yard. His lack of educational skills was not considered a hindrance to his becoming a part of that community. No more jeers from people his age. In fact, it was considered a bit of a recognized honor that he had been put back school year after school year and finally thrust forward so the system could rid itself of him. Prison had a different educational system, one in which he thrived.

From those he met and became friends, he learned how to pick a victim and how to enter their residences with ease, or how to take them down on the street. He was educated on how to attack and secure his targets with stunning speed. He learned his craft from professionals. But he, like they, failed to consider the forces working against them while teaching him how to pick and size up a victim, the important elements of the right neighborhood, and how to dress for the job.

They would class him about concealing his face during the attacks and how to avoid leaving any fingerprints or other means of identification at the scene. They told him that there would be confusion over his race based on appearances, if seen, and his voice, if heard. He learned what to say and when to say it. He was taught the importance of affiliations and how to control them.

He exited prison with the educational level of a doctorate in crime.

Even so, with all that he learned about being cautious to avoid leaving anything behind that could identify him, his error came by wearing clothing that caused him to sweat. For it was the discovery of ten tiny drops of perspiration that fell from his body that identified him as having been the person who assaulted and robbed Nicole Marshall.

As it was, Marshall was never given the opportunity to view his face or make a clear determination of his race. She surmised he was black because of the way he spoke, but agreed, when questioned by Delmer's defense attorney Ms. Bender, that the man on trial was visually white and not black.

Legally, however, because his father was black he is black. Nevertheless, that fact never came up in the trial. All that mattered was that he appears to be totally white and not black.

Delmer entered Marshall's home while wearing heavy dark clothing and gloves that were rough and cut Marshall's lip when he grabbed her. He became overheated while dragging Marshall around the house by her hair or her clothes and began sweating. The sweat turned into drops that fell from his face landing on the floor as he made his way through the home dragging Marshall along with him by her hair or her night clothes. The drops contained his DNA, and that provided the irrefutable evidence that he had been at that location.

Ten small drops that, at first appearance, according to Mike Dumer, looked like syrup. However, seeing them and not knowing what they were, he alerted his forensic specialist of their presence. She photographed them and took samples that were sent to the Florida Department of Law Enforcement's Crime Lab in Fort Myers for analysis.

The technician there confirmed DiFranco's suspicion that the drops were sweat and that they contained DNA. Those ten tiny drops spotted by Dumer, photographed and sampled by DiFranco nailed Delmer to the scene at the Carmilfra home the night of March 14th, 2009. The DNA pattern report was then sent to the FBI's CODIS program to see if they had a donor in file to match what was found at the Carmilfra scene and CODIS returned a negative match. After 15 ½ years in Federal Prison, CODIS had not put Delmer's DNA on file.

Had the FBI's DNA recognition system of CODIS not been backlogged, Delmer Smith would have been in jail within a week or two after the samples were sent in and not months later. Several violent attacks would not have taken place, and two women would still be alive today.

As it was, CODIS identified Delmer as the DNA donor well after he had already been arrested and charged for crimes in both Sarasota and Manatee Counties.

CHAPTER TWENTY TWO

All Rise, Day One

It was morning, December 6th, 2011, and the first of two trials was about to begin. Delmer had been charged with home invasion and kidnapping. In addition, he had allegedly had a gun on him which increased the penalty should he be found guilty.

"All rise," the booming voice of the bailiff began his announcement in Courtroom 5-C.

In response to his words, there quickly came the sounds of shuffling feet and bumps and thumps on the wooden benches as people stood respectfully. Their eyes were turned toward the door to the judge's chambers that had just opened.

"This Twelfth Judicial Court in and for Sarasota County is now in session," the bailiff continued. "The Honorable Rochelle Curley is presiding."

Circuit Court Judge Rochelle Curley is a mixture of two cultures. She is both African American and Japanese. She has long, black, flowing hair that extends past her shoulders and has a slight bounce as she walks. Her smile is quick, soft, and magnetic. She is known for her warmth and charm and an easygoing manner that helps relax those in her presence. However, she can also be tough when she finds the need.

The youngest of five children, Rochelle Curley grew up in a home with a father who was a career Navy man who taught her and her siblings that, "you have to give back." That is the hallmark of her career in public service, giving back to a society that has given much to her and to her family over the years. She enters the room holding a small collection of folders. Her black robes flow gracefully around her as she steps up to take her place at the bench.

She placed the folders on her bench, smoothed her gown, and sat in the large upholstered chair from which she had a clear view of the entire room. She looked up and smiled warmly at those present. Almost everyone in the room was known to her both inside and outside of court. "Good morning," she said with a slight smile, then added courteously, "Please be seated."

The sliding sound of chairs and shuffling feet filled the room as the gallery and attendant personnel resumed their seats amidst the few polite responses being made to the judge as she turned to the folders on her bench. She glanced up from them at the prosecution and then the defense tables. "Good morning State and Defense," she said, acknowledging the presence of the prosecution team made up of Assistant State Attorney Elizabeth "Beth" Scanlan and her associate Assistant State Attorney W. Earl Varn, and also that of the defense, Attorney Marjorie Bender.

Curly wastes no time in getting the trial off and running. She welcomes the Jury and thanks them for being there. She then begins by giving instructions to them and to the court in general. When finished, she then gives permission for Scanlan to start her opening statements to the Jury.

CHAPTER TWENTY THREE
Just another Day

"Thank you, your honor," Beth Scanlan replied rising from her chair to approach the Jury. She was conscious of how quickly she moved. Too fast might seem too eager, too slow might signal being uninterested, bored, or not prepared. However, she knew that between the two speeds there was a spot where, if she clicked on it just right, it would signify control over the issues as well as produce just enough dramatic flair that would draw the Jury in. She paused, a quick glance back and down at the neat pile of labeled folders, note pads, and writing instruments left on the table where her associate, Earl Varn, sat. She needed nothing, just her voice to make her opening statement.

She calmly approached the Jury.

She had a story to tell and was confident that her preparation would provide sufficient evidence, both in terms of physical confirmation as well as in the testimony provided by her witnesses to win a guilty verdict on all charges.

"Good morning, ladies and gentlemen," she said just loudly enough to be picked up by the court reporters, but intimate enough to cause the jurors to be drawn more closely into her web.

"Good morning," an individual juror responded.

Ms. Scanlan nodded acknowledging the juror's response and then, without skipping a beat, said "March 14th of 2009. That was just another day for Nicole Marshall for most of the day. She is a sixty-five-year-old snowbird. She resides down here for the winter, and she spends her summers back up in Canada where she's from. She was down here at the end of the season, March 14th of 2009. Her husband still travels quite a bit for work, and he happened to be out of town on that day [Saturday], so she was home alone." She paused for a moment to let that sink in.

"She likes to make jewelry from beads, and so that night that's what she was doing at about 10 o'clock. She was beading, and she was watching television." She paused again, took a breath, and then continued slowly.

"March 14, 2009 was not just another day for Delmer Smith. That was a day that he decided that he was going to rob and terrorize Nicole Marshall, a complete stranger, as she sat alone at home." Again, a brief and deliberate pause. She was focused and out to establish meaningful contact with each juror individually.

As she slowly moved past them, her eyes met their eyes. She held them for a moment in a commanding gaze, and then moved to the next person. She knew it was important to establish a connection early on in the proceedings with each member of the panel. Therefore, she spoke in such a manner that her message was delivered to each juror, individually and intimately, pulling them in, telling the story that needed to be told.

The smile was gone and a smoldering intensity could be seen in her eyes.

She was in prosecutorial mode, and the spotlight was on her at center stage.

In the meantime, her adversary, Defense Attorney Bender sat beside her cuffed and shackled client, Delmer Smith, at a table to the right of the prosecution's. Behind Bender and Delmer, and a bit to the right, stood a deputy sheriff. In front, and also to the right was a second officer. Near the doorway to the hall out of which Delmer had been brought was a third officer.

Bender was not watching Scanlan, nor was she paying any attention to Delmer sitting next to her showing no emotion. She focused on a pad of paper lying in front of her. She would take notes regarding what Scanlan would say in her opening remarks to the Jury. In this way, she was readying herself for her counterattack if and when she would go on the offensive.

Scanlan would methodically introduce the Jury to the details of the crimes for which Delmer had been charged. She would take them systematically from the beginning when he allegedly made entry into Marshall's rented home, through what took place once he was inside, to when he left the residence leaving Nicole Marshall hog tied, alone, and fearing for her life.

She would tell the Jury about some of the witnesses she would call upon. She told what each witness would testify about, what the Jury should expect to hear from those witnesses, and the importance of the testimony they would hear. She also spoke of the physical evidence to be presented, and the significance of each piece of that evidence. In the end, she would close her presentation of the facts with the statement that after hearing from the witnesses and viewing the evidence as presented, the Jury would have only one thing to do at that point, and that would be to return a verdict of guilty for the crimes for which Delmer was charged.

CHAPTER TWENTY FOUR
The Break-in

"At 10 P.M. he broke into her house," Scanlan told the Jury during her opening remarks. "He didn't bust in through the front door. He didn't throw a rock through a window so that she would be alerted and able to call the police. Instead, he broke the screen door on her lanai. Her lanai opens into a pool area, and then there are several entrances into the house through the lanai. Once on the lanai, he popped out one of the bedroom windows that opened onto the lanai, and he stealthily crept into her house without her knowledge."

No one knows why Delmer chose Nicole Marshall as a target. Delmer never said why. To this day, he still claims innocence. Nevertheless, the facts of the case would quickly prove otherwise.

The home rented by Marshall on Carmilfra Drive was set back from the road. In front of it was a collection of large boulders surrounded by a variety of broadleaved plants. The driveway was a semi-circle with the plantings and boulders occupying the center blocking the view of most of the front of the house. At nighttime, what little light afforded by the incandescent streetlamp across the street could not expose much of the home to view.

Behind the home was a screened porch with a small kidney-shaped swimming pool. Behind that, was a backyard of boulders painted white. They ended at a seawall where the Phillippi Creek opened up to a broad expanse making up a large bay. In the middle of the bay, near a bridge passing over it, was an island with several businesses located on it and in particular was a restaurant with lights that could be seen from the back of the house. The presence of those lights would be discussed during the trial.

This would be the sixth case in less than thirty days in which Delmer was suspected of having been the attacker. However, unknown to him, or anyone else that night, or for many days thereafter, Marshall would be the one who, with a strong display of emotional strength, would prove to be his undoing. That and the ten small wet drops of sweat he left behind found on an initial crime scene walkthrough by Detective Mike Dumer and Sergeant Rhonda DiFranco. Upon analysis, it was discovered that his DNA was within those drops. And, despite the objections and the storyline developed by the Defense, those tiny drops of liquid that easily could have been overlooked were it not for the sharp eyes of Dumer and DiFranco would be the evidence that connected him to the scene of the crime.

Scanlan went on to explain that DiFranco would testify concerning her belief as to where the point of entry had been. She would also speak about her finding footprints left behind in the loose earth "…on the corner of the house…" and that she photographed them. She was unaware, at the time of her testimony, if the shoes that left the marks had been located. She told the Court that the pool cage screen appeared to have been intentionally cut allowing someone to reach through and unlock the screen cage door allowing access to the pool deck. She then found what she considered as evidence of a forced entry to have occurred through the master bedroom jalousie window. Upon examining the window, she noticed the crank on it had been broken. She believed the suspect had made entry into the house at that point.

In my interview with Nicole I asked her, "Can you tell me something about that night, about what you were doing before you were attacked?"

"Yes." Nicole smiled. "Um," she paused. I was sure her thoughts were drifting back, reliving, feeling, dreading the trip but knowing this was a catharsis. A cleansing, clearing out of all the terror associated with the attack that hung on in her memories.

Each time she spoke of the event, she told me, something else peeled away, drifted off, leaving her feeling cleaner, more relaxed. It was not that she enjoyed doing it. Recalling that night was not fun for her. She told me it was a trip through painful, haunting doorways. They could have been shut tight, left to become dust covered, barred and bolted; but she said she knew doing so would simply allow what was there to fester and, over time, the pressure, always pressing outwards, would suddenly find the need to burst out, rupturing, rushing out, in an uncontrolled wave of pent-up memories and emotions. "No," she said, "this is better. Talk about it. Get it out." Just as she had done in the trial, in the depositions, and in the interviews with Mike Dumer and others. "Then walk away." There was fresh air waiting for her.

"This was one event in my life. I'll not let it destroy me," she said firmly. She was a survivor and her attacker would most likely never be free again. He would be confined for the rest of his life in prison.

"I had been in the kitchen. It was only for a short time." Nicole sat forward as she spoke. Her eyes danced right and left, her mind searching her memories of that night. "I had turned on the television to watch a program while I did some beading. That is one of my hobbies," she glanced up at me — a slight smile, "—beading, and I had a project I was working on."

During the trial, Scanlan produced interior and exterior photos of the home on Carmilfra taken the night of the attack. The prosecutor used the photos to orientate the Jury to the home with Nicole providing narrative. In this way, the Jury would better be able to follow Nicole's testimony regarding where she was in the home at any given time. Once done, Scanlan turned her questions to the attack itself. "Now," she began, "at 10:00 o'clock on March 14th tell the jurors what you were doing at that time."

"I was in the kitchen, and was putting some food in the fridge that had been sitting on the counter," Nicole answered.

Scanlan then asked Nicole about her awareness of the time of day. Nicole responded that just prior to her going to the kitchen she had glanced at the clock and it was "…precisely 10:03." Scanlan asked her about how she could be so positive. Nicole replied that for some reason the time just stuck in her mind.

She then recalled that while she had been in the kitchen, she heard a loud but muffled thump.

Scanlan questioned her about the noise. Nicole said she originally felt the sound had come from outside. She added that there was always a certain amount of noise in the neighborhood and so she disregarded it. She added that had she thought the sound had come from inside the house she would have gone and investigated.

During my meeting with Nicole, she suggested that perhaps it had been a wise thing that she had not gone to find the source of the noise. She felt that had she done so, Delmer might have attacked her at that point in a fury over his having been discovered and she might have been injured. I agreed with her.

Scanlan paused for a moment before she continued with her statement to the Jury, moving deliberately and slowly along the well-polished wooden rail behind which the Jury sat, pausing in her conversation with them repeatedly to place emphasis on some part of her comments. In a brief moment she would turn and face them, take a deep breath, and then continue with her telling of the attack, echoing Mike Dumer's report which was part of the evidence to be brought into the trial:

> And she turned and saw him standing right next to her in front of the front door. He immediately turned off the lights so that she was in the dark. She could not see his face. She believes he was wearing a mask, but everything took place so quickly. It started with an eerie feeling, a sense that someone was there in the room with her when she expected to be completely alone. Then the shadow seen from the corner of her eye, undefined. Turning toward it, the shadow became a person by the door, more defined than not, but then the lights went out. Suddenly, terrified, alone, she knew he was standing next to her; and then it happened —— he grabbed her.

"It happened so fast," Nicole told me as we sat drinking coffee at the Starbucks' coffee shop in Barnes and Noble. "I felt someone in the room with me. I turned and looked and there was this shadow, this person by the door.

Suddenly I was in the dark because he turned the lights out and the next thing I knew he grabbed me."

"That must have been very frightening," I said, trying to imagine how I would have felt to have been so suddenly confronted with someone who had invaded what I would consider to be the inviolability of a private residence. "It was," she said nodding slowly, her lips tightening. "It was very frightening."

"At first I thought my mind was playing tricks on me, but when the lights went out I realized that it was very real."

"He grabbed her. Her beads went flying everywhere," the prosecutor's voice rose on the word *everywhere* for emphasis. "The lamp she was using for better light went flying and broke on the floor. He pulled her off of her couch, and he pushed her down on the ground, and covered her mouth."

Delmer pushed Marshall down on her knees. She was facing the couch. He was standing over her.

"He was wearing some sort of a rough glove that scratched her face. He pushed her so that she was face down on the couch. The lights were off, leaving them in the dark," Scanlan said, then paused for a moment allowing the Jury to mentally digest the scene.

Detective Dumer wrote in his report, "Nicole Marshall stated that an unknown male came from the area of the front door and immediately attacked her, put his hand over her mouth, and put a black gun to her head. The perpetrator stated coldly and matter-of-factly, 'don't scream or I'll shoot you.' Nicole Marshall described the gun as a large black handgun with a square slide and a round barrel."

What Nicole saw would be a point of contention that the defense would argue.

Did Nicole or did not Nicole actually see a gun? That was the argument presented by Bender. The reason is that the display of a firearm during the commission of a felony in the State of Florida carries a mandatory prison term of 10 years. So, naturally, Bender would attack Nicole's recall of having seen a handgun as soon as she had a chance during her cross examination of Nicole.

"Okay." Scanlan approached Nicole who was seated in the witness chair. "Now, you said you felt this presence standing next to you, and you turned and you saw somebody. Tell us what happened after that."

"When I realized what was happening... well, I realized what was happening because this person grabbed me right away."

"How did he grab you?"

"The left hand over my face. And in doing so, I fell, and I was face down on the couch right here (she pointed at a photograph being used as an exhibit in the trial) and sort of on my knees, right there."

"What happened to your lamps and your beads?"

"Oh, everything went flying, of course."

"The lamp ... you can see the lamp here (she again pointed at the photograph) and it was ... actually, it was plugged here. So, of course, by coming toward me, the lamp flew, and I started screaming. And, of course, all my ... my tray and my beads went all over the place."

"And what did he do then?"

"Well, he grabbed me by the face, and he hurt me. And I was ... I screamed, of course. I got very scared, and I realized what was happening. And he hurt my face. I could feel he was wearing a very rough glove because my lip was torn, and it was burning, and the side of my face was burning. I had a hard time breathing, and I screamed."

Scanlan paused for a second to allow the jurors to absorb that part of Nicole's testimony and then asked, "And when you screamed, what did he do?"

"Well," Nicole spoke haltingly, "he actually whispered in my ear — but he was very demanding — and — and he said,' Shh, stop screaming or I will kill you.'"

CHAPTER TWENTY FIVE
Nine Missing Minutes

It is shortly after 1 P.M. on December 6th, 2011 when Sergeant Tutko, a 13-year veteran with the Sarasota Sheriff's office was called to the stand by Prosecutor Scanlan. Tutko was the supervisor at the Carmilfra scene.

"Were you working on the night of March 14, 2009?" Scanlan asked Tutko.

"Yes, I was," he replied, sitting forward in the witness chair.

Scanlan then questioned the Sergeant regarding his receiving the call concerning the robbery and his response to it. She asked how long it took him to reach the Carmilfra address from the time he received a call.

Tutko responded that he had "immediately responded to the area of the call" and that it was a "matter of minutes" before he reached the scene.

"Okay. When you first arrived on the scene, what was taking place?"

Tutko testified that upon arrival at the scene he located the victim at a neighbor's house and spoke with Deputy Kuentzel who had been the original investigating officer. He noted the crime scene had been cleared and sealed and that he had called the on call detective: Mike Dumer.

Scanlan finished her direct and Defense Attorney Bender stepped forward for her cross.

Bender had come across an error in the Tutko's reports. There was a discrepancy in the CAD[12] report where the time listed for Tutko's arrival was misstated. She felt it might be used to create an opening to establish doubt in the juror's minds concerning the State's case against her client.

"Do you remember, sir, exactly what time you are reported as arriving?" Bender asked.

"No, I do not. Because I'm — in the confusion of things, the computer-generated paperwork that shows what time people arrive, I was listed, I think, after midnight, and I actually arrived on scene prior to that. The only thing I could say is that in the confusion of things with two supervisors responding to the scene they didn't show me as being on scene. Because if you look at the CAD report, it shows dispatch and arrival at the same time."

"Now, your dispatch log shows an incorrect time of your arrival at six minutes after midnight; correct?"

"Yes."

Bender questioned the Sergeant if he knew why there was a discrepancy and again he stated that there was confusion and that he could not state as to what caused the discrepancy. She then approached him about the contamination sheet and the fact that there was a discrepancy on arrival time between the CAD report and the contamination sheet for two of the officers, Deputy Swinney and Deputy Thomas. According to the contamination sheet, there was a nine-minute discrepancy.

"Okay. What is the discrepancy, Sergeant?" Bender asked.

"I can't explain that."

"You can't?"

"No."

"And during that nine minutes of discrepancy, you are inside a neighbor's home with Deputy Kuentzel; correct?"

"Yes."

---

[12] CAD is short for: Computer-aided dispatch used by law enforcement.

Bender approached Tutko on the stand. "You're familiar with what's called a contamination sheet; correct?"

"Yes."

"And if I may, I know it's hard to remember specific times, but does— can you just tell the Jury what the contamination sheet is."

Tutko nodded, and looking toward the Jury said, "The contamination sheet is a sheet that we fill out on the crime scene where it shows everyone that has entered the crime scene and the time that they have entered that crime scene and the reason that they went into that crime scene."

Bender felt that the time discrepancies were important. She was using these errors as a way of planting in the jurors' minds that just maybe the officers had not properly managed the scene. If that were the case, then possibly it was contaminated. That would bring in a hint of doubt that would be unacceptable in a criminal trial. That could lead to a not guilty verdict.

"All right," Bender continued. "What time, sir, did Deputy Thomas, Mrzuack, and Swinney arrive at the Carmilfra address?"

"Deputy Thomas arrived at 2336 hours, Deputy Swinney arrived at 2336 hours, and Deputy Mrzuack, it states 2353 hours."

During the deposition of Detective Mike Dumer conducted by Bender, Dumer testified that Officers Thomas, Swinney, and Mrzuack were the three deputies who entered the home. He further confirmed that two of them then refused to give DNA samples citing privacy rights.

This is not only a concern with local law enforcement but has come up in other jurisdictions. Bender would have like to enter it into the trial, but it was ruled as not being relative. Regardless, the officers' actions resulted in a major shock wave passing through not only the Sheriff's Office but the whole judicial system.

"Okay. Now, you're getting that information from your CAD report; right?" Bender questioned.

"Yes, I am," Tutko replied.

"Okay. So turning to the contamination log — and we don't know who wrote it — but does that show when people entered the home? That is the purpose of it; right?"

"Yes."

Bender went on to develop another discrepancy of nine minutes between the two logs.

"Okay. Can you explain to us what the discrepancy between those times would be? Because they're arriving, they're entering the home right away, right, but the contamination log isn't begun until later. And then the time that they're supposedly entering is on that log. So we've got, what, between 2336 and 2345. What is that, 11 minutes?"

"Nine. No. It's almost 9 minutes."

"Nine minutes?" Bender paused looking at the papers before her. "I am not a math person. Nine minutes?" Bender looked up at Tutko.

"I believe, yes," the sergeant replied.

"Okay. What is the discrepancy, Sergeant?"

"I can't explain that."

A wisp of a smile slipped across Bender's lips as she stole a glance at the Jury. "You can't?"

"No."

"And during that nine minutes of discrepancy," she paused to let that fact sink into the juror's minds, "you are inside the neighbor's home with Deputy Kuentzel; correct?"

"Yes."

"And Ms. Nicole Marshall?" Bender added.

"Yes."

"And as you said, in the confusion you've got a lot to take care of; right?"

"Yes."

"You've got the K-9 guy; he's already there. But you've got possibly the helicopter; you have got to set up a perimeter. And what does a perimeter do?"

"The perimeter would be trying to contain someone, if they were still in the area, so they wouldn't get away from the scene," Tutko explained, directing the answer toward the Jury.

"And that would be — so that means that you have to make sure that other deputies are, like, on adjacent streets so if someone is running or someone is driving, those deputies are going to see a larger area; am I correct?"

"Yes."

"Whether one comes or goes?"

"Correct."

"Okay. And how many people — how many deputies were on the scene, I would say, before the detective [Mike Dumer] arrived."

"It appears to be approximately 15."

"And you don't know where, with specificity — or can you tell us with specificity during that nine-minute gap in the time between the two reports where any of those particular officers were? You can probably account for some; right?"

"Yes. I can account for Deputy Kuentzel and — "

"He was with you?"

"— the recruit that he had with him, yes."

"And who was that?"

"Deputy Josh Pelfrey. And, obviously, you have Deputy Wineka; he's the helicopter pilot. So he's really out of the mix."

"Sure."

"The other deputies could have been on perimeter positions, all right, so that's why you have so many listed here, and then you have the victim's assistance, Miss

Farnsworth. So you can take a few names off that list, but there's still approximately 12 on there."

"Okay. The contamination log has how many people on it?"

"Seven."

Bender then questioned what time it was that Detective Dumer showed up. Tutko again advised that he did not know and that was not on the CAD report. Tutko said he believed that Dumer arrived shortly after midnight. He believed it was around 0030 hours.

Bender's line of questioning was to bring a degree of uncertainty into the minds of the jurors in regard to the record keeping of the Sheriff's Office. She pushed further. "Okay. What I'm gathering from what you are telling me is that it's very difficult to track down and keep records of who goes where and what; correct?"

"Yes."

Her questioning shifted to the activities that took place when Sergeant Tutko called out on the radio to seal the house. "Do you know when you called that out in this nine-minute discrepancy time?"

"I would have done that after they had taken care of the residence in clearing it and got on the radio at that point when they said it was clear, that I told them, 'Nobody go into that house' at that point."

Bender then asked Tutko if he knew what time it was that he radioed the message to seal the house.

"I can't give you a time, no."

Bender went on to say that Tutko was also not in the position to be able to know if anybody actually heard him over the radio. Tutko agreed with that. He also agreed that he was "assuming" that everyone would follow the order to stay out of the house. On further questioning, he granted that he did not know who it was that had written and maintained the contamination sheet. Bender pushed further trying to establish uncertainties by questioning when the crime scene tape had gone up. Tutko did not know. He actually did not recall seeing any at all. At that point

Bender concluded her cross and Scanlan stepped up to redirect and repair any damage that Bender had done to the case regarding law enforcement's credibility.

"When the officer," she paused to rephrase her question, " — when the deputies arrive on scene, there is a small amount of time that's spent assessing the situation prior to entering the residence; is that correct?" Scanlan asked Tutko.

"Yes."

"Okay. And then they enter it together?"

"Yes."

"Whether or not that took exactly 9 minutes, do you know?"

"No, I do not."

Scanlan paused, her mind working, and then asked, "Okay. Is that approximately the length of time that it would take or is that long?" She knew she was treading on the "object to" button but took the shot, hoping her response to the opposition's position would be strong enough to prevent a "sustained" from the Court.

Bender rose from her seat, hand in the air, "Judge, I'm going to object to speculation."

"Sustained."

Scanlan immediately fired back, "Everything she [Ms. Bender] asked him was speculation."

"Sustained," the Court replied with finality in her voice.

Scanlan was incredulous but ready with a backup question. "Well," she glanced from the witness to the Jury and then back to the witness, "let me ask you the question this way: You were on the scene, and we have what is recorded on the contamination sheet. Are you aware of anybody else who entered the residence for any reason?"

"No."

"So whatever length of time," she paused to let that sink in to the Jury, "it took for the deputies to go in initially and clear the residence, those are the only people that were in there?"

"Yes."

Scanlan said she had no further questions. The Court looked to Bender who said she had no recross. Tutko was released and Scanlan called the prosecution's next witness: Detective DeFranco.

CHAPTER TWENTY SIX
Ten Mystery Droplets

On the 6th of December 2011, Assistant State Attorney Beth Scanlan is in the midst of addressing the Jury with her opening statement.

She tells them that following the attack by Delmer, Marshall, "had bruises everywhere, on her wrists, on her ankles, around her neck, from the electrical cords, and she had a terrible pain in her chest. It turns out that she was so terrified she had a heart attack." She paused to let the Jury absorb that fact. She would return to Nicole's condition later that same day when she called her as a witness.

"What about your heart?" Scanlan asked Nicole. "Tell me what happened."

"Well," Nicole testified, "my heart was beating, and I started feeling a very—like a very—heaviness in my chest. And I was rubbing my chest, and that's when my friend said, why are you rubbing your chest? And I said, I just feel a heaviness. And she was very concerned, and she said, 'We have to take you to the hospital now.'"

"And what did you find out at the hospital?"

"At the hospital I was told after they did the first exams that I was having a heart attack."

"Little over an hour later [after the break-in and robbery]," Scanlan continues:

Sergeant DiFranco responded to the scene. She is the Criminalistics technician who responded. She will tell you what processing the scene means. She will tell you that… means…she went through the entire house, that the first thing that she did was take photographs of everything before she touched anything so that she would have a record of where everything was located, where anything was found.

"I arrived about four minutes," she paused, reflecting back, "— I believe it was four minutes before 1 A.M.." DiFranco would testify.

Scanlan asked DiFranco about what all was included in the "crime scene."

"The entire house," DiFranco said.

"Both inside and outside?"

"Yes."

When Detective Dumer testified, he said that when he arrived on scene he first met with Sergeant Tutko and Deputy Thomas. They advised him that the scene was secured. Tutko told the detective that he could enter it at any time he wished. Dumer told Tutko that he preferred to wait for his forensic person, whom he knew was in route.

Tutko testified that he had placed a call to forensics at "11:34 P.M." and that DiFranco, the specialist on-call that night, arrived a few minutes before midnight.

Tutko replied to Scanlan's questions, informing the Court that both Dumer and DiFranco arrived at the scene shortly after being phoned, and that he was aware that DiFranco had been sleeping when he called her.

"She got there maybe 5 minutes to one in the morning," Dumer testified. "I met with her at some point [soon after her arrival] and told her that when she was ready to go inside the residence to let me know." He knew that she would want to take photographs of the exterior of the crime scene before moving inside.

"So," Scanlan asked, tilting her head slightly to the side "you didn't go with her as she documented the exterior of the residence?"

"That's correct," Dumer answered. He did not feel his presence was needed by her at that point.

However, prior to their entering the house together, DiFranco approached the detective with a request, and the two "checked the perimeter," as Dumer called it. Scanlan asked what he meant by that. Dumer responded that DiFranco "wanted to point a couple things out to me."

"I found footprints on one corner of the house on the outside," DiFranco testified. "There was a cut in the screen lanai that went into the pool area." She felt they could possibly be of significance to the investigation.

"How do you document the footprints?" Scanlan asked DiFranco.

"Scale and photograph."

"When you say 'scale,' explain to them [the Jury] what you mean."

"You put a measure, a paper measure, a ruler that will document the size of the foot."

"Okay. Now, is a footprint by itself that's left in the dirt or in the sand or anything, is that alone evidence, or do you need something else?"

"Clarify, I'm trying to —"

"Do you need the shoe to match it to?"

"Yes."

"It was dark inside the residence, as I recall," Dumer testified.

DiFranco also testified that it was dark when questioned if the lights were on when they entered the residence. She did not remember using her flashlight but did recall that Dumer had one and used it.

"Once inside the residence," Scanlan told the Jury in her opening statement that:

> DiFranco and Dumer had observed a knotted wire located on the floor in the living room. They would later learn that Ms. Nicole Marshall had initially been attacked in that room, and that, prior to her assailant leaving, he would tie her up in that same room and leave her lying face down where she would fear the possibility that she might accidentally strangle herself.
> He left her alone hog-tied on her living room floor, heart beating so fast that she didn't know what she was going to do. She laid there completely still for at least five minutes thinking that if she couldn't get herself untied she was going to remain on that floor and she wouldn't be found until the next day. She didn't think that she would stay alive until the next day. She thought her leg would cramp and that she would choke herself.

"I had my flashlight with me" Dumer testified, "and we were looking around together. She [DiFranco] had gone beyond—when we came into the house, the living room is on the left side of the house, and there was a hallway to the right," Dumer replied to a question put to him by Scanlan.

"That led to the two bedrooms?" Scanlan asked.

"Right."

"Okay. And what of significance happened there?"

"Well, I was walking through that hallway — and I think Sergeant DiFranco had gone beyond me — and I was

looking
with my flashlight and I noticed something on the floor that caught my attention."

Dumer had discovered a series of fluid droplets that were scattered about on the floor throughout the residence.

"Okay," Scanlan said, aware that after looking at them that the two officers had concluded the drops appeared to be fresh, in a "fluid state rather than dried."

"And I called her back to it and asked her to take a look at what I thought initially was drops of syrup because of the discoloration of this fluid, but Sergeant DiFranco had taken a much closer look at it and told me that — "

Bender quickly stood. "Judge, I'm going to object to hearsay."

The Court sustained the objection "if he's going to say anything that Sergeant DiFranco said."

Scanlan quickly shifted her questions around, arriving at another objection from Bender when Dumer responded to Scanlan's question, "Did you come to believe it was something other than syrup?" And his response was, "She indicated that she thought it might be —"

Scanlan made a third attempt which brought another objection for hearsay, but Scanlan countered stating she was asking what his belief was. However, the Court responded saying that Scanlan had included in her question the words, "What did you think it was after your conversation with Sergeant DiFranco?"

Scanlan paused for a moment, regrouping, as she calmly looked over at Dumer who sat in the witness chair watching and waiting for her next move. The detective knew the attorney was locked in a courtroom version of "musical chairs" with his testimony at that point, and that she had two other players, Bender and the Court, who were controlling the music. Every step she took had to be calculated to impact the Jury. She needed Dumer to respond, to slip into the seat as soon as the music ended, to get into testimony what she wanted him to say. Even if it was objected to after he said it, and the Court then told the

Jury to "disregard" what he said. Her job was to get him to say what she wanted him to say.

It was quite simple really, Scanlan knew that once spoken, along with the entire complex and mysterious drama (as viewed from a juror's perspective) associated with the objection being made and the Court's response — good or bad — aided the juror's retention of the question and the response. The objection and associated drama would keep the comment anchored in each juror's mind. But, she also had to remember that the Jury was watching her and she needed to remain absolutely calm and in control.

"The Jury must believe you are in control," she told me in an interview. "Even the paper and files on the table or the lectern must be kept together and organized. If I, as an attorney, start searching and spreading papers out on the table or begin to hastily flip through things I will telegraph to the Jury that I am confused and not prepared. That will severely damage my credibility before a Jury and actually could cause me to lose the case."

And so, after a moment in which her mind quickly crafted a plan to make another pass at getting the detective to give her the answer she wanted, she calmly pushed forward again, "What was your belief as to what it was?"

Dumer replied, "After speaking to her [Scanlan sensed he was on thin ice, but showed no outward sign, and waited for the objection], I believed it to be potentially sweat droplets because of my discussion with her." For a brief moment there was silence. Scanlan waited expecting Bender to rise from her chair again. He had gotten into testimony what she wanted him to say. But, would it stay?

Surprisingly, no objection was sounded from the defense and Scanlan, content that she had gotten past that hurdle, went on quickly. "Did that effect in any way what steps you took after that?"

"It most certainly did. I basically stopped dead in my tracks at that point and I told her, I said, Rhonda, this is your scene. I'm going to back out of here. I don't need to walk through here any further to contaminate this scene. I'm going to go to the hospital and speak to the victim."

Earlier that day, Scanlan turned from the overhead projector that displayed a photograph of some of the droplets being entered as evidence and crossed to the lectern to resume questioning of Sergeant Rhonda DiFranco. "When you saw this," she referred to the droplets with a waving motion of her left hand in the direction of the screen where the photo was displayed, "What did you believe it was?"

"Sweat," the Sergeant replied without blinking an eye.

"Why did you believe it was sweat?"

DiFranco sat forward in her chair. "Well, I've — I've seen this before many, many times before. I used to work as a nurse in the VA, and I wore gloves pretty much my whole career at one time or another, latex gloves. And I have had experiences with sweat coming from gloves. So when this was presented, that's what I had initially believed it to be."

"And that conclusion," Scanlan asked as she moved to the side of the lectern and glanced down at her notes, "that you made, that was your initial conclusion based upon your life experience?"

"Correct."

"Okay. Does this need to have additional scientific testing done to verify whether or not that was, in fact —"

Ms. Bender suddenly stood, lips slightly pinched, "Judge, I'm going to object. She's not authorized to say whether it should be done or shouldn't be done. It calls for a legal conclusion."

The Court, "Sustained."

"That wasn't the question I asked," Scanlan said, minutely shaking her head. She paused for a moment, folded her arms across her chest, then calmly restated her question. "Can you tell," she began again, "by looking at that whether or not that is, in fact, sweat, or is there additional scientific testing that needs be done in order to determine that?"

"Well, yeah."

It was an obvious question. The objection and its being sustained had a hollow effect on preventing a logical inquiry and explanatory answer. It simply forced Scanlan to maneuver a bit momentarily. She still got the answer she wanted.

DiFranco had taken steps to secure samples of a substance that she, based on her experience, believed was human sweat. However, she was not trained to be able to state with absolute certainty, based upon scientific fact, that the droplets were indeed human sweat. Her belief was simply founded on her experience with viewing sweat over the years.

DiFranco found numerous droplets on her walkthrough with Detective Dumer. After they viewed the house inside and out, she returned with her camera and forensic supplies to document what was there. She photographed, sampled, and labeled what she considered as important to the investigation.

Scanlan returned to questioning DiFranco about her arrival at Carmilfra and her activities once there. She went over specific details moving from the outside of the house to the inside. "Now," Scanlan said, "as far as processing the inside of the house, explain to me how you went through and what you did specifically as you walked through this house."

"Well, once I photographed the front and the exterior of the house, at that time Detective Dumer and I made a walk-through together to determine what was significant and what wasn't significant."

"So, how quickly are you going through the house?" Scanlan asks.

"Not real quick. It takes a little bit of time to go through." DiFranco replies.

"Take a step; look in front of you. Take a step; look in front of you. That sort of thing?"

Scanlan's approach is met with a quick objection for leading from Bender and the Court sustains.

Scanlan rephrases her question. "Okay. Tell me how you do it."

"Okay," DiFranco begins. "What we do is we both walk together, and we discuss each area as we're walking through."

The overhead projector is turned on by Scanlan and a photo displays the front room of the house. Scanlan hands a pointer to DiFranco so she can trace their path from the front door through the house. "When you arrived there, do you remember, was the door open like that?"

DiFranco did not recall.

"Okay." Scanlan thought quickly and rephrased her question. "Well, let me ask you the question this way. If the door had been closed, would you have gone and opened the door and photographed it that way, and or would you photograph it the way that you found it?"

"Photographed it the way I found it."

"So, you were looking at the entire house?"

"Yes."

The questioning and responses then established that Dumer and DiFranco had entered the darkened house together, what was originally seen by the pair, and how they advanced into and through crime scene. Scanlan asked if DiFranco remembered turning on any lights. DiFranco said no. Scanlan showed some of the photographs taken by DiFranco, including one showing a collection of mysterious dark particles on the floor and on a table found in the master bedroom.

"And in the master bedroom at that time, did you note anything of significance," the Prosecutor asked.

"The master bedroom closet was in disarray."

"And what else is of significance that you noticed as you're walking through the residence?"

DiFranco replied that as she moved into the room, she noticed what appeared to be flecks of pepper spread about on the floor. She found an open, damaged window she believed was the burglar's entry point and on a desktop surface located in the master bedroom while she was taking photos of the damaged window located in that room which had been the access point for the attacker.

Nicole testified that after she freed herself, she walked barefoot through the dark house and thought she was walking on sand.

"And did you find out what it was?" Scanlan asked.

"I was told it was pepper." Nicole went on to add that the substance was everywhere.

Ms. Bender on cross examination asked DiFranco, "How do you know it's pepper, the substance that you had next to Identification Marker –10 and that you indicated on the desk you believed that it was pepper? How do you know that for certain?"

"It looked like pepper."

"And we all cook; right?" Bender replied, question like, as she slowly moved around the lectern with her hands clasped in front of her, keeping her focus on DiFranco.

"Yes." DiFranco answered, not sure if Bender was being sarcastic or not.
"Did you taste it?"
"No, I did not."
"Did you smell it."
"No, I did not."
"Did you collect it?"
"No, I did not."

Detective Dumer was notified by Sergeant J. Blessee, the Patrol Supervisor District Two, at approximately 1300 hrs. on the 15th of March that a neighbor had located a black pepper box in his swimming pool as well as a pair of reading glasses which were located outside the probable point of entry. These items were collected by Sergeant Blessee's patrol deputies and submitted to North County Property evidence, where they would be stored until needed or released.

Having displayed and reviewed the photographs taken by DiFranco and projected on the screen on the back wall of the courtroom, Scanlan returned to the lectern where her notes were and, after a brief pause, returned to questioning about the droplets. She wanted to know where DiFranco had found them.
"We saw them in the living room, we saw them in the kitchen, the pantry room, the master bedroom, and I believe—I can't remember another place I believe that's it."

When it was time for the defense to cross-examine DiFranco, Ms. Bender went back through the photographs with the Sergeant and then focused on the droplets. "Am I correct that you started processing it about an hour and a half after the call, started taking your photographs? You didn't start collecting the Q-tip swabs until a little bit after that; correct?"

"Yes."

"But are we safe in assuming or estimating that it's at least, what, an hour and 40 minutes, an hour and 45 minutes after they could have or would have been placed there?"

"Could have."

"Have you done any type of," she paused, "or do you have any experience as a nurse, as a forensic officer in doing any kind of time analysis as to how long sweat or something similar to that stays on the floor in a wet condition?" DiFranco answered that she had not.

However, Scanlan had already put forth several questions regarding the condition of the droplets that DiFranco found, photographed, and from which she had taken samples. Her actions were in anticipation of probing by the defense for any weakness that might be found concerning the droplets.

"OK. Now, with regard to those swabs that you marked with numbers, the items number one through nine, right there in the various locations of the house, what is the process that you use as you go about collecting those?" Scanlan asked.

"I followed the protocols that are mandated through FDLE and collection and what I was trained in at Institute Police Technology and Management and that wet items are collected with a dry swab and then placed in paper."

"Okay. Now, this may seem to be an obvious question but: How is it that" she paused, "can you tell that it's still wet?"

"Well, as you were looking at the picture there, you could see, like, a 3D. And when you look at anything that's wet versus it dry, dry is stained, of course, and wet has a more 3-D appearance."

During Bender's deposition of Dumer, the attorney, recalling a prior part of the conversation, asked the detective, "And then we discussed; what was fresh about those droplets when you went into the house?"

"They appeared to be viscous to me, but I will tell you that I didn't actually sit there and touch them —."

"Well," Bender broke in, "I hope not—."

"Of course not. Because when I went into the house with Sergeant DiFranco, umm, you know as we started to do our, our walk through, it did not take us very long to discover, 'cause remember it's dark, and frankly that probably worked to our advantage, because she and I were in there with flashlights. So I didn't want to disturb the scene, and left it as it was found."

"So you left the light off?"

"Left the light off, walked in, started looking around, I'm looking around, and I say to her; at first I thought it was syrup. I said to her,' what the heck are these things on the floor?' And we started looking around and they're all over the place."

CHAPTER TWENTY SEVEN

It Splats and the Codis Crisis

On the Monday before Jury selection began in the Carmilfra home invasion case, Delmer Smith, after learning of the backlog problem with CODIS and how the DNA evidence had been collected, made an unusual courtroom move. He would speak directly to the Court claiming that the State had manufactured evidence against him.

Facing a potential life sentence in the case, Delmer sought to delay the trial. He was aware that the major evidence connecting him to the Carmilfra site was his DNA. Because of that, he crafted an argument that the DNA developed from sweat droplets was inadmissible. He believed it was impossible for sweat to have remained in a moisture state for the length of time indicated by the detectives prior to it being collected.

People on trial rarely address the Court directly; however, Delmer decided to argue his point, "It's impossible," he began. "I tried it over the weekend. I ran in place for a whole hour and I was dripping with sweat and I put the drops on the floor, and I looked at the spot … twenty to thirty minutes tops and it's completely gone."

Delmer would continue his argument adding, "Whatever this substance was, whatever the State says it is it's not. It's just false." He would bring into question how anyone would have been able to recognize that the substance was that of being human sweat, particularly when the forensics technician and the responding detective supposedly made the discovery some ninety minutes after the first Sheriff's Deputy had responded to the site.

"I'm not no lawyer," Delmer said. "I'm just explaining the best way I can. The detective testified last week he got there an hour and a half later. An hour and a half later there are drops on the ground?" Smith would then continue by telling the judge that a chemist would support the validity of his weekend tests. Sweat, he would claim, could not be able to remain moist for so long at a crime scene. It could also not be there in a "droplet" form as the forensics detectives described it to be.

"It splats," he said. "I tried it; I tried it every which way. I got down on the ground, I'm like, this is crazy, how can they say this is how it is?"

Judge Curly listened attentively and patiently. She was appreciative of his argument and thanked him for it. She then politely dismissed his position and moved on with what needed to be done, the selection and seating of the Jury.

FDLE Analyst Shayna Hayter phoned Detective Dumer just before noon on March 23rd, 2009. She reported that the analysis of the DNA samples was complete. She stated that she was able to obtain a DNA profile and that the profile was of a male. She told him she planned to have the profile uploaded to the FBI by Friday March 27th, and that she hoped they would have an answer back from CODIS within a matter of a few days or less.

She added that four of the five buccal swabs were from the same male contributor. The fifth buccal swab contained a mixture of DNA from the same male and an unknown female contributor.

Because of the presence of the unidentified female donor in the sample, Hayter requested that a buccal swab be obtained from Nicole Marshall. She also requested one be obtained from Nicole's husband for comparative analysis as the male donor had not yet been identified. Per her request, Detective Dumer and Sergeant DiFranco met with Nicole and her husband and took buccal samples from each which were then submitted to the FDLE in Fort Myers, FL for DNA analysis.

On March 31st, Hayter phoned Dumer and told him that CODIS found no match. Yet the subject later on who was arrested and who received a life sentence for the Carmilfra home invasion; and then the death sentence for the murder of Kathy Briles, had been in the federal prison system for fifteen years prior to moving to Sarasota, Florida. Because of that incarceration, his DNA should have been well established in CODIS.

"Something was wrong," Dumer told me. "How can this be?" He was certain they were dealing with a hardened criminal and yet, all they had was the CODIS report denying any match on the DNA found at the Carmilfra crime scene with any DNA records held by CODIS. There was nothing contained in the report to indicate there was a problem with the system. That revelation would come later on much to the shock and dismay of many in law enforcement and in the courts.

Had the system been working properly, Dumer later told me, "…two, possibly three, women's lives might have been saved."

Delmer also attacked the timing of the DNA matches. He had been in federal prison for bank robbery serving 15 years. He was released in 2008 and was placed on parole. "They had my DNA," he said. The prison system would not have let him out of jail without having taken a sample of DNA. "My DNA was in the system before I got out. It says so right here in black and white!" He waved a report from the Bureau of Prisons around. "They had my DNA. They are saying it [CODIS] was backlogged?" He wanted to know how it could be that if they had his DNA in CODIS, when he was released from prison, that they did not find a match when Hayter sent in her sample on March 27th, 2009. Why, he wanted to know, was his DNA only discovered on file after he had been arrested and a sample taken while he was in jail.

"Oh," he snarled, "it's backlogged. My DNA was in there before I got out [of prison for bankrobbery], for them to say it wasn't in there, show me."

Delmer's position was simple: the evidence was manufactured or contaminated.

Responding to the concerns of local law enforcement over the DNA crisis, the Bradenton Herald filed a report on October 8th, 2009 in which it disclosed alarming evidence of a major logjam within the system that effectively was putting the ability of law enforcement resources in suspension.

The newspaper's investigation reported that the FBI had not logged a considerable body of DNA evidence. In fact, it was discovered that there was a backlog of over 250,000 samples. This fact drew immediate calls for action from shocked local politicians and law enforcement personnel. U. S. Representative Vernon Buchanan began an investigation into the handling of the DNA. In particular, he was concerned with the handling of the DNA belonging to Delmer Smith who was later convicted in the break-in at Nicole Marshall's home.

"Unfortunately," Buchanan said in a release statement regarding the problem, "…in our community a violent criminal remained at-large and was able to keep committing crimes."

In fact, Sarasota County Sheriff Tom Knight remarked that Smith would have been arrested earlier on had his DNA been properly logged into the FBI system. Smith's DNA was found at four separate crime scenes in Sarasota in which women were attacked in their homes with two of them being raped. It was seven months after DNA was discovered at a crime scene in Sarasota before the link was made to Delmer Smith. During that time span, Smith may have been responsible for attacks on eleven women and one or two men. However, Sheriff Knight was kind enough to acknowledge the fact that the problem was due to limited resources and not the FBI's handling of the evidence.

On July 28th, 2010, only a few days before the anniversary of Kathy Briles death, the FBI publically disclosed that it had cut in half the convicted offender backlog from its peak in December 2009 of 312,000 samples to a then-current backlog of approximately 165,000 samples. In that report, the FBI stated that it was on track to eliminate the backlog. The report went on to state that it had shifted vital laboratory resources from casework to CODIS to address the massive growth of convicted offender samples which was largely in response to legislative changes in 2001, 2004, and 2005. Shifting the resources, along with other laboratory initiatives, gave the FBI the ability to address the backlog due to the skyrocketing demand.

In August 2009, the month Kathy Briles was murdered, the national DNA index system contained more than 7.3 million offender profiles. Within that number were 470,000 from Florida along with 280,000 pieces of evidence.

Even though there has been a push to eliminate the backlog, there have been cases where, due to the lack of speed in obtaining results, additional crimes have been committed before identification could be made of the perpetrator. In some cases, where it is warranted due to the need of a quick turnaround in identification, agencies will use private labs that may charge as much as $1,500 per sample.

Shayna Hayter had, through her testing, determined that the liquid drops found by DiFranco were sweat, and that they came from one man. Sweat contains sloughed off skin cells as she will testify about. The process is called "shedding."

It's December 7th, 2011, and Mr. Varn has called Shana Hayter as a witness for the prosecution. "Have you ever heard of a term called 'shedding'?" he asks her.

"Yes."

"Can you explain to the Jury what 'shedding' is?"

Hayter responds by telling the Jury that we all "shed" skin cells all the time. She testifies that if someone is sweating that the shed skin cells may find their way into the sweat and that skin cells contain DNA.

"In fact," Scanlan told the Jury in her opening remarks, "… it [the sample taken at Carmilfra] contained what FDLE analyst Shana Hayter will tell you is a complete profile. That means that the sample contains 13 genetic Markers that can be used to identify somebody, 13 separate things. When a sample contains all 13 of these Markers, it is enough to match it to someone and determine that that person is the one who left behind that DNA. Some samples don't have that many Markers. Some only have two or three or something like that, and that's what's called a partial sample. This was a full sample that could be used to identify the person who left that DNA behind at Nicole's house."

Sadly, it would not be until October 2nd, 2009, 60 days after Kathy Briles' murder, that Dumer would receive an FDLE report stating that a match had occurred and the man who was the DNA donor at the site of the home invasion on Carmilfra was Delmer Smith III, a convicted bank robber who had been out on parole. At that point, Delmer was sitting in jail in St. Petersburg for having violated his parole due to his involvement in a bar fight. When Delmer was informed that a substantial part of the evidence against him was because of the sweat he had deposited on the floor at the Carmilfra residence, he decided to complain that in his opinion he was being framed.

It was just slightly past 2 A.M. on March 15th when Detective Dumer left the scene on Carmilfra Drive and drove to the Sarasota Memorial Hospital in hopes of being able to meet with and interview the victim, Nicole Marshall. When he arrived at the hospital, he found her being attended to by medical personnel and that her neighbor was present as well in the room. He would soon learn that the neighbor was also Nicole Marshall's landlord.

While there, he took a recorded statement from the victim while she received treatment for her injuries. During the course of the recording, Nicole told Dumer her attacker had a gun. It appeared to be an automatic from what little she could see of it. She described it in one of their early meetings as being a "a large black handgun with a square slide and round barrel." The simple matter of how much of the weapon she was able to see, if in fact it was enough to be able to establish a handgun being involved in the crime, would be a point of contention that the defense would use. In Florida, there is an automatic sentence for use or display of a gun in a felony: displaying the weapon during a felony nets the criminal 10 years, fire it and it is 20 years, injure someone and it is life. No exceptions. No arguments. Automatic.

She went on and told Dumer that her assailant moved quickly to subdue her by striking her and forcing her face down onto the couch. She told the detective that she was aware that her attacker was wearing dark clothing that was rough to the touch, and that he had some type of heavy plastic-like gloves on that damaged her face when he grabbed her. But she was unsure if he was wearing a mask. She did recall, during the detective's interview with her at the hospital, that he had dark features about his face, what little she could see. She also said he sounded as if he were African American, but that she never saw any of his skin so she could not say positively that he was black. This would become a point the defense would use against her in its cross-examination of her on December 6th, 2011.

In addition to statements made to Dumer, when the initial call had gone out alerting Sergeant Tutko and others about the break-in, the question of race was raised and Bender was quick to seize on that and brought it up while questioning Tutko.

"Okay. Do you recall that the victim first reported that it was an African-American that had attacked her?"

"I believe that's what it says on the screen, the CAD screen."

Bender's main attack on race would occur during her cross-examination of Nicole Marshall. It was an attempt to introduce doubt that her client committed the crime. But the reality was that Nicole was unsure of her attacker's race and based her comments on what she heard him say and what she could see, which was not very much of him, physically.

"Now, is it not true," Bender asked, "that you believed, given the accent that you heard this assailant speak in, that he was an African American male?"

"Yes, I believed so."

"That means a black man; correct?"

"Yes."

"And not seeing any white area or any pale area of skin and the accent of the voice, you assumed it was a black man; correct?"

"I went by the accent, yes, and the voice."

"Okay. Nothing in what you were able to see or heard told you it was a white person; correct?"

"Correct."

Ms. Bender turned and pointed to the defendant. "Ms. Marshall, is Mr. Smith white or black?"

"White."

Nevertheless, technically and legally, Bender was wrong. Delmer is black as far as the law is concerned. He may look white, but he is 50 % black and so considered black by everyone except, in this case, Bender. In fact the term used to describe Delmer's racial status is: Mulatto.

This term is considered by many to be offensive. A better description would be racially mixed. But from a visual standpoint, Delmer can pass as white. From a bloodline standpoint, which takes into account identification on documents we all need to complete from time to time, he would claim that he was black. He would then be considered a member of a minority, thereby denying he is clearly half-white as well.

The State questioned witness Michele Quinones about Delmer's use of slang and ghetto-style talking as a counterattack on Bender's maneuver to establish doubt of Delmer's involvement based upon race. At least an attempt was made to introduce that to the Court by Scanlan on a redirect examination. "Okay," she began as she slowly walked across the courtroom speaking carefully as she did. "Tell me about what you called, 'the bubble.'"

Instantly, Defense Attorney Bender sat upright, the note taking pencil in her hand frozen between her fingers pointing outward away from the tablet she was writing on. She immediately wondered where Scanlan was going and was starting out of her seat when Michele answered. "Now I see things differently. And, like, you live in a bubble where you don't really see what's going on in the world around you."

Bender, sensing Scanlan was steering into an area that would be dangerous in regard to her client, was on her feet. "Judge."

"Is that how you felt?" Scanlan continued, ignoring Bender.

"Judge, can we approach?" Bender dropped the pencil.

The Court, "Sure."

The opposing attorneys approached the bench.

"Judge —," Bender started.

Judge Curley leaned forward. "What's the objection?"

"The objection is…" she paused for a moment thinking of how to word her complaint and then continued, "is that I think that she's going to be leading into an area where she's going to talk about part of the bursting of the bubble was when this battery incident happened —"

"Not going to talk about that," Scanlan replied quickly overriding Bender while shaking her head and looking down at the floor.

Bender continued, "— and all of that."

"But why is —"

"I don't know what the bubble —" Bender began, shaking her head, but was interrupted by the Court

"But why is it relevant to what she thinks now versus what she thought then?" Judge Curley asked, shifting her eyes from one attorney to the other like a spectator at a tennis match.

"She got interrupted," Scanlan said softly, nodding toward where Michele sat. "So I'm going to have her completely explain —"

Judge Curley leaned forward. Her curiosity pushed for a needed explanation from which she could make an informed decision relative to the objection, "How did she get into the bubble?" Her eyes wide, eyebrows lifted, looking for an answer from either woman.

"She," Scanlan said dryly, a bit mildly testy, as she nodded toward Bender, "got into whether or not Ms. Quinones believes that any of this property was stolen back when it happened. She looks back now and she thinks that maybe it was. Ms. Bender got into it. I'm just going to have her finish explaining that issue. That's all."

"All right, I'm going to sustain the objection." Judge Curley sat back in her seat and watched the opposing attorneys move back away from the bench.

Bender went back to sit beside Delmer content that she had won the challenge. Scanlan moved to stand near her table where State Attorney Varn sat watching the proceedings and taking notes. Scanlan looked down at the floor thinking how to adjust and recover quickly. She was not happy that she had been stopped in her logical pursuit of the facts. Quickly she came up with a different approach.

"The fact that you didn't know where all that property came from certainly means that it could have been stolen, doesn't it?" Scanlan asked.

"Correct."

"Okay. Let me ask you about one other area." Scanlan slyly began to maneuver her questions toward Delmer's style of speech. "When," Scanlan paused for a second, rethinking how to phrase her question. She then went on, "The defendant's normal demeanor, how would you describe the way he was with you normally?"

"Oh, he was great with me. He was very sweet, buy me flowers for no reason, wash my hair every day. Make my mother tea when she was sick."

"How did he speak to you? What was his manner of speaking to you ordinarily?"

"Slang, fun, if not," Michele stopped suddenly, unsure of the question being asked, then added, "it all depends what we're talking about."

Scanlan looked directly at Michele and asked calmly, not wishing to expose the direction she was taking to

Bender who was listening intently, "Okay. When the defendant gets excited does his manner of speech tend to change?"

Bender started to stand.

"Yes."

"I'm going to," Bender started, but only to be cut off by Scanlan who continued her question sequence.

"Tell me how?" Scanlan quickly asked, ignoring Bender hoping for an answer that the Jury would hear before the challenge was issued forcing her to stop midsentence. The seasoned attorney learned years before that an objection may be lodged but if the Jury heard the answer, regardless of whether or not the objection was sustained, they would recall it during their deliberations. So, it was important to push forward and ignore the opposition.

"Judge, I'm going to object to relevance as to —."

Before Bender was able to complete her objection, Curley stopped her by requesting that both women approach the bench once more. As the Judge sat forward, she calmly asked for an explanation.

In response, Scanlan told the Court that Bender had "… asked Ms. Marshall if she assumed that her attacker was a black man based upon the way that he was speaking and the manner that he was speaking." She went on to argue that Michele was about to testify that when the defendant became "anxious or excited or angry" that he tended "to speak …'ghetto.'"

It was Scanlan's argument that Bender had opened the door to the prosecution being able to use Michele for rebuttal against Bender's questioning of Nicole Marshal relative to her racial identification based on the sound of Delmer's voice during the time he was holding her captive.

Scanlan continued her argument, "I believe that this will link it back to," she paused, "Ms. Bender specifically asked Ms. Marshall about the manner in which her attacker spoke, and then she made Ms. Marshall specifically point out that Mr. Smith is a white man. So I'm going to have

Ms. Quinones from her personal knowledge explain that issue —"

"Okay."

"— only because Ms. Bender brought it up."

Judge Curley looked from Scanlan to Bender. "Your response?"

"Judge, I don't think it's," she paused, then continued, "her interpretation of how he behaves at different times in different arenas through her interpretation whether he's excited or angry or whatever is relevant to this, and just because her interpretation is something ghetto, I think that that is a derogatory term that —"

Scanlan looked from Bender to Judge Curley as she interrupted the defense attorney. "That's the term she uses," she said pointedly. "That's not my term."

Bender continues with a stammer, slightly startled by Scanlan's interruption, "— is— but it's wholly her personal opinion, and I don't think that that's relevant —"

Scanlan responded quickly, defending her position, "Her opinion is based upon eight months of her daily observations of the defendant."

Judge Curley said quickly, "Objection sustained." She sat back in her chair and quietly waited for any response to occur from either of the attorneys. Then Scanlan said, "Judge, if we can come back —"

Judge Curley nodded, agreeing to a continuance of the discussion at the bench.

Scanlan said, "I will make a motion in limine[13] for closing arguments that Ms. Bender not be allowed to argue any inferences based upon those questions that she asked Ms. Marshall."

The Court looked over at the prosecution and replied quietly, "We'll deal with that at the time."

---

[13] A motion in limine is used to exclude evidence by a party who believes the introduction of such evidence would be prejudicial to them. An example would be the making of a motion to prevent a Jury from knowing of prior crimes.

Assistant State Attorney Varn stood and jumped into the discussion. "The issue is," he began, "and I always go back to this whenever we're talking about a relevancy objection — does the relevant information tend to prove or disprove the material fact in issue? Okay. Ms. Bender did bring up the fact that he — that the defendant — that he was black based upon the manner of speaking."

Judge Curley frowned. She clearly was not buying the prosecution's argument. "Do you realize that all of what you are saying right now is so stereotypical? Because what you failed to do — what you failed to do is you failed to establish that through your witness. All she said was African-American. You're taking a leap and going — it's ghetto or slang. None of that. Uh — uh. I'm laying the record. Ms. Marshall testified to none of that. Ms. Marshall did not say anything that he uses particular — I want crack, I want money; I'm going to kill you — X, Y, and Z. That's not — okay?" The look on her face drove the point home.

Scanlan took several steps back into the center of the room. She was startled that she had been blocked once again. However, she refused to let it bother her or to allow any hint of her frustration while she set about to mentally regroup. It was a place in her courtroom life to which she was well attuned and no one could suspect her feelings or thoughts. She then turned and faced Michele while asking her question quickly, "Does the defendant's demeanor change when he gets angry or excited?"

"Yes."

Walking back to take her seat next to Earl Varn, she knew the answer received wasn't 100% what she wanted, but she managed to get her position into the trial and it might have mattered to the jurors as it was obvious what she was trying to submit to them.

CHAPTER TWENTY EIGHT
Mike Dumer

Scanlan, in her examination of Sergeant Tutko, addressed his remark about the need for one person who would be in charge of a case.

Responding to her questions regarding the Carmilfra case, Tutko had testified that once the crime scene was under control he then had received a brief synopsis of what had taken place from Deputy Kuentzel. Following that report, he requested the on-call detective to come to the scene and take over management of the case.

"And why would the investigation be turned over to a detective?" Scanlan asked Sergeant Tutko, as the Jury looked on.

"Because he is the person who is going to see that case through to the end. He is responsible for all the follow-up. So per policy, he would be the one handling that case from then on."

That person, for this case, was Detective Mike Dumer.

In a meeting with Beth Scanlan and Susanne O'Donnell, Beth told me, "Detective Dumer spent months working on the Carmilfra case and those related to it. He was extremely focused on solving them and bringing the person responsible for these crimes to justice." As she spoke, Susanne O'Donnell nodded her head in assent. Both attorneys cited Dumer, "… because of his attention and dedication to solving the cases, as being largely responsible for the arrest and prosecution of Delmer Smith."

On March 15th, 2009, Nicole Marshall remained in the hospital for observation following evidence that she had suffered a cardiac event. Later in the day, her husband flew in from Montreal, Canada to be with his wife and to assist in the investigation. In the meantime, Detective Dumer continued speaking with her regarding her credit cards and other items that were stolen.

Almost immediately after visiting his wife in the hospital, Marc Marshall went to work at the Carmilfra Drive address. There he combed through Nicole's belongings to discover what things he knew were missing. While doing so he wrote a more comprehensive list of stolen items than he had before.

While searching through the disheveled mess, Marc found his wife's wallet. Everyone was relieved to find it still held her credit cards.

Detective Dumer and his supervisor, Sergeant Walsh, became determined they would solve the Carmilfra Drive and Osage Terrace cases. Carmilfra was believed to be the case of the highest worth in terms of evidence because of the sweat droppings. Delmer Smith was very adept at not leaving any evidence behind that would identify him, but it was hoped that the sweat found at Carmilfra would be his undoing. Walsh told Dumer to focus on Carmilfra, a fact recognized by the prosecution.

Scanlan asked in trial if Dumer had returned to Carmilfra Drive after visiting with Nicole Marshall at the hospital. He responded that he had and that he had met with Sergeant DiFranco again, but he had nothing more to do with the processing of the scene as that was DiFranco's area of expertise.

"Okay," Scanlan said. "In the next few months, did you spend that time following up potential leads trying to find the perpetrator of this crime?"

"Yes, I did."

"Was there anything in particular that you thought would lead you to a break in the case?" Scanlan stood next to the lectern and waited for the answer that would introduce critical evidence that linked Delmer Smith directly to the crime.

"There was three items in particular that the victim had told me were taken during this particular crime. The first was her computer, an HP laptop computer; the second was the television that was taken off the wall. It was a 55 inch Phillips plasma TV. It's one of the old plasma TVs that change color on the back drop of the wall. So that was just something that I was very interested in, as well as an old generation Cassiopeia PDA. It was green in color."

"What is a PDA?"

"Personal data assistant." Dumer went on to explain that PDAs were developed and sold before Blackberries and iPhones and were not as capable as the later devices. He knew that, if found, both the computer and the PDA would have data that would be traceable back to the Marshall's. The television was a bit out of date and might also stand out if pawned or attempted to be disposed of at a collective garage sale location such as the Red Barn in Manatee County.

"What sorts of things did you do to look for these three particular items?" Scanlan asked.

"Well, I know that there was some searches on Craigslist. We had checked some pawnshops. I visited many of our— many persons that are in the county that may have taken possession of these kind of items to see if they talk to a lot of different people to see if they had any knowledge of these types of items that might have been sold for money or any other exchange."

"Fair to say that from the middle of March until the middle of September you followed up on a lot of the leads that pretty much went nowhere?"

"Yes," Dumer responded. "That's correct."

Dumer continued to meet on and off with the Marshall's for several days about the missing items.

The 16th of March, 2009, proved to be a busy day for the detective. He went back to the pawnshops in the area, where he again spoke to the owners describing the stolen property he was searching for. He was told by those he interviewed that they would keep an eye out and if any items were brought to them that they thought resembled what he was looking for then they would immediately be in touch with him. As a follow up to a prior conversation, he then spoke with Marc Marshall on the phone to advise him of the actions taken. He also met again with Nicole Marshall. in the hospital briefly and, as he had done with her husband, brought her up to date and asked her if she could remember anything else that might help him with the investigation.

He then drove back into the neighborhood where the burglary had happened and stopped at Suncoast Motor Sports. Suncoast is an automobile sales business specializing in foreign cars. The business backs up against Carmilfra Drive and part of the Phillippi Creek. Knowing it had security cameras focused in a variety of directions, Dumer thought it might just have a video of the night of the break-in.

However, after he reviewed the video tapes from that night, he realized, unfortunately, that the videos were useless to him. The distance and the angle filmed brought about such a distorted view of the street and the Creek that the detective knew it held no investigative value. He then drove to where Palos Verde Drive intersects Carmilfra Drive and spoke with the neighbors who lived in that area.

While doing so, one of the residents reported that she had seen a suspicious white male in the neighborhood either on March 11th or 12th about 2030 hours. Nothing else was learned except that he wore a "green hoodie," and he appeared to be in his late teens.

At one point in the day, he received a phone call from forensic technician Jessica Sawyer. She wanted him to know that she was in route from Sarasota to the FDL offices in Fort Myers. She had five of the DNA samples that had been collected by Sergeant DiFranco at the Carmilfra Drive location. Following that conversation, and wanting to insure that the DNA samples would receive priority processing, Dumer then contacted Rochelle Gateman, the supervisor for the FDLE Bio-lab in Fort Myers. Gateman advised him that her staff would expedite the processing of the DNA connected in this case per his request.

On the 17th, Marc Marshall phoned Dumer to advise him that the missing computer had Webcam software installed and that they had Skype accounts. Marshall told the detective that his son had noted his mother's Skype account had been activated shortly before midnight on the 16th. He said the son had attempted to make contact but there was no response and the Skype session was terminated immediately.

Dumer knew it was a longshot, but there was a chance the thief might unwittingly expose himself via the Skype account, and so he decided to contact the company for assistance. On the 18th, he made a call to Matt Flinders of Skype in Salt Lake City. The Detective gave an overview of the information required from Skype and Flinders directed him to the Advanced Technical Support Unit located in Luxemburg, Germany. Following that conversation, Dumer sent a "Preservation Letter" to the company requesting that all data regarding both Marc's and Nicole's Skype accounts be protected.

On the 19th, he followed up by sending two subpoenas to the home office of Skype in Luxemburg requesting all service and account information. However, neither Flinders nor the home office in Luxemburg were able to help him as there had been no use of the Skype accounts since when the computer had been stolen.

Early afternoon of the 19th, Dumer saw to it that all known information regarding the case was entered into the FBI's database: Violent Criminal Apprehension Program or VICAP. The VICAP system is used to determine if there are similar cases that have been entered. He found no matching entries.

On the 21st, he met with his supervisor, Sergeant Walsh, along with detectives Lefebvre, Kaspar, and Colonna at the Sarasota County Sheriff's offices in downtown Sarasota. There the team of officers put together a plan to visit the area along US 41 (The Tamiami Trail) from Bahia Vista Street to Stickney Point Road. The plan was to look for anyone appearing suspicious or to locate known individuals with whom they could speak regarding some of the activities in the area. The operation went into effect at 1900 hours and concluded at 2400. Although the team made numerous contacts, they were not able to develop any information regarding any of the attacks in the area.

On the 22nd and 23rd, Dumer rechecked for activity on the Skype accounts and was informed there had been none. Shayna Hayter phoned him before noon on the 23rd and told him she definitely had DNA from a male. She also had found in one of the samples a mixture containing DNA from a male and female. "What I would like for you to get for me is a buccal swab from both the victim and her husband," she told him. "That way I can eliminate the husband and confirm the DNA on the wife.

"I'll get it right away," Dumer replied.

"Fine. While you do that I am going to upload my findings to CODIS and see what we can find there."

Dumer immediately phoned Mrs. Marshall and requested a meeting. He also contacted forensics officer DiFranco. She agreed to meet with both he and the Marshalls to obtain buccal swabs from the couple that were then submitted to the FDLE lab in Fort Myers. A few days later, he learned that evidence collected at the Bougainvillea address had been submitted to the FDLE in search of any DNA that might be there.

On the 25th, Dumer was notified by Detective DeNiro that the Sarasota Police Department had forwarded to the FDLE evidence collected at the Bougainvillea scene for DNA analysis.

On the 30th, he met again with Nicole Marshall. This time she provided him with a pillow sham. She told him that, "He used the comforter to cover the large screen TV when he took if off the wall." She also supplied him with an updated list of the items that had been stolen.

On the 31st, Shana Hayter called Dumer to tell him that the DNA sample uploaded to CODIS had resulted in no identification being made.

On April 2nd and 3rd, Walsh and Dumer reviewed case reports from Sarasota and Manatee counties to see if there were similarities and several were found. It became more certain that this was the same person operating in both counties.

Then, on the 6th of April, Dumer was notified of a homicide at 2150 Jo An Drive in Sarasota. The victim is Georgann Lee Smith. Georgann was a 37-year-old nursing home worker who was also a holder of a black belt in Karate. However, her advanced degree in Karate was no match for the attack. It happened quickly. She was stunned with a blow to the face or head immediately upon coming into contact with her attacker who, most likely, had met her at the front door to her home. A strong possibility was cited that she might have known her killer.

A trademark of Delmer Smith was that he always attacked quickly and his focus was on instantaneous control. He achieved that by striking the face or head stunning the victim. A close friend of the deceased found her body in the midst of a blood spattered front room. The wounds were consistent in appearance and extent of damage to that of someone having been beaten to death with a blunt object.

Additionally, Georgann had been sexually assaulted both prior to her death and following her death with foreign objects. The ruthlessness and brutality of those attacks were so severe that internal organs were perforated and ruptured.

The incredible blood spatter was evidence that Georgann's struggle to remain alive moved room to room through her home. She had been beaten to death with a baseball bat. The very same one she kept next to her front door for self-protection. Her fight to live ended where her naked body was found lying on the blood-spattered mattress she slept on in the front room of the house.

Her friends told me that the rear of the house was too hot to sleep there and she had moved a mattress to the front where it was cooler. That was where they found her corpse, beaten to death.

Amid the wreckage of broken furniture in a hauntingly quiet room—they found Georgann Smith's body. All about her battered remains was blood spatter. She, herself, was blood covered, raped, and left lying partially on her mattress in a pool of drying blood; her eyes open wide in the shock and horror of the last fleeting moments of her young life.

CHAPTER TWENTY NINE
Dark Clothes and a Gun

In Detective Dumer's July 26th, 2011 deposition taken by Marjorie Bender, he explained that Nicole Marshall was surprised by the attack. When questioned by the attorney if Nicole was able to define her attacker, the detective responded, "Nicole described the unknown perpetrator as male." He then went on to say that, according to Nicole, the man was, "large in stature. Wearing dark clothes. Unknown if he was wearing a mask but he had dark features about his face." He added that Nicole had told him that, "… the perpetrator sounded like an African-American."

"Okay," Ms. Bender said. "But nothing else."

"That's all she could tell me," Dumer said sitting forward slightly with his hands folded, his focus calm and intent on Bender.

"Okay."

"Because you have to understand it was dark," he continued.

"Uh, hmm." She was listening but, at the same time, looking at her notes and wanting to get back to the direction she wished to move in and so his response was basically overruled as it had no relevance to the area she was interested.

"Um, she was watching TV sitting on her couch knitting or doing some sort of a bead project. She was, she saw something come out of the corner of her eye and the next thing you know wham. Somebody is on top of her. The lights turned off. She's got her head thrown onto this; into the couch," Dumer continued without prompting.

"Uh, hmm."

"She's under significant physical control and being told don't scream or I'll shoot you."

"Uh, hmm."

"You haven't met Ms. Marshall yet but she is all of about ninety-five pounds."

Bender looked up from her notes. She had decided to question the presence of a handgun. So she went on to question details about the gun that Nicole said she had seen, "The gun that was described with a square slide and round barrel."

Dumer replied, "As far as she described it, yeah."

Ms. Bender continued, "Okay, I think she was; it might have been heard that said something akin to a nine millimeter. Maybe that was someone else."

Dumer replied, "Um, I don't think she would know."

Having read the deposition and noting the comment about the presence of a handgun, I decided to track down Mike Dumer and ask him about it. I stopped by his home one Saturday and spoke with his wife who told me that he and his son were at the local recreational baseball fields. Finding him there, I told him I was curious about his deposition regarding Nicole and the weapon used by Delmer to threaten his victims. "Nicole," he began with a slight smile as he crossed his arms and leaned up against the side of his car, "is not a gun owner." He looked over to where his son had disappeared with his friends to a refreshment stand. "She wouldn't know a .45 from a shotgun." He laughed.

I knew he was joking, but the point was made. There was no way that she could have identified the weapon as to its make or caliber even though Delmer exposed the weapon to her at one point as he threatened her life. The fact was that it was done while she was under incredible stress, fearing for her life. She was not thinking that she might need to be able to provide a description of the firearm to anyone in the immediate future. Her mind was focused on survival.

In court, Bender strategically probed Nicole's memory regarding the pistol carried by her assailant. "The situation that the State described that you went through in," she paused for a moment as she walked slowly toward the witness, "I believe it was the master closet where you were kneeling on the ground …"

"Yes," Nicole answered, not knowing there was more to the question."

"… was that the only time when you were in this person's presence that you caught a slight glimpse of the barrel of that gun?" She placed heavy, purposeful emphasis on the words: slight glimpse.

"It was not a slight glimpse," Nicole quickly returned. She sensed the direction the questioning was taking. "It was **not** a slight glimpse!"

Bender was startled by the sharp return. "What was it?" she asked.

"It was shown to me. He showed me the gun!"

"How much of the gun did you see?" Bender was looking for an opening to trip up Nicole. It never came.

"She was a great witness," Scanlan would later say.

During the deposition of Detective Dumer taken months before the trial, Defense Attorney Bender sought information about the gun then too. She needed to come up with a rational reason in order to convince the judge in the case why it was necessary to prevent any inclusion of the gun owned by Delmer into the trial. Looking across the table at the detective, she regarded him thoughtfully as she continued with her questions. "Okay," she began. "But that's the extent of the detail you recall her being able to give. And that's a very important part for you to get from the victim as soon as possible, correct?"

Dumer sensed that Bender was seeking a hole for her to probe. "Well and," he began, "and again that's why I put at the very end refer to the DVD for the full account of her statement."

"Right."

"I'm pretty sure that we transcribed all the statements as to what she said." He picked up a folder filled with papers and glanced at the contents.

"Uh, hmm."

"And here it is right here. It's in this report." He tapped the file with his index finger, his gaze straying from the file to Bender's eyes that were focused on his. "It's sixty pages long and we go exactly what it is that she told us so as to how she described that gun." He sat back in his chair grateful that the remarks had been well documented and that Scanlan had seen to the file being present for the deposition.

Ms. Bender continued, "No other features regarding the clothing you stated?"

"No," Dumer replied.

"Okay."

Dumer decided to clarify the situation regarding what Nicole had told him and how he had recorded it. "My report is a consolidation. It is not a, not a, um, blow-by-blow description so to speak. Right? You, you, we agree on that? It's this report, this investigation …"

Ms. Bender replied looking down at her notepad, "Um, Detective …"

Dumer continued, "is contained in about five different binders not just one …"

"I know sir," Bender said speaking on top of Dumer.

"… report."

Bender would continue to probe as the deposition went forward, hoping to find a weak spot in Dumer's report on or his memory of the case. Notwithstanding her attempts, the detective would continue to hold his own place and not be rattled by her.

CHAPTER THIRTY
Home Invasion

Scanlan continued with her opening presentation to the Jury of how Delmer had moved quickly to gain control and silence Nicole Marshall. "She screamed in terror. He told her that if she didn't stop screaming, he would kill her. She believed him, and decided that from that moment on she would do whatever he said. She desperately hoped that she could stay alive." To make sure she did not cry out, he covered her mouth with a rough textured glove that cut and bruised her face leaving visible marks.

Nicole told me that immediately after he had turned the lights out, she found herself suddenly face down on the couch, pressed there by the strength and weight of the man leaning over the top of her. "I don't know how it came to me," she said as she looked up at me from her coffee. "But he had me down on my knees. I was facing the couch. My face was down on the sofa cushion and he was holding me that way. My hands had dropped to the floor as I was trying to support myself and it suddenly dawned on me that I could reach up under the couch and take my rings off.

"I don't know what made me think of it, but I knew I had one chance to save my rings and I immediately pulled them off my fingers and left them on the floor beneath the couch where he could not see them. That's the only reason I still have them." She held up her hand for me to see.

"He made her turn off the television," Scanlan continued with the narrative of the attack in her opening statements:

> He dragged her through the house, checking out each room to see what was in it that was available for him to steal. They went room to room. He stayed behind her. He was holding onto the back of her hair or maybe the back of her robe. She had very long hair at the time. You'll see her testify today. She's cut her hair short, but her hair was almost down to her waist at the time.
>
> Because he was behind her, she wasn't able to see anything about him other than to get a sense of him as being a stocky strongman. She knew he was not huge, but he was definitely bigger than her husband, the one man she was most familiar with, and he was certainly much bigger than she. She is 5'2" and weighs approximately 98 pounds. He is 5' 11" and weighs in at just slightly above 220 pounds.
>
> He had on those scratchy gloves that he kept over her mouth, and, like I said, she believes that he had on a mask. She still to this day she cannot tell you exactly … who he was. He kept saying things to her like he needed money, he needed crack.
>
> He's dragging her around the house. They got into the bathroom, and in the bathroom he showed her the barrel of his gun and told her that he would kill her. She was trying at that point very hard to pay attention to all the details about what would happen, but her heart was racing fast, and she was terrified. The defendant had the gun in one hand, holding up to her head, and he was holding her with the other hand by the back of her hair or the top of her robe.
>
> They left the bathroom. They went into the second bedroom where the light was still on. He

told her to turn the light off. He looked around, and he asked her what was in the room, what was in the room that he could take. Pointed out certain things. He asked questions about her headphones, her Cassiopeia which is an old-style PDA type device.

They went through the living room. They went into the kitchen. He saw her computer set up in the kitchen. He made her pack it up for him and her computer bag. He demanded that she tell him the password so they would be able to get into the computer. Her computer was not password locked, and she kept telling him this. He didn't believe her and he demanded, 'Give me the password. Give me the password.'

At the Starbucks in the Barnes and Nobles in Sarasota where I met Nicole Marshall four years and one month following the break-in at her home, she paused in our conversation. Her eyes slipped from mine to the coffee cup held securely in both hands. She licked her lips and then said, almost in a whisper, "He kept demanding that I tell him the password. I kept telling him there is no password." Her eyes, grown large, suddenly rose and met mine, her voice taking on strength. "He didn't believe me. I was terrified. I was afraid he was going to kill me because I couldn't tell him the password, but there was no password!"

She paused again, remembering, her fingers growing tight about her coffee cup. "I put everything in the bag," she said quietly, slowly. "Everything that had anything to do with the computer, just like he told me to do, I put it in the bag." She would later plead with him to "please leave the computer" with her because of the personal information she had placed on the laptop.

He said he would.

He lied.

"When he left," Scanlan continued with her opening remarks:

> He took with him her wallet that had around $250 in cash in it that was on a shelf in the master bedroom. He took her watch. He took her big screen television. He took her computer. He took the speakers for her computer. He took a Bose docking station and her iPod. He took some of her crystals which weren't worth anything, but he asked her if they were diamonds, and he took those too. However, he did not get her wedding rings.

While in the kitchen, Delmer rummaged through every cabinet, opening every drawer, looking for something to steal. He did all this in the dark. He even looked in the refrigerator.

Scanlan told the Jury that there was another bathroom in the house, and that Delmer, having found it difficult to work in the dark, ordered her to go into that room and to turn on the light to help him see. "When she did that she was hoping at that point that she would be able to get a good look at him. She tried when they were in the bathroom to get a look at him in the mirror, but it was too fast, and she couldn't. He dragged her from the bathroom back into the living room, and he told her to lie down on the ground. He was going to take her big screen, flat screen television off the wall.

"He realized that he needed tools to be able to do that, so he demanded that she tell him where her tools were."

CHAPTER THIRTY ONE
I'm from Canada

"I told him I didn't know where the tools were. I didn't know where they were kept." Nicole said recalling the moment when he had hold of her, his hidden face but close to hers. She spoke unhurriedly with a low voice and slowly sipped her coffee.

"What?" he hissed, pulling her closer. "You don't know where the tools are? You live here, don't you?"

"No," she explained quickly, "I'm visiting from Canada. I'm renting this house. I don't know where everything is at."

His grip on her tightened as he leaned in closer to her. Then, after what seemed a long time, he said to her coldly, "Well, after tonight you won't be visiting again."

She was startled. What was he telling her? Was he indicating he intended on killing her? Deep terror grabbed at her and her throat tightened as her mouth went dry. But then she took charge of herself.

Nevertheless, regardless of the fear, a calm strength lay deep within her that resolved to not let him have the day — no matter what lay ahead.

She had been through enough in her life that, regardless of the height of her fear, she refused to simply lay down her life without making sure he knew that he could take all from her but he could never take who she was, and so she replied evenly and thoughtfully, "Why?" she asked. Then she added honestly, without any tremor in her voice, "I like it here."

She steeled herself for a response. However, all that occurred was the presence of an ominous silence that engulfed them for what she felt was hours and yet it was only moments. She thought she felt him tense and then relax slightly, not enough to release her but enough to notice the difference in how he was holding onto her.

He continued to stand close next to her breathing heavily.

Had she endangered herself, she wondered by making such a comment? Had she spoken with too much confidence in her voice, too loudly?

She did not know. She could feel him staring at her, but did not dare look up and over at him sensing to do so would unleash a fury she did not wish to expose herself.

A long moment passed while he stood near to her — menacingly close. The only sound she heard was his breathing, and her own heart hammering the blood through her veins. Then, without another word being said between them, he tightened his grip on her and forcibly led her into the garage.

He knew that was the most logical place for the tools he sought.

She did not fight him. She did not resist him in any manner. She let him take her where he wanted to go choosing to be compliant, not argue, and especially to not show any signs of panic. Her life had been filled with a series of events from early childhood that had taught her how to act in such a case as this. "Don't panic!" She told herself. "Don't show fear or anger. Try to be as normal acting as possible. It is your life that's on the line."

"Hoping to keep him calm she (Nicole) thanked him for not hurting her, and she told him he was being kind." Scanlan continued with her opening remarks.

"He replied to her by saying, 'No, I am not kind, and I will kill you,'"

"In the garage, he found several tools he said he needed. He handed them to her and he told her to carry them for him. He then led her back into the living room. Once there, he took the tools from her telling her to face away from him so she could not see what he was doing."

Scanlan continued her presentation to the Jury:

> He got her back into the living room and he made her get back on the floor. He tied her up with electrical wires. She was hogtied. He tied electrical wires around her hands, behind her back and then to her feet and then tied that same wire and looped around her neck. She's lying facedown on the floor. She kept as still as possible. Her biggest concern was that she would have a leg cramp and she would choke herself and die there on her living room floor.

"I was extremely frightened that I would get a leg cramp," Nicole told me. "The wires were tight across my throat. I was afraid to move for fear I would choke myself. I could hear him moving about the house. At one point he told me I was being watched by a partner. He even said, 'she's cooperating.'" However, at no time did Nicole hear or see anyone else in the house.

She told me that another wire was run from the wires around her neck to the wires around her feet and that he had also gagged her with one of her t-shirts.

Scanlan went on with her opening, as she made purposeful eye contact with each juror:

She's tied up on the floor, trying to concentrate just on breathing and staying as still as possible. She's got her head sideways facing the pool, looking out on the lanai. Out of the corner of her eye she can see him lifting the television off the wall. She heard him going through her house as she lay there tied up on the floor. She hears him taking different things from different rooms, all of the things that he had walked around and looked [at], all the things that were valuable that he could take. He even stole the bedspread off her bed so he could put everything on the bedspread and take it all out in one bundle.

When I met with Detective Dumer to discuss this case, he said:

> Nicole told me that after Delmer had her hog tied; the perp went back through the house searching for the items he wanted to take with him. While her attacker was roaming around the house and ransacking it, he would act as though he was speaking to someone else advising this other person that Nicole was cooperating. He would then occasionally advise her that she was being watched. He came back several times to check on her asking if she was okay prior to searching further for other things to steal.

"Before he left he told her he was going to untie her, but he didn't. He said that when she was gone [Scanlan paused and corrected herself] when he was gone she can call the Police, but he also told her that he had a partner who was watching the house and the partner was going to stay behind and keep an eye on her," Scanlan told the Jury. She added, "She would tell you that she thinks that he was trying to scare her. She never got the sense that there was another person. You're not going to hear any evidence that there was another person involved. And when he left, she did not hear anyone."

Marshall told me, "I asked him to please, please leave my computer. It had a lot of personal data on it, beading information, and other things. He said he would, but he lied." Nicole looked at me and shook her head. "He lied. He took it with him."

She recalled he mentioned something about a van; and he told her he had to return, which he did before driving off, to cover his trail by pouring something around the house (it was later discovered the substance was pepper).

"Thankfully," Scanlan told the Jury during her opening remarks, "when he first came into the house, she had the presence of mind and was able to take her wedding rings off and throw them underneath her couch as she was pushed face down on the couch. He did not get her wedding rings."

Scanlan paused for a moment to let the Jury absorb the picture she was painting, and then added:

"He left her alone hog-tied on her living room floor, heart beating so fast that she didn't know what she was going to do. She laid there completely still for at least five minutes thinking that if she couldn't get herself untied she was going to remain on that floor and she wouldn't be found until the next day."

Scanlan paused once more and then continued:

"She didn't think that she would stay alive until the next day. She thought her leg would cramp and that she would choke herself. She started to wiggle around a little bit, terrified that she was going to hurt herself even worse, but she managed to wiggle around just enough to get the wires a little bit loose, looked around, did not see anyone in the house, did not sense anyone in the house, and she kept wiggling little by little until she was able to get herself out of those electrical cords."

"Once you got yourself free and out of the cords, what happened after that?" Scanlan asked Nicole as she sat in the witness chair.
"Well, my mouth was very dry and my heart was beating so fast and my face was hurting so much that the first thing I did was to go to the bathroom and take a look at my face…."
"Were you bleeding?"
"Yes." She then drank a little water because she was so dry.

Scanlan continued, "When she finally got herself released, she looked for her cell phone. She didn't have a landline in the house. She just had a cell phone. She found that her cell phone was broken in half and left on her couch, so she was not able to call for help from her home."

"So once you found that [the broken phone], what did you do next?" Scanlan asked.

"Well, for a little while I thought if I go outside through the front door, maybe somebody's watching me, is it wise to do so?" Smith had done his best to give the impression that a partner was close by and keeping watch on her. "She's cooperating," he said once, but Nicole never sensed another person's presence. Still, common sense called for caution. Therefore, she hesitated on the idea of running for help.

She thought about going out the back. However, behind the house was an area covered with rocks and boulders. At the far end was a fence. Beyond the fence was the Phillippi Creek.

"I was so shaky that I thought I'd fall in the water. So I took courage, and I ran out the front door."

"She ran out the front door, and she went to her next-door neighbor's house to beg them to help her."

"I rang the doorbell quite a bit. They were just about to go to bed. And they all came out, and I was greeted by the owner of the house. And she took me in her arms, and I told her what had happened, that I had been robbed."

"I was crying quite a bit at that point," she testified.

"But there she was," Scanlan continued with her opening remarks. "She is in her robe. She's barefoot. She's got marks around her neck. She's got marks around her ankles. She's got marks around her wrists. She's terrified. She tells them, 'I've been robbed.' They call the Police. It takes the police only two minutes to arrive to the house to see — to respond to the scene."

Scanlan explained the actions taken by officers upon arrival. She spoke of how they secured the scene. She tells the Jury that the officers visited briefly with Nicole at the neighbor's house and found her in critical condition with an ambulance on the way.

"She had bruises everywhere, on her wrists, on her ankles, around her neck, from the electrical cords, and she had a terrible pain in her chest." Scanlan paused, taking a deep breath, and then said slowly, matter-of-factly, looking into each juror's eyes, "It turns out that she was so terrified that she had a heart attack."

CHAPTER THIRTY TWO
Spilled Pepper

On March 15th at 0023 hours, Detective Dumer arrived at the Carmilfra Drive address where he met Sergeant Daniel Tutko and Deputy J. Thomas. These officers provided him with an initial update on the home invasion robbery. Dumer noted the residence had been taped off with crime scene tape and that it was secure to which he would later testify in a deposition conducted by Delmer's defense attorney, Marjorie Bender on July 26, 2011.

"Okay, so when you arrived, they [the other officers] were already on the scene, but you didn't go into, you believe, the crime scene?" Bender asked during her deposition of Detective Dumer on July 26, 2011. She was seeking a hole in Dumer's investigative methods. She had earlier lightly probed the detective's background in forensics. She was looking for an opening to introduce doubt about the investigative methods regarding prevention of crime scene contamination.

"No, I know that I did not." Dumer responded. "Because … one of the things that I do routinely, particularly on a … major crime scene … is I don't want to contaminate the scene. So the very first thing I'm doing is, I'm going to wait, 'cause I'm not in a rush …. I'm going to wait for my forensics people to get there …." Dumer went on to explain that he wants to allow the forensics person to have access to an uncontaminated scene.

While speaking with the other officers, Dumer learned that deputy Thomas had conducted a limited canvas of the neighborhood that did not reveal any witness information. Dumer then asked where the victim was. Sergeant Tutko said that she was at the neighbor's house and Deputy Thomas pointed to that location.

Dumer walked over to the neighbor's residence in hopes that he would be able to speak with the victim; however, once there, he learned she was suffering from chest pains and that she was being prepared for transport to Sarasota Memorial Hospital. The neighbor would accompany her as they were close friends.

"I walked back to Nicole's home," Dumer told me. "I knew that I was not going to be able to interview her then. I would have to check in later after she received medical treatment. By then it was a little after one o'clock in the morning, and I met Sergeant R. DiFranco from forensic services." The detective wrote in his investigative report:

> Sergeant DiFranco and I conducted a walkthrough of the crime scene. In our initial walkthrough we noticed a lanai screen in the rear of the residence that had a tear in the screening next to the entrance door. We also located several shoe impressions on the east side of the house that were photographed.
>
> I noted that the house was a single story residence with a circular drive. The front door entrance opened into a living room area. Once inside the residence, I observed a knotted electrical wire located on the floor of the living room. Sergeant DiFranco and I located fluid droplets on the floor throughout the residence. The droplets appeared to be fresh, that is, in a fluid state rather

than dried. I backed out of the residence in order to preserve any additional evidence that may be located. Sergeant DiFranco photographed and documented the scene.

By then it was about 0200 and the detective drove to the hospital to meet with the victim. "While there," he told me, "I took a recorded statement from Nicole while she was being treated by medical personnel."

Bender was curious about the pepper being spread about in the house, and asked Dumer during his deposition, "Um, were you able to, and this is a completely different topic. Were you able to determine why, um, the suspect used pepper? Was it simply to put a K-9 off-track or do you not know?"

"I don't know," Dumer replied. "Here's the problem, there are many questions I would like to," he paused, "to, ask Mr. Smith. That would be one of them."

"Well my...." Bender tried to continue.

"Because the first question I'd ask him would be did you see *Cool Hand Luke?*"

"Why?" Bender sat forward, head titled slightly, her curiosity tweaked.

"Because in the movie, *Cool Hand Luke,* that's what they did. They threw pepper down to try and cut off the dogs. We don't know. We don't know why the perpetrator put pepper down. We don't know."

Dumer went on to say that he had spoken with several people concerning the pepper issue related to tracking dogs. One such person was a deputy at the time of the Carmilfra home invasion, Tracey Ross, who volunteers his time with the Sarasota dog search and rescue team. "He's been doing it for a long time. He has several bloodhounds that he uses," Dumer said referring to Ross.

Dumer said he had questioned Mr. Ross about whether or not the use of pepper could affect the olfactory capability of a K–9. Ross told Dumer that, in all the tests conducted that he was aware of, there was no proof that the use of pepper could cause confusion where a K-9 was involved.

"I guess Delmer Smith thought that spreading pepper around would throw off any tracking dogs we might bring in to search for him. He obviously got the idea from the movie *Cool Hand Luke*." Mike smiled at me. "It doesn't work."

Dr. Terry Clekis, a Veterinarian at Braden River Animal Hospital in Manatee County, told me he had never heard of any proof that pepper would slow down a search dog. Ted Kraft, a dog trainer in Georgia, agreed.

Spilled pepper was found at only two crime scenes known to have been where Delmer had been. The first was at Osage Terrace and the second was at Carmilfra.

CHAPTER THIRTY THREE
Shana Hayter's Droplets

While conducting an initial walkthrough of the crime scene with Sergeant Rhonda DiFranco, Detective Dumer initially spotted two drops of brownish liquid lying on the floor. Their brownish tint made him think they might be syrup. He brought them to DiFranco's attention who then counted ten such drops. She determined they likely were droplets of human sweat and took samples for analysis. Five of the samples were then taken by Jessica Sawyer to Florida's crime-lab in Fort Myers for analysis. The lab confirmed DiFranco's belief. It also found a complete profile of male DNA in the drops that were then sent to the FBI's CODIS section hoping for a match.

Those ten tiny drops that could have been easily overlooked, except for Dumer and DiFranco's experienced eyes, would be significant in the investigation. They confirmed that the suspect, Delmer Smith, had been in the residence.

Upon his request, Smith was granted the right to appear before the Court had seated the Jury in order to argue his belief that the State could not use the sweat drops as evidence. His strategy was to slow court action, if not prevent it entirely. The Court listened to him, and then proceeded with the trial.

His defense attorney, Marjorie Bender, would follow up during the trial by trying to prove the samples were contaminated and thereby inadmissible. She called Shana Hayter, the State of Florida's analyst as a witness. Hayter had extracted the DNA that linked Smith to the crime.

Bender began her dispute of the DNA/sweat issue by attacking what, for some, would be obvious. "Ms. Hayter, how long does sweat stay on the floor in Florida?"

Hayter is relaxed. She looks directly at Bender and replies, "I'm not sure. I've never done any testing on that or it would be dependent on many factors, I would assume."

Bender questions a comment that Hayter had made during her testimony about the samples being discolored. Hayter replied, "The swabs I received in my custody did have some staining present, yes."

"And you never did any testing to figure out what caused that coloration, am I correct?"

"No. FDLE does not perform any of those tests."

Perfect, Bender thinks. She feels she has an opening to bring some discredit to the sampling process. "So you do not know what caused that particular color for that liquid; correct?"

"Correct."

Bender then asked Hayter if she had reviewed any of the photographs of the droplets prior to their being collected and then sent to her as swabs. Hayter said she had not. Bender followed up by asking Hayter if she would be surprised to find that the drops had been round and discolored at the time of collection.

"I'm not sure what you're referring to." Hayter frowned slightly as she answered hesitantly, unsure of where Bender was trying to lead her.

Bender took a step forward away from the lectern and said, "Would you be surprised," the attorney said slowly, adding a bit of tease and tension with a thin but cocky smile. She was relishing the direction her question would take them. She stood just to the side of the lectern and clasped her hands together allowing her fingers to form a steeple just in front of her as she continued. "Would you be surprised if the droplets as they were collected by Sergeant DiFranco on the floor, if they were also discolored when she collected them, sent them to you, the swab was discolored?"

Hayter replied that she was not sure; she had not seen the samples and therefore "… did not know how the color, if there was a color, of the liquid would transfer on the swab."

Bender pushed further feeling confident in the direction she was taking. "Would it be more disconcerting of what was picked up on the floor was clear and then by the time it got to you, you saw a brown discoloration?"

"Not necessarily." Hayter was sinking Bender's ship. "Again, I don't know what the samples looked like and I can't testify to how the color changed on the swab."

"Okay," Bender knew she had taken this as far as she could, but needed to confirm that the color was there. "But it was definitely there; correct?"

Hayter confirmed that it was and Bender slyly moved onto other issues. She had done what she needed to do to introduce to the Jury the possibility that the samples had been contaminated. However, she was not done with the direction she was moving and would come back again in a few minutes. However, just then she changed directions questioning how the lab was accredited and then a bit more about Hayter's background and experience. She slowly moved the questions to an area about contamination referring to the prosecutions own discussion of that topic.

"Let me ask you a couple questions regarding the specific definitions that you gave the state in response to his questioning about contamination."

"Okay."

Bender began carefully choosing her words as she continued her questioning. Her issue was to try to get Hayter to agree that there was contamination that had occurred with the sweat samples taken at Nicole's residence. Her argument was that because the samples had a discoloration to them that that was evidence of contamination.

Hayter fenced back calmly and professionally that the discoloration had occurred prior to her having contact with the samples and that contamination from her standpoint had to do with any such event occurring after the samples arrived in her custody and not before. However, Bender continued bringing the word "contamination" into the discussion. She discussed the possibility that perhaps there was a "more specialized term 'contamination,' the way you are using it through definition." She asked if she could simply look in the dictionary for the word and use that in reference to what they were discussing and Hayter replied, "I did not review the dictionary prior to testifying but it's usually the term we consider during or DNA testing."

Bender pressed again trying to use the fact that there was discoloration in the samples as evidence of contamination. "Well," she began, "it's very clear that there is a discoloration in what you tested and what is the result of ...."

Varn abruptly spoke up. "Judge, I'm going to object to the form of that question because it mischaracterized the evidence."

The Court responded, "I didn't hear the full questions."

Bender responded, "I didn't finish the question yet."

"Okay." The Court waved assent for Bender to continue.

"I think it's clear," Bender began again, "what I was saying is we established and you said through your notes that there was discoloration in State's exhibit 35, 36, 37, 38, 39 and that's as far as I got. I think we already covered that. That was the preface to my question."

The Court nodded and replied, "All right. Go ahead."

Bender turned her attention back from the Judge to the witness. "So, Ms. Hayter, my question is: Do you not then look at that discoloration or something else as a quote/unquote 'contaminant'?"

"Not necessarily to me because that's how the sample arrived into my custody."

Again the problem of not being able to get Hayter to agree. "Right. Okay." Bender stepped back to the lectern her mind searching for another path to bring discredit on the DNA collection and sampling process. Not to be deterred she adds, "That's what I understood your testimony to mean because your definition, as an analyst for FDLE to contamination, means something that gets into your process, something that isn't supposed to get in; right?"

"Yes."

"Right." Bender's eyes stray momentarily to the Jury as she slows her speech just slightly to bring attention to what she is about to say. "And it came to you with discoloration?"

Of course, Bender hopes that will just about seal the deal. "And it came to you with discoloration?" The whole issue right there on the floor. It was discolored. It didn't matter if it was not done in Hayter's presence. The fact is that the discoloration, according to Bender, was evidence of contamination. But did the Jury subscribe to the same channel of thought? That would be learned when the verdict came in.

In a later section of testimony, Prosecutor Scanlan called Sergeant Rhonda DiFranco to the stand for her testimony of what took place the night Nicole Marshall was assaulted. Sergeant DiFranco was an investigator in the forensics department of the Sarasota County Sheriff's Office. She documented the Carmilfra crime scene. During her initial walk through, she was accompanied with Detective Dumer.

She testified that the pair moved cautiously through the house noting the condition and location of items throughout the residence. After she discovered the droplets on the floor, she placed markers next to them, photographed them, and then took samples from them for analysis.

Scanlan began displaying for the Court and Jury photographs that have been taken by the forensic specialist.

She explained to the Jury the difference between walking through a scene and processing the scene. "Okay. So let's go back to — will start at, you walk through this scene; right?"

"Right."

"And then document everything with photographs without the markers. And then you put the markers down, and you document that as well; right?"

"Correct."

Scanlan focused on the first two markers. "And what was it that you are marking there at number 1 and number 2?"

"They were droplets."

"Okay. When did you first notice that there were droplets on the floor?"

"When we were doing the walk-through."

Following the walk-through, Dumer left Sergeant DiFranco to process the scene. It was at that point that she put Markers down where two of the droplets had been found.

"Okay. So you marked these droplets that are on the floor; right?"

"Correct."

Scanlan then asked where DiFranco had found droplets. The detective answered, "We saw them in the living room, we saw them in the kitchen, the pantry room, the master bedroom, and I believe— I can't remember another place."

Scanlan asked DiFranco what she believed the droplets were.

"Sweat," DiFranco answered without hesitation.

"Why did you believe that that was sweat?"

DiFranco explained that she had once worked as a nurse for the Veterans' Administration. While so employed, she wore gloves and found that she sweated in them. So having seen these droplets, she felt they were reminiscent of what she had seen in the past.

"And that conclusion that you made, that was your initial conclusion based upon your life experience?"

"Correct."

Convinced that the droplets were bodily fluid, DiFranco collected samples by using a Q-tip designed for such purposes and sent it off for analysis. The lab confirmed that the liquid was composed of sweat that belonged to a single male contributor. However, at the time, CODIS was backlogged and did not have Smith's DNA on file. It was not until much later in the year that the FBI reported the donor was Delmer Smith.

To counteract any possible arguments that might arise from the defense, Scanlan wanted to know how DiFranco knew the sweat was wet. The answer, "Well, as you were looking at the picture there, you could see, like, a 3-D. And when you look at anything that's wet versus its dry and stained, of course and wet has a more 3-D appearance."

CHAPTER THIRTY FOUR
Nicole Marshall

At 1230 hours on March 15th, Detective Dumer drove back to the Sarasota Memorial Hospital. Once there he met again with Nicole Marshall victim who, he soon discovered, had been admitted for observation because of the severity of her injuries and the rapid beating of her heart that had occurred while she had been attacked. Nicole told him that the attendant physician had explained to her that she had suffered what they termed to be a "cardiac event." He felt it was best to keep her until they believed it was medically safe for her to return home. Nicole, at the time, thinking her wallet had been stolen, provided him with information concerning her credit and debit cards.

An hour later, Sergeant J. Blessee, the Patrol Supervisor for Sarasota County Sheriff's Office District 2, phoned Dumer. Blessee told the detective that a neighbor of the victim had contacted him advising the sergeant that he, the neighbor, had discovered a black pepper box in his swimming pool. The sergeant thanked the neighbor and took the box into his possession.

The sergeant added that while he personally had been searching the grounds behind the house, that he had located a pair of reading glasses. He told Dumer that he found the glasses just outside the point of entry and was securing them as being possibly related to the crime.

Shortly after that discussion, Dumer drove home to get some needed sleep. It had been a long night. He knew there would be a lot more work to do on the case and needed to rest before going back out. When he did return to the field, it was early afternoon and Nicole's husband, Marc, had arrived by air from Canada.

The men met at slightly past 3 P.M. in order to review the details of the home invasion and to determine what had been taken. Marc was quickly able to provide the detective with specific details concerning items that were missing from Nicole's belongings. Then, while searching through the mess left in the ransacked house, and to everyone's relief, he located his wife's wallet with her credit and debit cards still inside.

Later that day, Jessica Sawyer drove five of the DNA samples collected by Sergeant DiFranco to the FDLE's bio-lab in Ft. Myers. In the meantime, Dumer was on the road visiting the various pawnshops in Sarasota County providing them with descriptions of the stolen articles to which Marc added more items later in the day.

After visiting several of the local pawnshops, Dumer then drove back to the hospital where he met with Nicole and her husband. Dumer explained the circumstances of the fluid that had been located on the floor and that it was being taken for DNA analysis. He wanted to know if anybody else had been in the home that might have contributed to the sweat drops.

Nicole told him no one else had been in the home that week except her. She told him she had cleaned her floors using a swifter mop on either Monday or Tuesday before the weekend of March 14th. Dumer made note of that and went back into the field searching for information.

Questions concerning the use of the Swifter would arise during the trial, but nothing was developed that hindered the prosecution as several days had passed from the use of the cleaning device to the time of the attack.

The Sarasota Police Department and the Sarasota Sheriff's Office were beginning to see similarities in several cases being looked at by both agencies.

Simultaneously, the City of Bradenton and Manatee County were sharing similar thoughts concerning several break-ins in their communities.

Could it be that the perpetrator was the same person in all these cases? It was obviously worth a meeting between the Departments and the sharing of information in the hopes that if it was one person, or even two, that the likelihood of locating and arresting the thief or thieves would be increased by having local, State, and federal Departments cooperating with one another.

In the meantime "Craig's List" was checked to see if any area sale's items were popping up that might be from either the cases at Bougainvillea or Carmilfra. There were none. Dumer drove back to the pawnshops in the area to recheck them and to remind the stores to be on the lookout for the stolen goods.

Later that day, Detective Dumer walked the short distance from his office to the Sarasota Police Department's offices for a multi-jurisdictional meeting. The meeting was called regarding the growing list of cases in both Sarasota County and Manatee County that had similarities. It was believed they were all related. The agencies represented at the meeting included the Sarasota Sheriff's Office, Manatee Sheriff's Office, Sarasota City Police, Florida Department of Law Enforcement, and the Federal Bureau of Investigation.

The FBI reminded everyone there that the federal agency has a database known as the violent criminal apprehension program. The purpose of the program is to search for similar cases in other jurisdictions that may be related. By March 19th, all known information to date on this case had been entered into that program but no ping backs occurred and the mystery continued.

On March 21st, Dumer joined with his supervisor, Sergeant John Walsh, Detectives LeFebvre, Kaspar, and Colonna to discuss the emerging situation and to determine an approach which might yield needed information regarding the break-ins which would lead them to the person or persons involved. The Department, as a whole, recognized the growing fact that something significant was taking place within the County in terms of these home invasions. An operational plan was needed and so they determined to construct and conduct a surveillance in the area of us 41 from Bahia Vista Street to Stickney Point Road looking for suspicious persons or incidents which might be related to this particular case as well as other possibly related home invasions in the area. Multiple contacts were made throughout the operation which they put into play on the evening of the 21st, but no relevant information was obtained which would aid them in solving the then current cases.

On March 22nd Detective Dumer received a report from Xavier Lamour in Luxemburg that there had been some activity on the Skype account belonging to Nicole and her husband. It had been brief but provided no real information as to location.

March 23, Detective Dumer met with Nicole Marshall and her husband Marc while Sergeant DiFranco obtained buccal swabs from both individuals for submission to FDLE lab in Fort Myers. "It was necessary for us to do that because we needed to eliminate them from any other possible DNA that was obtained," Dumer told me.

On March 25, Detective Dumer received information from detective DeNiro that the evidence collected by the Sarasota Police Department from Bougainvillea Street had been submitted to the FDLE for DNA analysis.

Five days later, Dumer met with Nicole again. She provided him with a pillow sham that matched the comforter used by Delmer Smith to cover the large screen TV when he removed it from a residence. Nicole also provided Dumer with a detailed list of stolen properties.

On March 31, Dumer received a phone call from Shana Hayter, crime laboratory analyst at the FDLE offices in Ft. Myers. She was sorry to report that the DNA samples submitted for analysis resulted in no identification of any known individuals. It would later be determined that the lack of identification was caused by the massive and inexcusable backlog in CODIS which, when discovered, would send ripples of anger throughout the law enforcement community. It also generated numerous newspaper articles condemning the failure of the trusted system and the danger imposed on the public resulting from it. A local Congressman, Pat Buchanan also became involved and added his voice to the growing ranks of criticism regarding the management of CODIS and the resulting danger to the public and law enforcement.

On April 2 and April 3, Sergeant Walsh and Detective Dumer reviewed case reports from the Sarasota County Sheriff's Office, Sarasota Police Department, the Manatee County Sheriff's Office, and the Bradenton Police Department looking for similar crimes and patterns in order to develop potential suspects.

Then on April 6, at 10:43 P.M., the detectives were notified of a possible homicide at 2150 Jo An Drive. The caller identified herself as a close friend of the deceased, Georgeann Smith.

On April 7th, Shana Hayter called Mike Dumer and confirmed that the female DNA collected the night of the attack at the Carmilfra address matched the DNA of Nicole. However, her husband's sample did not match that of the suspect DNA.

On April 9th, Sergeant Walsh assigned Detective Dumer to participate in a multijurisdictional effort to review cases that appeared similar in nature regarding the recent string of home invasion robberies in both Sarasota and Manatee counties. During the meeting, the detectives of each respective agency reviewed their cases. The group recognized similarities between their cases. Similar geographical locations of the crime scenes, race, gender, age of the victim, the suspect's physical description including ski mask, gloves, other clothing, the suspect's verbal elocution, similar statements made by the subject, the level of violence perpetrated upon the victim, and the manner in which the victims were bound, including the type of knot used were disturbingly similar.

CHAPTER THIRTY FIVE

Almost Caught

"I have a question," Defense Attorney Bender began during her deposition of Detective Dumer. She looked up from her notes and focused her gaze on the man seated across the table from her. "The Crime stoppers tip that you received regarding Delmer Smith in April, um, do you have any recordings of that? Any information with specificity on that?"

"We have the actual crime stoppers tip," replied the detective. "What would you like to know?"

Ms. Bender was interested in learning how it came to be that Delmer Smith had come to the sheriff's office attention, when and why. "Let me take a look," he said and turned to the documents. "Here it is April 23, 1300 hrs."

"Anything you know about it."

"Sure, no problem." Detective Dumer went on to state that Delmer Smith had become a person of interest because of a crime stoppers tip that came to them on April 23. It had to do with a suspicious vehicle report that was prompted following hearing and reading about several local violent home invasions. The woman caller reported seeing a vehicle slowly cruising about her neighborhood and acting oddly in late January or February:

> I came home from work and a car followed me. I noticed him so I drove past my house and I lost him. Returning to my house I found him hiding behind a tree about three houses down. And when I entered my house he was at my front door trying to get in. I called 911 but nothing was searched. Upon my

boyfriend arriving at my house we found the man about three houses down in his car. He fled once he knew we noticed him. I called 911 again but again nothing was done of this.

Dumer said that the caller said she was aware of problems in the area and hoped her report would assist law enforcement. As this was a crime stoppers report, it was confidential and the reporting person's identity was protected. The license plate, Dumer recalled, was found to be registered to Delmer Smith. However the car, which was reported to be a '92 maroon Honda, was not the car the tag belonged on. Likewise, the male identified as being seated in the car, and who drove off when he discovered he was being observed, was determined to not fit the description of Delmer Smith. "So Delmer Smith was placed on our person of interest with an eventually need to contact and, and follow up with among the —" Dumer began to answer but was interrupted by Bender.

"Because of the tag?"

"Because of the tag," Dumer replied. "And so Delmer Smith was placed on a list of persons of interest but that was about all we did with him. I think we tried to make contact. He had a North Port address at the time. I think we made one attempt to speak with him. We didn't locate him and we moved on. We didn't dismiss it. We never closed it. But we had a ton of other things to do."

CHAPTER THIRTY SIX

Handgun as Evidence

It is early afternoon on the 6th of December, 2011. Outside the main Sarasota County Courthouse, known as the Judge Lynn N. Silvertooth Judicial Center, the city is beginning to prepare for the Holidays. Workers are hanging decorations on streetlights while pedestrians and traffic stream along beneath them. Passing faces look up at the workers perched in lift buckets curious about what the utility workers are doing and then disappear as everyone hurries on their separate ways.

It is a cloudless Tuesday, and warm with a high of 89 degrees Fahrenheit. The temperature will dip during the night to a chilly 58 degrees. However, those in courtroom 5-C are not concerned with the weather, nor are their thoughts on or about the upcoming holidays. A man's life is on the line for a violent crime that had been committed, and in the secured and quiet atmosphere of the courtroom, an intense debate is underway over the admissibility of a handgun, bullets, and holster into evidence. The defense and the prosecution had researched similar cases and were presenting them to the Judge. Both were set to defend their positions with Bender taking the lead when a side door opened to the courtroom.

Judge Curly, Bender, and Scanlan stopped their discussion and looked in the direction of the door. There subdued voices could be heard giving instructions to a bald man wearing a blue jail shirt and trousers. He stood at the center of a swarm of burly deputies who dwarfed the 5'11" 220-pound career criminal. The man nodded his understanding, and then turned to face the courtroom shuffling his feet as he did causing the leg chains he wore to rattle.

As he came into the room, hampered by the locked restraints on his legs and arms, Delmer Smith could be seen blinking from one officer to another as they led him slowly toward the defense table. The courtroom environment was not unknown to Delmer. He is forty-one years of age and of that number he has spent eighteen years in lockup starting at age fourteen leaving him with only nine adult years of freedom. The chains hamper and he moved gradually forward in a shuffle. The shackles only allowed half the distance of a normal step.

His head was down, eyes focused on the carpeted floor immediately in front of him. His face wore a compliant masklike look; but his lips were tightly sealed as he followed the directions given him nodding his understanding and agreement with each order he received. Then, while Delmer Smith was helped into his seat at the defense table, his chains still rattling, the three court officers resumed their debate.

Bender's position was simply that Nicole Marshall had stated a handgun had been presented to her by her assailant during the commission of the crime. However, the fact was that she could not identify the weapon, as she had never clearly viewed it. Nicole had testified that all she could remember seeing was a square object with a round circle in it as it was presented to her in a threat. The victim was not familiar with firearms and could not tell the caliber or the manufacturer of the weapon.

Bender believed two things. In the first place, she felt that as the victim could not identify the gun it should not be introduced into evidence. Secondly, because it had been hidden away for months, it could be argued that it might not even be the weapon Delmer was accused of having carried with him during the break-in.

She used a then recent case, *Downs vs. State*, which took place in July of 2011. There the question of "relevance" had been brought up regarding the introduction of a firearm as evidence in that trial. She wished to use that case to bar the introduction into evidence of the alleged use of a gun found in Delmer's belongings.

"Whether the gun was properly admitted into evidence," she began reading from the prior case, "presents a question of relevance...."

"Where are you? Where are you?" the Court interrupted, suddenly sitting forward in her chair, frowning and flipping through several pages of the prior court case laid out before her. Her mouth fell open as she raised a hand in question and looked to Bender seeking guidance.

The attorney jerked her head back and moved quickly to respond by pointing out where she was in the lengthy transcript.

The Court then, having found where Bender was in the case, replied, "Right." She nodded her head in indication that Bender could proceed.

Bender calmly resumed her reading from the case:

> Generally, where the evidence at trial does not link a seized gun to the crime charged, the gun is inadmissible as evidence. A gun different from the one used in the crime is not relevant to prove the crime occurred. Any marginal reference to this type of testimony is substantially outweighed by the danger of unfair prejudices....

Therefore, Bender felt the handgun should not be introduced as evidence against her client.

"In part," she presented, "this motion was heard by the victim's testimony, or lack thereof, regarding her ability to identify the handgun.... They," she went on speaking about the prosecution, "intended on introducing ... a Walther handgun ... ammunition ... an ammunition clip ... listed as exhibits, also a holster to the gun. These are items ... found in a duffel bag ... in the attic of the home of

Martha Tejeda[14] ...." Ms. Bender added, stating several cases by name as the foundation for her position, "... there is an insufficient link and identification ... it was found six months after the crime itself, in a completely different location, in other possessions, that even the State's evidence is going to show was in the possession of other people. There's no forensics on the gun. There is no identification by the victim of this gun. We don't know if it's the same gun. That is our argument."

She paused for a moment, shuffling some papers on her table, building the intensity of the argument she had in play, readying herself for the move to attack the case that the State was going to use. Looking to the copy of the case in front of her, she began slowly:

"Now, I know we don't need to know it's the exact same gun. The state's case law, *Counsel*, which also cites a number of my cases I've presented to the court, I think the gist of *Counsel* is that if there is sufficient evidence to prove a link or a nexus, then it's a matter of weight and credibility of the witnesses and identification that's posed by the admitting party for the Jury to determine.

She glanced at Scanlan who was waiting patiently for her to finish, knowing the Court would then turn to the Prosecutor for her side of the argument. Sensing by the relaxed appearance of her opponent, Bender knew that she was well prepared to argue it. Bender was doing her best to keep the firearm out of the evidence pool. Of course, she had no way of knowing if the Court would agree with her position, but the attempt was worth the energy. Additionally, her presenting the argument would also give her a foundation for an appeal if warranted. She continued:

---

[14] Ms. Martha Tejeda was a neighbor and girlfriend of Delmer Smith. She was rumored to be carrying his child. She will be a major witness in the Kathleen Briles murder case.

Here, I believe that there was ... simply based on the evidence that's been introduced in the trial at this point, there is insufficient evidence for introduction of that in order to link it. In other words, just because someone is stopped in a car later on and has a bullet-proof vest or has ammunition in the car in the crime that they are charged with, say, happened a month before hand and it was a shooting incident, but there's not identification of the gun, right, you can't ... the State can't introduce evidence that, oh, well, you know it was a drug deal, that's why the shooting occurred. And he was wearing a bulletproof vest, because that's oftentimes what drug dealers do. Any ammunition that is found in the car, of course, shows that he's had a weapon or ammunition in the car. It's simply not enough.

And the fact that, in our case, Ms. Marshall can identify just a very limited part that she can of the firearm is no substantiation that this pistol that they seek to introduce into evidence, especially the ammunition, was involved in the crime itself.

Bender looked from Judge Curley to Scanlan, signaling she had finished, and was awaiting Scanlan's reply.

She had done her best, but would that be enough? A courtroom is a strange place where verbal battles play out. The end of these skirmishes is never truly known. Time can decay the passions laid out so eloquently. Issues and items planned and presented as facts and counter facts, circumstantial provisions, case law, and, in some cases, just flat out bull shit, can lift one side above the other to establish a win.

But, is a small win a true victory overall?

In this case, her job was to protect and defend her client to the greatest extent allowed her by law, realizing that not all battles are needed to be won in order to win a war, but each verbal firefight was a crucial part of the whole. And, so she took a deep breath and looked back at the Judge waiting for the Court to make the necessary call for the prosecution's argument, if any, and she knew there would be a response. There was always a response.

The Court turned to the Prosecution, "All right. Response, Ms. Scanlan?"

Ms. Scanlan smiled politely and stepped up to bat:

> Judge, this case is factually indistinguishable from *Counsel*, which is why I provided that case to your Honor and to defense counsel last week on this issue.

She nodded in Bender's direction and began her explanation of the facts:

> In *Counsel*, there was an armed robbery that occurred at a doctor's office. The gun was found in the home of the defendant three weeks after the armed robbery. I note that in *Counsel*, several witnesses gave descriptions of the gun that was used in a robbery. There were discrepancies in their descriptions of the gun and the gun that was found underneath the mattress but there were also many similarities.

"I will note also from *Counsel*," she looked to the file in her hands:

> I'm going to read this part from paragraph five on the second page: 'Contrary to defendant's assertion, the fact that the State failed to display the gun to the witnesses and elicit testimony from them concerning whether the gun admitted was actually the robbery weapon used, or even had similar characteristics, is not determinative of on the issue of admissibility. Such testimony was not necessary to establish the gun's probative value.

She lowered the file and looked at the Judge:

The gist of Ms. Bender's argument is that there is no nexus between the gun that was used and the crime that occurred, and that is simply not the case. The gun can be linked to the defendant himself in two different ways:

> He asked Martha Tejeda specifically to get 'that gun' and to… and it's identified as 'that gun' because he tells her exactly which duffel bag it is in when she is at the storage unit in picking up his property. He asked her to get 'that gun' and to take it and hide it and to not give it to anyone else.

Tejeda's testimony, linked to seven recorded phone calls that took place between Tejeda and Delmer, while Delmer was being held in the Pinellas County Jail for violating his Federal probation, would be prove to be extremely damaging to the defense's case. In each call, Delmer worked at getting Tejeda to go and retrieve several bags he had placed Scanlan asked her if she had discussed the gun with Delmer during their seven phone calls.[15] "Yes," was the reply.

"And tell me," she asked, "what it was that he told you during that conversation."

"To throw out the gun. But," Tejeda frowned, "I would say to him. Did you kill somebody? And he said, 'Just throw it out. I have not killed anybody. That was Michele's and she put it there.'"

Scanlan continued wanting to know what Delmer had told her regarding the gun and the police and Tejeda

---

[15] These phone calls are covered extensively in *The Woman in the Pink Top*

replied, "He told me not to give it to the police, the gun; to throw it out."

Scanlan continued:

> It can also be linked to the defendant himself because the duffel bag in which the gun is found has numerous items that are not of the criminal nature that can be identified as the defendants, most specifically, a prescription bottle that has his name on it. That is in the same duffel bag in which the gun is found.
> It can be linked to the crime in two ways.
> Also in that duffel bag in which the gun and that prescription bottle with the defendant's name on it is found is the Bose docking station, which Ms. Marshall is able to identify because she found the serial number for it and she has the warranty card that has a serial number for it. That matches the serial number that is on the Bose docking station. That is found in the exact same duffel bag in which the gun was located. It can also be linked to the crime by virtue of the fact that when Ms. Tejeda in a later phone call tells the defendant that she has been visited by the police, he tells her that she has to throw that gun away, and she has to not turn that over to the police or anyone else. That is evidence of defendant's consciousness of the guilt with relation to that gun, which leads to the inference that it was used during the commission of a crime. So for those reasons, the gun is relevant, it is admissible, and any issues that the defense wants to bring up should go to the weight of the evidence to be considered and not the admissibility of it.

Sensing the conclusion of Scanlan's presentation, the Judge looked over at Bender. "Response?"

Bender then reminds the Court that there were two items found in the duffel bag that could be referred to as being a "gun." One is a pistol and the other is a BB rifle. Her position was simply that there was a need to define which of the two items was being discussed when the term "that gun" was used. She also said she did not recall that statement actually being used in the phone call between the defendant and Tejeda. There was also the issue of how long had it been since the crime took place to the discovery of the gun: six months. Plus, she argued, that the duffel bag and, therefore, "the gun" has been in someone else's possession and so should not be admissible as evidence.

The Court thought for a moment and then said the gun would be allowed entrance into the evidence pool but not any ammunition. Curly determined that the gun was relevant based on statements made by the defendant that would be introduced during the trial and denied the defense motion holding that *Council* provided the foundation for her decision.

The Jury was then brought in and Scanlan called her second witness for the day: Michele Quinones.

GORDON KUHN

CHAPTER THIRTY SEVEN
State's Exhibit 42

It is day one of the trial. Scanlan is in the midst of her opening statement. She has just finished her comments about the collection of DNA found in sweat left behind by the defendant at the Carmilfra crime scene. She now turns her attention to an item of evidence that will be numbered and introduced by her later. Her requirement at this point is to provide background for the Jury so they will be prepared for when she does introduce it fully:

Detective Dumer spent the entire summer investigating the case in following up lead after lead after lead. He needed to find that one person from whom he could take a DNA sample and compare that to the DNA that was left at the scene.

He focused on trying to track down the stolen property. Having investigated many crimes before, he knows that when this kind of property is taken, it's possible that it will be located at a pawn shop or somewhere else. So he's looking for specific property than he knows that he would be able to identify if he found that property. And he knows that if he can find that property, that will probably lead him to the person who left the DNA.

He did that all summer long, and in September he finally got a break. He got information that the Venice Police Department had recovered a computer, and he had been focusing all summer long on finding that computer. He was told that the computer that the Venice Police Department had found was the same make and model as the one that was stolen from Nicole during the robbery. He got the name of Delmer Smith as a person who had taken the computer.

Detective Dumer went to the Venice Police Department to look at the computer. He turned it on, and he instantly — when the screen came up, he saw that the files in the desktop were labeled 'Nicole' and 'Marc.' Now, Nicole's husband is Marc Marshall. He instantly thought, 'This is the same make. This is the same model. These are Nicole's and Marc's. He opened up the email program, and he saw that the email was all going to the email address that he knew to be Nicole Marshall's.

He also found that there was some software on the computer that showed that it had been used to DJ in a bar, and he found that there was a folder on the computer that was labeled "D's Music."

So he spoke to Michele Quinones. Michele Quinones is a woman who used to be the defendant's girlfriend. Throughout most of 2009 she and the defendant were actually engaged. She will be here to testify, and she will tell you how she works as a DJ in a bar, and that's what she was doing for most of 2009. She has a program on her computer were she keeps all the music that she plays.

She will tell you that one night shortly after Nicole was robbed, she was working, and the computer that she was using to work crashed. The defendant was there with her at the bar, as he was on most nights that she worked, and he gave her a laptop that he had with him. She will tell you that she loaded all her music onto it, and for the next few months she used that laptop until hers was fixed. That laptop was the one that was stolen from Nicole Marshall.

That computer becomes State's Exhibit number 42. A great deal will be said about this exhibit during the course of the trial.

CHAPTER THIRTY EIGHT
Michele Quinones

Beth Scanlan quietly watched as her next witness took the stand and was sworn in. "Good morning," she greeted the woman.

"Good morning," the witness replied.

"Would you introduce yourself to the ladies and gentlemen on the Jury, please."

"My name is Michele Quinones," the witness said, turning and looking directly at the panel of men and women who, some of them, acknowledged her comment with a slight smile and/or nod.

Michele had been the closest of Delmer's several girlfriends after having left his wife, Donna, for her. They had become engaged at one point. Then the relationship began to fail as they grew distant from one another. By the time of the fight at TOTI's, Delmer and Michele were still together but the relationship had become extremely difficult and fragile, so fragile that the fight and resulting arrest would break whatever thread was there between them and cause its death.

"Do you know the defendant in this case, Delmer Smith?"

"Yes." Michele glanced over at Delmer who, dressed in a yellow jump suit, was sitting placidly next to his defense attorney. His head was turned slightly face down as if looking at the table. His eyes glanced in her direction and then away. He appeared impassive over the events taking place around him.

"How do you know him?"

"He was my fiancé."

"When was he your fiancé?" Scanlan asked.

"In '09."

"When did you meet him?"

Michele stumbled over '08 or '09. After a confused moment, she finally settled on '08 for an answer. She went on to explain that they had met when she was working for Black and Decker and DeWalt in a Home Depot store in Bradenton. He had approached her, flirted with her, she flirted back, and they were soon living together with his moving into her home in North Port. Within 2 to 3 months, they were engaged but no date for a marriage had been set. Michele was also suddenly laid off from work, but being resourceful, she became self-employed.

"Okay, what did you start doing for work in January of '09?"

"DJing," Michele replied quickly, sitting forward in her chair.

"And explain to the jurors what DJing is, just in case they don't know," Scanlan requested with a nod of her head toward where they Jury sat.

Michele explained that she was a disk jockey working at a bar playing music to entertain others. She told the Court that she was playing, "Pop music, '80s music, '90s music. Dance music mostly; not bar music, I guess."

Scanlan asked about Michelle's need for equipment.

"Digital DJ. I don't do CDs or vinyl. It's very digital: MP3, digital files. So computer and mini-players that look like record players but not, smaller."

"Okay. Is it essential that you have a computer to do this work?"

"Yes."

"Okay. So did you always have a computer while you were working as —"

"At that time I had a tower," Michele broke in. "It looks like your desktop computer with the tower and the monitor."

Scanlan then shifted her questions to the whereabouts of Delmer when Michele was working. "When you would work, what did the defendant do? Would he come with you?"

Michele explained that he would drive her to work, set up her "rig," and then sit at the bar with his computer while she worked. If she needed to go to the restroom or take a break he would fill in for her. Then he would help her dismantle the equipment and drive her home.

"Did that pretty much always happen —"

"Yes," Michele again answered quickly without letting Scanlan finish.

"— and he was always there when you were working?"

"Absolutely."

Scanlan then asked if there came a time when Michelle's computer crashed and what happened soon thereafter.

"Yes," she replied. When it happened, she said she was confused and looked to Delmer for help. Delmer reminded her that he had backed up her music and software to a computer in his possession, a laptop. He exchanged his laptop for her tower so she could continue to work. That piece of equipment would prove to be a central piece of evidence as Delmer's possession of it linked him to one of the early robberies in Sarasota.

Both Scanlan and Bender would spend time questioning Quinones about the machine and about Delmer's computer knowledge.

When the defense began questioning Quinones, the former fiancé of Delmer found Bender closely questioning her about Delmer's computer knowledge. "Aren't you the one who told me that Delmer was computer stupid?" Bender asked her regarding a statement made by Quinones during her deposition.

Quinones responded in the affirmative, adding, "To some extent, uh-huh."

Bender wanted to know whether Quinones or Delmer had installed the files used by Quinones in her DJ job. The witness claimed that she had installed the files. However, Bender continued to press concerning her client's access to or use of the laptop in question. The attorney wanted to know who had placed the music files on the computer. Quinones said that she had placed the files on the computer.

"Right," Bender pressed, "And you are not a computer expert?"

"Not at all."

Bender continued questioning the witness about her ability to install files on the computer. Quinones testified that developing files on a computer is a rather easy thing to do.

Bender again asked the witness if she was a computer expert who understood how to figure "out the diagnostic forensics of when files can be transferred, moved, put back into a computer, moved from another document, and whether those dates that show then as the created date —"

Slightly antagonized, and fully anticipating the question before Bender could finish, Quinones immediately attempted to answer and stepped on Bender's inquiry before the attorney was able to finish. But then, she herself was cut off by Bender quickly asking once again, "You're not an expert; are you?"

Again, Quinones said that she was not.

Scanlan jumped in, "Judge, I'm going to ask that Ms. Bender allow the witness to finish her answer before she asks another question."

"Okay," the Court responded, "One person at a time speaking." She nodded her head slightly. "Go ahead."

Again, Bender asked Quinones if she were an expert. Again the witness said no. Once more Bender asked if she had ever studied "the forensic analysis of how to move files from one computer to the next ...." Quinones replied that she had not.

Bender continued to probe until, feeling she had exhausted that line of questioning, then asked the witness if she had ever questioned the defendant on how he had come to have the laptop.

Michele responded that she had not.

Bender then questioned if Quinones had ever looked around at other files in the computer other than the music files. Bender wanted to know if Quinones had noted any foreign languages being used to which Quinones answered that she had not. Bender asked , "When you opened up that computer, you didn't see anything unusual in the way of French? French music? Other people's names?"

"No."

"Other people's email?"

"No, ma'am."

Quinones testified that when she was playing music she was working and not using the computer for anything other than that. She had her files installed and they were the ones she opened, not any others. "You don't have to open anything to download a file," she said.

"But you have to open the computer," Bender shot back, upping the pressure.

"Yeah."

"Right." Bender had just then had the laptop connected to a projector that placed the laptop's display on a large screen for viewing by the Court and Jury. She pointed at the screen. "People have — like, right now people there's a picture." She was referring to a photograph that had been placed on the laptop by Nicole Marshall in replacement of the standard computer screen.

"Just what — yeah, that," Quinones replied pointing at what was shown on the display.

"Is that yours?" Bender looked over at the witness and then added slightly sarcastically, seeing a bit of confusion in Michele's face. "No? Don't know?"

Michele frowned.

"Have you ever seen it before? On the desktop?"
"You mean just now?"
"No."

Quinones pointed at the image. She looked from it back to Bender. "That's always been like that as far as I can remember."

"So that's always been —"

Michele cut in, "That picture has always been there, yes."

"Did you put it there?"

"No." She went on to say that, she did not use the laptop for any recreational use as she had her own computer at home. For her, the laptop was solely used in her business as a DJ.

Quinones had a cold that day and obviously not feeling well. Bender noted that she was uncomfortable and asked if she was okay. "Do you need a glass of water?"

"No. I'm good." Quinones forced a smile.

Feeling not being able to drag anything substantial out of the witness, Bender told the court that she had no further questions. Scanlan stood and conducted a short re-cross and then Quinones was allowed to leave.

CHAPTER THIRTY NINE

Detective Dumer Testifies

It's the afternoon of December 6th, and Scanlan calls for Detective Dumer to come to the stand. She begins by having him introduce himself to the Court and the Jury.

"My name is Michael Dumer. I'm a detective with the Sarasota County Sheriff's Office."

"And how long have you worked for the Sarasota County Sheriff's office?"

"Since 2004."

Scanlan had informed the Jury during her opening statement that Dumer had picked three items from all that had been stolen from Nicole Marshall. He felt those three articles would stand out if taken into a pawnshop or bartered somewhere. "The first," he testified, "was her computer, an HP laptop computer; the second was the television that was taken off the wall. It was a 55-inch Philips plasma TV. ... So that was just something that I was very interested in, as well as an old generation Cassiopeia PDA. It was green in color."

To show the Jury the extensive time and energy spent on the investigation Scanlan asked, "What sorts of things did you do to look for these three particular items?"

Dumer sat forward in his chair recalling all he had done. "Well, I know that there were some searches on Craigslist. We had checked some pawnshops." He went on to say that he had visited many of those living in the county that he felt might have come into contact with the items sought."

Scanlan waited for a moment after he finished his comment before calmly asking, "Fair to say that from the middle of March until the middle of September you followed up on a lot of leads that pretty much went nowhere?"

"Yes. That's correct." While that was true, there were several arrests made resulting directly from his investigations that came about because of Carmilfra.

Scanlan stepped forward, moving slightly to the side of the lectern where she glanced down at her notes. She looked up at the detective and asked, "On September 15th of 2009, did you get what you believe to be a potential good lead on one of these items?"

Dumer clasped his hands in front of him as he recalled the trip to Venice. "I did."

Scanlan reached out and rested one hand on the lectern, her eyes on the detective. "And tell me about that."

Dumer sat back in the witness chair, cleared his throat and began. "On the night of the 14th I was working late, and I get notification that the Venice Police Department has made an arrest and that there were items at the Venice Police Department that I might be interested in."

"What was one of these items?"

"One of these items was an HP 17-inch laptop."

Scanlan then showed the detective what was labeled as State's Exhibit 42. "Is this the laptop?"

"Yes, it is."

"And now, did you turn this laptop on?"

"I did."

"Okay. And what information, if any, did you get when you turned it on?"

"I was able to identify several files on the desktop there were provided to me as information during one of my interviews with someone. And I also took a look at the file structure on the hard drive, and under the C-drive and the users' folders there were two file folders that were there one was called Nicole, and the other was Mark ...."

"And did those two names have significance to you in the context of this investigation?"

"It did." Dumer sat back in his chair. He unclasped his hands and gestured, "Obviously, the victim is Nicole Marshall and her husband is Marc, also spelled with a C."

"You met him?" Scanlan asked.

"I have."

"And what, if anything, else did you find?" Scanlan asked.

Dumer testified that he had noted the model number on the computer and it matched the number given to him by the victim once before. "What I found interesting was it also had a CA designation on it, which is a Canadian—out of HP Canada." That label identified the computer as being of Canadian manufacture and he knew that the Marshalls were from Montréal and were, in fact, Canadians.

Scanlan asked him where on the computer he found the designation. Dumer replied that it was on the backside of the computer.

"On this side?" Scanlan asked pointing.

"Yes. It's right here, DV9618 CA," Dumer pointed at a metal plate attached to the rear of the computer.

Scanlan asked if there was anything else he noted, and he replied that he found Nicole's personal email account.

"Did you know at that time what her e-mail account was?" Scanlan asked.

"I knew her e-mail address, yes. And when you take a look at the file structure and the e-mail account, you will see that all the e-mails that she was sending back and forth to her friends, many of which were in French."

Dumer then told the Court about the iTunes account and the music that Nicole Marshall had on file there. "Ms. Marshall had identified several artists that she had on her iTunes account, and I looked to verify that those were, in fact, present. I have those names here, if you would like them."

"Go ahead," Scanlan said.

"They were, indeed, present on this particular computer, this iTunes software: Georges Brassens; Georges Moustaki; Gotan Project...." He continued to list several others before stopping.

Scanlan then asked if there was anything else he had found to be of significance on the computer. He replied that there "was a sticker on the front of the keyboard that was written in French" that Nicole and her husband recognized immediately when he showed the machine to them.

"All right. Was there anything on the computer that indicated somebody other than Nicole Marshall may have been using it?"

"Yes. I mean, there were—there was software that had been installed called virtual DJ that was not resident on the computer when it was owned by Ms. Marshall and these desktop files that I spoke of. There were two word documents and a PDF file called *Midnight Sun* that was on there that wasn't part—it wasn't installed. And I think Ms. Marshall told me also in December that the desktop picture had been changed as well from when she saw it last."

"Do you know what virtual DJ is?" Scanlan asked.

"I've never personally run the program, but I understand that is just a DJ program that will play, you know, digital music in either genres or—probably much like iTunes does."

Scanlan then told Dumer she had no other questions for him at that time. She stepped away from the lectern and returned to her seat at the prosecution table next to fellow prosecutor Earl Varn.

The Court then nodded to Ms. Bender indicating she was allowed to start her cross-examination of the detective. The attorney stood and approached the lectern with several sheets of paper that she placed before her. "Good afternoon, Detective Dumer," she said dryly.

"Good afternoon, Ms. Bender."

~ 205 ~

Bender then began her cross-examination by first focusing on the contamination log and the CAD report. This was an attempt to discover discrepancies as she had done with Sergeant Tutko. She asked Dumer about his recording of time. He told her that when he left his home he radioed dispatch. "When I did that, they logged me on, and they showed me en route. But when I arrived there, I didn't call out the car. In other words, I got there, put it in park, shut if off."

Bender then asked him if he had knowledge of events occurring before he arrived, but not something that he had been told which would have been considered hearsay. She was interested to know if he had any personal knowledge of who had entered the home or what might have been recorded on the contamination sheet. He told her he had no personal knowledge only what he had been told had taken place.

Bender then moved to his involvement with DiFranco.

"Now, when you went into the home with Sergeant DiFranco, you said you saw what you believed were drops of syrup; correct?"

"That was my initial," he paused and then started again, "I said to her, what in the world is that? You know, it looks like syrup on the floor here and it was —"

Bender broke in quickly stepping on Dumer's testimony. "You said it was syrup because it was brownish; right?"

"Yes. It appeared to me to be so, yes."

"Okay. Did you make any other observations about it at that time when you're looking at it for that first few moments with your flashlight? In that hallway, I assume?"

"You mean as to whether it was dried or wet? Is that what you're asking me?"

"Sure. Well, anything: shiny, dry, wet, round."

"It appeared to be shiny. You know, it would reflect some of the light from my flashlight, as I recall."

"Okay. I know," Bender said, recognizing the fact that this one night had been a long time before the trial, "two years ago."

"And a half, yeah," Dumer corrected.

"You certainly didn't test it; correct?" She smiled dryly at him. The question was a sneer suggesting that as it appeared to be syrup to him that he might have actually tasted it.

"No, ma'am." Dumer's reply was equally dry.

CHAPTER FORTY

Jail House Confession

Prior to the start of the trial, State Attorney Scanlan had been notified by the Sheriff's Office that a prisoner being held by the State of Florida wanted to speak to someone in her department regarding Delmer Smith. Scanlan followed up on the request and learned that an inmate named Phillip Casciola wished to report a conversation that had taken place between he and Delmer while in jail.

The inmate, who was serving a 22-year sentence for four felonies, told the Prosecutor that he wished to discuss with her something he felt would be significant to the case. She decided to meet with him; but she was cautious as many of these meetings take place in an environment where the inmate is seeking something in return for whatever he or she is offering. From the start, she made it clear to Casciola that talking with her was not going to result in anything in return from her or her office except a thank you.

She realized, from experience, that her proposed introduction of his testimony into the trial posed potential issues for which she was prepared to address knowing both Bender and Judge Curly would have concerns. In order to get Casciola's testimony before the Jury she must present a proffer[16] to show to the Court and the Defense what her questions will be and what Casciola's answers will also be.

---

[16] A proffer is when something is proposed as evidence. To offer to the court something that will be or may be considered as evidence.

Bender has already lodged an objection to the testimony.

It is shortly after a lunch break on the afternoon of December 7th. For the moment, the Jury is purposely absent in the courtroom because Scanlan is having Casciola called to the stand for the proffer.

Casciola is sworn and Scanlan begins with introductory remarks and then shifts to questioning Casciola on why he is in prison and what he did there for work.

Casciola stated that he was a State Certified Law Clerk. He worked in the jail law library. There he assisted other prisoners with their legal research. One prisoner who met with him was Delmer Smith. Scanlan wants to explore the conversation that took place between the two men.

"At the time that you and the defendant were housed in the same jail, did he approach you and ask for assistance from you in that capacity [of Certified Law Clerk]?"

"Yes, ma'am."

"And when he did that, what if anything did he tell you about the crime that he was charged with that occurred in Sarasota?"

Casciola replied, "That he committed it."

Scanlan turns to face the Court. "Those are the only questions I'm going to ask him with regard to that."

The court begins to respond but Bender jumps in with a renewed objection. "Your honor," she begins, "I think she's going to say did he approach him and ask for assistance? Yes. And what did he say? That he committed the crime in Sarasota?"

Scanlan immediately responds, "That he was charged with in Sarasota, yes."

Bender replies, "That he was charged in Sarasota. I renew the objection that I made before because, given the whole context of the conversation which the Court has now heard, that it is absolutely impossible to ask any factually true questions in order to examine his testimony …."

The defense attorney's objection was based on her belief that it would be impossible for her, in her attempt to shield Delmer, to ask Casciola questions without pulling in additional information about cases that Delmer had not yet been convicted. She felt exposing the Jury to that other information would be extremely prejudicial to her client.

The Court understood her position and replied with a nod, "Okay." Curly then looked to Scanlan for a response.

Scanlan took a step forward and quickly replied, "And that is the very reason why inextricably intertwined evidence is admissible."

The Court momentarily thought over both arguments. The judge was acutely aware of the danger of potential contamination of the trial by revealing untried cases involving the defendant. Awareness by the Jury that other cases may be brought against the defendant could color their opinion in an injurious manner. To protect him, to prevent a mistrial, or a reason for an appeal, the Court advises the opposing attorneys that it is imperative that they will have to be cautious of what he is asked and he will have to be cautious of how he replies. The attorneys and Casciola all agree to the cautionary position of the Court and Scanlan is allowed to have him testify in front of the Jury.

The Court agreed that while the course being taken was relevant, it was also "possibly dangerous."

The concern was that this case was a Sarasota case; however, there was the pending murder case in Manatee County. To accidentally introduce anything in connection with that case would not only be prejudicial to the defendant in the Sarasota case, it could, by inclusion, jeopardize the Manatee County case as well.

After a brief comment made to the attorneys, Judge Curly concluded that there was only one question she was going to allow in connection to any statements previously made. That question was simply, "Did the defendant admit to a robbery in Sarasota." She leaned back in her chair and looked at both attorneys. "He can reply yes," she said with finality.

The Jury was brought in and the Court asked the normal questions concerning anyone approaching them about the case, and did anyone of them discuss the case with anyone else, or had they seen anything or read anything about the case. The responses were all negative and so they were seated and advised that Mr. Casciola was a witness that was on the stand. She then told Scanlan to proceed with a cautionary look in her eyes. Scanlan nodded and stepped to the podium.

She welcomed Casciola and he responded to her in like fashion. She then asked about his being in prison and he replied that he had been convicted of four felonies and he had received a sentence of 22 years as punishment. She asked what it did in prison for work. He explained he was a State Certified Law Clerk and that it was regarded as an official position. That done, Scanlan asked about his encounter with Delmer Smith. "At the time that you and the defendant were housed in the same jail, did he approach you and ask for assistance from you in that capacity?"

"Yes, ma'am."

"Okay. And when he asked you for your assistance, did he admit to you that he had committed a robbery in Sarasota?"

"Yes, ma'am."

As Casciola testified, Delmer sat quietly at the defense table. His head was slightly at a downward tilt. His face expressionless. Occasionally his eyes would drift toward the witness, but they held no emotion or betrayal of his thoughts. Later, when Delmer testified, Bender attempted to invalidate Casciola's testimony.

"Delmer," the attorney began slowly, "did you know that gentlemen, Philip Casciola, that came in here in the orange?"

"No, I didn't." Delmer said firmly.

"Did you ever tell him that you," Bender paused, thinking of a better way to ask her question, and then continued, "or did you ever admit to him that you committed a life felony here in Sarasota?"

"No, I have not."

"Did you ever ask him for legal advice?"

"Most definitely not."

Scanlan said she had no further questions, and Judge Curly nodded at Bender.

Bender stepped forward to cross exam the witness, but unfortunately stumbled over her briefcase. Recovering her footing, and her composure, she made light of the misstep by quickly asking dryly, "Mr. Casciola, are you awake now?" There was no humor in her voice.

Bender questioned the possibility that Casciola was expecting some benefit from the State for his testimony. The direction of her examination was an intelligent move on her part. She simply had to slip into the prosecution's case reasonable doubt. Once established, she could use it to her advantage.

He responded calmly that he did not. He told her he expected to live out his life in prison because of his age, the length of the sentence, and his family's history of a variety of diseases that accounted for many of his relative's early deaths.

She shifted her questioning to asking the witness how it had been possible for the two men to have met. Both were in an area referred to as a confinement pod. "Now, you were never in the same cell with Mr. Smith; correct?"

"That is correct."

"And when you allege that this statement, when he asked you for help, right, you the nonlawyer, that it was while you were in jail; right?"

"While I was in Manatee County, yes, ma'am."

Bender pointed out that the activity of prisoners in the confinement pods are closely monitored.

"I don't know what you consider monitoring," Casciola replied. "I mean, you're locked in a cell for 24 hours a day."

"Okay. Great. And you have deputies there 24 hours a day."

"Yes, ma'am."

"Okay. And there are cameras above you; right?"

"Yes."

"Monitoring the activity on the floor whenever you are allowed out of your individual cell; correct?"

"Yes, ma'am."

"And, in fact, in that confinement pod there is a whole bank of television cameras where each and every person's activity is monitored and the correctional officers are there 24/7; correct, Mr. Casciola?"

"Yes, ma'am."

"And you are shackled by your ankles, right, whenever you walk?"

"Yes, ma'am."

"Right. You do not get the privileges in a confinement pod that you get anywhere else in that jail; correct?"

"No, ma'am."

Bender continued to question Casciola developing a scenario in which it would have been most unlikely for the two men to have met and discussed anything.

"And you have no witnesses, right, to corroborate your claim that he said I admit to a robbery in Sarasota; right?"

"That is correct, ma'am."

"And you have no documentation, no letters, no written small notes back and forth between the two of you tucked into your socks or anything of that nature; right?"

"I do not have any, ma'am."

"Right. And fact, when you are and that confinement pod, you were never anywhere else near Mr. Smith other than when you were in the confinement pod; correct?"

"That is correct."

"So magically," Bender suddenly accusingly remarked, "you have a conversation about legal issues, so much so that you get an incrimination from him that now you're coming forward to tell us so that a miracle can possibly happen for you; right?"

"No, ma'am."

"No," Bender repeated his negative reply with a hint of disbelief in her voice if not sarcasm. "Okay. All right," Bender paused. She looked at the floor then back up at Casciola and then said, "Then I assume, Mr. Casciola, it's just out of the goodness of your heart; right?"

"A consciousness, a conscious decision, ma'am."

"I'm glad you finally attained that, sir."

Scanlan immediately spoke out, "Objection, argumentative."

The court sustained and Bender withdrew her question. Then, saying she had nothing further, the Defense took up her place next to Delmer as Scanlan stood to begin her redirect.

No sooner had Scanlan asked, "Explain exactly why it is that you decided to come forward with this information?" than Bender objected and requested that she and Scanlan meet with the Court for a Bench conference. Bender stated her concern was about the witness possibly mentioning other crimes that Delmer had not yet been prosecuted for, namely the Briles' murder case.

The conversation between the three women was brief. It was decided that Casciola had said earlier in his testimony why he had come forward. Scanlan said that he had told her that knowing he was going to face life in prison, he wanted to do something good in his life and this seemed to fit that requirement.

CHAPTER FORTY ONE

Delmer Smith Testifies

It's December 8th and Delmer Smith has requested that he be allowed to testify. Bender notifies the court that Delmer is shackled and will not be able to walk in front of the Jury. The Court replies that she will address that once she has confirmed that the defendant wishes to testify and has him stand to be sworn in. Once done she questions his intention. "Sir, this is an important point in time in which you decide whether or not you want to testify for the Jury or if you want to exercise your right to remain silent. Do you understand?"

"Yes, I do."

She then tells him that any conversations with his attorney are private. However, she wants to make sure that he had time enough to speak with Bender and that he was certain of his decision. He tells her he wishes to go forward and testify and that all of his questions put to his attorney were answered by her.

Scanlan stands and introduces a request that Delmer be advised by the Court that he cannot introduce any remarks about the two deputies who refused to submit DNA samples as he had made remarks about his being "very anxious" about that issue.

The Court turns to Bender who responds that Delmer is well aware of the Court's decision about the lack of relevancy to the case regarding Deputies Swinney and Thomas's refusal. However, Bender adds that she does not agree with the Court's ruling on the issue and felt that it should have been explored previously.

The Court asks if Bender has anything else to discuss and Bender says she does not.

The concern then turns to his being able to walk to the stand without shackles on. The Court advises that if the bailiffs are okay with that Bender can proceed. Getting a nod from the officers, the Jury is brought in and seated. The Court questions them concerning having read about the case or discussed it with anyone. Satisfied with the jurors' responses, she then informs them that the prosecution has rested and that it is now the Defense's case. She looks to Bender nodding her permission for attorney to proceed.

Bender calls Delmer as a witness. He walks to the stand unshackled and takes a seat. The Court swears him in and then immediately requests that the Jury be removed. Once done, Delmer is shackled again. However, there are problems that need to be addressed before the Jury can be returned to the Courtroom.

The first concern is over the possibility that some jurors will be able to see the shackles. A discussion takes place about concealing them from any potential view of the Jury. The other issue is where the bailiffs will stand. Once this is solved, including the placement of a trashcan as a visual block, the Jury is brought back in.

Scanlan enters a concern about if the defendant moves his feet and exposes the shackles it will create a possible appellate issue that Delmer can bring up as a complaint citing that such viewing by the Jury would be prejudicial to his case. Bender asks if they could shackle his knees instead of his ankles. The bailiffs reply that the shackles will not fit around his legs that high up.

Struggling for a resolution to the dilemma posed by the possible exposure of the shackles, the discussion then shifts to the placement of deputies in the room related to where Delmer is sitting if he is to be unshackled.

There are three officers in the room. Bender is concerned that having the bailiffs close to Delmer will be as prejudicial to him, from the prospective of the Jury, as it would be if the Jury were able to view his shackles.

Delmer finally solves the problem. "I'll leave them on."

"Just leave them on?" Bender asks him.

"Yeah."

The shackles are replaced and the Jury is returned.

Bender asked Delmer the normal questions for identification purposes: his name, date of birth.

"July 19, 1971," he replied.

"How old are you?"

"I'm forty."

She then asks about where he lived and with whom in 2009. He replied that he lived with Michele Quinones in North Port until August of 2009. She does not ask why he moved out or where he moved. Others had already covered that ground.

"What did you do for a living?"

"I'm a licensed personal trainer, any and every kind of odd jobs I can get. I can come across, or whatever." He further explains that he worked for cash doing pressure washing of homes, cars, installing car burglar systems, and that he did a lot of bartering.

"Were you paid by a company?" Bender asks.

"No."

She then produces copies of three documents and asks Delmer if he recognizes them.

"They're my certification and my CPR and my business card."

Bender notes that they are not originals. "Why are they copies?" she quizzes him, slightly tilting her head quizzically.

"I don't have the originals."

"Tell me about the business card," she calmly askes and steps forward pursing her defense strategy.

"The business card was printed up so I can pass it out to people and get publicity and, you know, hopefully somebody would call me and hire me." Delmer explains, suggesting that the business card was a way of his advertising his services.

"And where would you give these cards? How did you get your clients?" Bender continued.

"Numerous places, in the club where Michele DJed at, Venice Island at the beaches, restaurants, stores, I would place them inside of, like, Publix. You know, they have a board."

"Where did you do your work?" Bender asked.

"Everywhere. Backyards, houses, Lifestyles, Bally's."

"The beach?"

"Of course, the beach."

"People's houses you said?"

"Yes."

Bender questions him if he had ever been in the area of the Phillippi Creek.

"I have been around there several times in the area."

Bender then questions him about photographs shown to him of Marshall's rented home on Carmilfra Drive. Did he recognize the house? Had he ever been there?

"You know, I can't say for sure because I had been in and out of different homes, so I can't say for sure, but I mean, I know the area."

"Do you have any memory of ever being in her home at all?"

"I can't say for sure."

Delmer's position is simple. He did not recall ever being in Marshall's home. Nevertheless, he told the Court, he might have been there at some point to provide a free consultation and that could account for his DNA being there.

Bender asked if he kept records.

He told her he did not. He explained, "I'm used to doing free presentations. You know, I would give people like 4 to 5 different, you know, free sessions. Then we will talk about maybe a payment plan and because of the way the economy is and people not being able to afford a personal trainer because we do charge a lot in certain areas in our time is expensive, you know, what we do."

"Right. What I'm saying is, did you keep a list of all of the clients you say you had or no?"

"No."

Bender asked Delmer if he contributed to the finances that supported him and Michele while he resided at her home with her mother. "Did you help pay the rent?"

"Yes, I did."

"And how much a month did she want you to have by the end of the month?"

"It was $500 for the mortgage and then you've got to think about the car payment, the insurance, and the cell phones. So I have to—a little over 500."

"Would you say you are doing fairly well during that period of time or just making it at the end of every month?"

"Some months it would be just barely making it. Some months it would be doing good."

Bender asked him what he did with his money. He told her that he was investing in equipment to sell.

Next, Bender brought in as evidence copies of receipts purported to be purchases for several pieces of computer equipment already admitted as evidence. Showing him the documents she asked if he recognized them as being sales receipts.

"Yeah."

"Are they yours?"

"Yes, they are."

Each of the receipts listed a variety of software and computer equipment as well as a dollar amount that Delmer said he had paid Cellecz. One receipt was dated February 24, 2009 and the other was April 6, 2009.

"And on the first receipt from February," Bender asked, "how much money did you spend buying that equipment?"

"$3,465.70."

"And where did you get that money to buy?"

"Money that I saved up from items that I had. Wheeled and dealed and jobs that I went on to."

Bender asked about the second receipt, "And how much did you spend in April?"

"A total $1,139.55."

Delmer testified that he met Cellecz several times at the Red Barn in Bradenton.

"Was he one of your main property suppliers?"

"Oh, yeah." They would meet several times a week. He said he never asked where Cellecz obtained the computer items. However, on one occasion he did ask him if they were "hot," and he said Cellecz assured him they were not.

"This is my business," Cellecz said, according to Delmer. "I used to own a computer place. This is my business. Everything is good." However, Delmer said he insisted on being given a receipt.

Delmer confirmed that he was aware after the fact that the items brought into the trial as evidence that had been in his possession had been stolen. However, he continued to say that he had obtained it all from Cellecz.

Bender then questioned him on his ability to use computer equipment. Delmer testified that he was embarrassed to say that he was computer illiterate and that he relied upon Michele Quinones to program the computers.

Moving away from the subject of the computers, Bender questioned him on where he had stored his equipment. He testified that he had several locations. One storage location was in North Port. Another location had been in Michele Quinones home. A third location was in a trailer he kept at a property location owned by a man named Watmough.

She then asked him about the rifle found in his possession. Delmer had felony convictions. He could not legally own a gun. Bender asked why he had one when he knew he was in violation of the ruling against his ownership of any firearms.

"Well, the reason why I bought the rifle is because I have five Chihuahuas, and when I would let my dogs outside, I seen snakes." Delmer was afraid that one of the snakes would make off with the puppy. Because of that he bought the BB rifle.

"Did you," Bender asked, "have any other guns in your possession?"

"No, I did not."

"You saw and you heard the testimony about this small gun, this black and silver gun that they showed the other day, is that your gun?"

"No, it is not."

Scanlan began an aggressive cross-examination. "You sort of danced around a lot of issues. Let me ask you a few things straight. You denied having committed this crime; is that correct?"

"Yes, I'm denying it." Delmer calmly watched Scanlan.

"Okay. You say that you were not in Ms. Marshall's home on the night of March 14, 2009?"

"I was not in there," Delmer replied dryly.

"You did not, "Scanlan paused momentarily, then began again, "you do not have any explanation for how your DNA was left there?"

With a slight shrug, Delmer responded, "The only explanation and what I answered with Ms. Bender was, I'm a personal trainer. I mean, I go from home to home, jobs as far as with the gyms, beaches, parks, backyards. I train people."

"Okay. So you are charged with this crime two years ago?"

"Yes, I was."

Scanlan recited the list of items introduced as being evidence. She also developed that in her thinking he had help in disposing of the stolen items by pawning them with the help of a man named James Cellecz, a man who Bender would attempt to pin the burglary charge on saying that Cellecz had committed the crimes and not Delmer.

Delmer continued to respond of his lack of knowledge that those items were stolen. "I purchased them legally," he said. However Scanlan went after the receipts that had been included into evidence by challenging dates and his memory of exactly what and when he had purchased computer equipment from James Cellecz.

Focusing on one of the receipts, Scanlan attempted to get Delmer to identify the computer the receipt applied to. "Okay. So you had Nicole's computer from February 24 up until the time it was found at Shannon's house?"[17]

Delmer knew he could not have had the computer in question in hand prior to the date of the burglary. "No. That's not when I bought that computer."

"I'm sorry?" Scanlan was fully aware of the timeline.

"That's not when I bought the computer," Delmer said again.

"When did you buy the computer?"

"I bought the computer March sometime."

Scanlan looked at the document and frowned. "Why does the receipt for the computer say February 24th?" She looked up at the witness waiting for a response.

"I have no idea," Delmer replied. "This is the receipt that James Cellecz gave me. I didn't even look at the date until I got a chance, that was in your guys' discovery, and I was telling Ms. Bender about it."

"Okay. But you definitely had it on March 17th of 2009, because that is when the files were being created."

Delmer began a long description about Michele's computer crashing and that he had to step in with the one purchased from Cellecz. "You know," he began, "Michele's computer crashed and she is, like, well, what am I going to do? She is crying. She is hysterical. This is my baby; it's my baby. I want to make sure that she

---

[17] The burglary on Carmilfra Drive occurred on March 14th, 2009.

stopped crying. So I said, look, let's just use this one. She said, okay. So she downloaded all her programs into this computer and she started DJing with this computer."

"Okay. But none of that answered my question. Did you have the computer on March 17th when it shows that the first files were created?"

"Yes."

"Yes," Scanlan repeated. "Thank you." She paused and then added, "The other items that you purchased from James, you said that you got all of those from him at the same time," she paused, "am I understanding that correctly — the iPod, the Cassiopeia, and the Bose sound docking station?"

"Yes."

"Okay. So your testimony here, essentially, is that James Cellecz is the one who committed this crime?"

"No. My Testimony is," Delmer stiffened, his eyes widened, he sensed a trap, and his mind began to spin, "I'm saying that I bought, I purchased the items from James Cellecz. I never said that he committed the crime. I'm saying I bought these items from James Cellecz."

Scanlan continued calmly yet aggressively, "But if your testimony is to be believed, then it's far more likely that it was him than you because he had the property before you; correct?"

"No. That's your statement," Delmer knew he was in a fight. "You're saying that, I'm not saying that. I'm saying that I bought it from him."

"All at the same time?" Scanlan was relentless.

"Yes."

"All obviously, sometime within two days of the crime having been committed; correct? Because we know that you had it on March 17th, and we know that it wasn't taken until March 14th."

Delmer carefully shifted in his seat remembering the importance of not showing the shackles. "I could not tell you if it was a crime committed two days or a week before.

I do not know. All I know is that when he had these items, he sold them to me. I bought them."

"Right," Scanlan continued. "And that necessarily had to be sometime after the crime was committed; right? Because we agree that they were originally Nicole's items; correct?"

"We agree that," Delmer paused, thinking, "yes. We agree that they were her items, yes."

CHAPTER FORTY TWO

Bags, Guns, and Phone Calls

Scanlan continued concerning the computer equipment, "You agree that you had them on March 17th; correct?"

"Correct," Delmer replied.

"So sometime between the date of the crime, which was March 14th and the date that you purchased it, which was sometime before March 17th is when you purchased them from James, according to you?"

"I can just tell you I purchased them, and I can't tell you exactly what day it was, I know the day that Michele started downloading her music in it."

Regarding the burglary on Carmilfra Drive, he went further to say, "As far as when the crime was committed, I still," he paused, "I can't answer that and tell you that, yes, I knew that he took this on a particular day or he did this on a particular day. How he [Cellecz] came about having this in his possession, I have no idea. I just know that I purchased them on a certain day and that was it."

"Do you have any reason to doubt the testimony that the crime was committed on March 14th of 2009?"

"No," Delmer replied, "I don't have any doubt about that."

Scanlan then asked, "Okay. Do you have a reason why it is difficult for you to follow the logic that you received that property sometime between March 14th of 2009 and March 17th of 2009?"

Bender immediately objected and the Court sustained.

Scanlan followed up with, "You would admit that you're not actually answering the question; correct?"

Bender again objected and the Court again sustained as an improper question.

Scanlan then shifted to questions about the two guns found in Delmer's bags. One was a BB gun and the other was a handgun. Delmer said he was aware of the BB gun but wasn't about the other. Yet, he claimed he had personally loaded the bags and that, admittedly, within the bags were articles belonging to the Marshall's. When pressured he said, "I don't know anything about a gun being in my bag."

Scanlan countered, "Did you hear the testimony from Technician Hendrickson yesterday?"

It's December 7th of 2011, and Scanlan flipped the light on for the projector which lit a large screen display visible to all in the courtroom. She had been examining Hendrickson who was one of the detectives who went to Martha Tejeda's home in North Port and retrieved items from bags belonging to Delmer that Tejeda had, at the request of Delmer, placed in her attic. She adjusted the focus while placing a document, a property receipt, in position to be viewed. The form described what Hendrickson and her colleague, Jessica Jarecki, had found while searching through bags belonging to Delmer Smith and kept by Martha Tejeda at her home in North Port at the request by Delmer.

Next, Scanlan picked up a gun and placed it on the projection table. "What is this?" she asked looking up from the machine towards Hendrickson.

"This is a handgun. This is a Walther 380 semi-automatic handgun." She further testified that the gun had been found in one of the bags that Delmer had stored at Tejeda's home.

"And when you found it, it was actually inside of the holster?" Scanlan asked.

"Yes," Hendrickson said, nodding her head.

"I did not have a handgun inside of my bag," Delmer's face hardened as he continued with his argument.

"Okay. So you deny knowledge of the handgun?" Scanlan asked.

"I'm saying there was no gun, period, inside my bag."

The Prosecution had introduced a tape of a phone conversation that took place between Delmer and Tejeda when Delmer was working on getting Tejeda over to the storage facility to retrieve the stored bags. During that conversation, Delmer mentioned the BB rifle to Tejeda, but he then began talking about the necessity of her locating "that other thing" in the bag.

For several days after his arrest, Delmer had worked on getting Tejeda to drive to American Storage in North Port and to retrieve several duffel bags and a backpack placed in a locker there.

December 7th, 2011. Martha Tejeda is on the witness stand. Scanlan has introduced to the Court a recording of a phone call between Tejeda and Delmer. The phone call was one of several made during September of 2009 while Delmer was being held in the Pinellas County jail for violation of his Federal Probation Agreement. In those calls Delmer pushed for Tejeda to remove and hide several large duffle type bags that contained his "clothes" he had stored at American Storage in North Port.

When curiosity drove her to ask what was in the bags, he told her that they just had his clothes inside of them. He told her that his former girlfriend, Michele Quinones, had taken most of his things and that was why he had put what was left in the bags and was storing them and for her to not say anything to Quinones about the bags or the clothes. However, it didn't make sense to Tejeda because at one point, he told her he had prepaid American Storage for 3 months' use of the locker where the bags were stored. So, in her mind, the question was simply why would he want to move them right then? Why was there such a rush as was evident from Delmer's increasing push for her to get them and put them in her house and not tell anyone where they were? She didn't understand.

Finally, she asked and he told her there were some things in the bags besides the clothes but wouldn't elaborate.

On December 7^{nth}, 2012 during the Manatee County murder trial, Tejeda was on the stand once again and was being questioned by Delmer's defense attorney, Mr. Hernandez, who asked, "Now, the conversations that you had with Mr. Smith about the storage, did he have concern that he was in possession of property that could be stolen?"

"He was like frightened, I don't know," she replied frowning, face tense.

There were 7 phone calls that were introduced to that case. In each call it was clear that Delmer was becoming more stressed, more desperate, pushing Tejeda to get the bags, with one more important than the others. "It's the big bag," he told her. "The big red one."

During the phone call to Tejeda on September 12th, 2009, Delmer was becoming increasingly concerned about her getting the bags out of storage. "All right. Okay," he said to her, "listen, baby, I need you to," he paused, "I need you to go the storage today." His voice stressed the word "today."

"Baby, when I picking up the car," Tejeda replied softly, "I need the keys, I go to storage, okay, relax."

"No, no. I tell you why, it's very very important. You know that; right?" His voice was tight, climbing.

"Why very important?" Curious, relaxed tone. She felt she needed to know.

That question stopped Delmer for a moment. "Huh?"

"You have something — (the rest of the recording was unintelligible) —."

"No," his voice dipped in volume as he hesitated. Then, "Yeah, it's something in there that shouldn't be in there"

"What happened?" she asked.

"Mira," he began slowly, reluctantly, volume low. The sound of a shuffling movement entered the recording. He was speaking very close to the landline's mouthpiece. "I can't tell you that, you'll see." His voice sank.

"I know," her voice sank, became softer, more complaint and accepting, understanding, "I think—(unintelligible)—okay, when I pick up the keys I go pick it up—everything."

December 7^{nth}, 2011. Scanlan asks Tejeda gently, "Did you take all of those items out of the storage unit like he asked you to?"

"Yes."

"Where did you take them?"

"Home."

"And where in your home did you put them?"

"I put them in the attic."

Scanlan has Tejeda look at a piece of evidence. "Is that the red bag you were talking about?"

"Yes."

"Okay. What was inside that bag?"

"There was a big gun."

"Okay. Was there a smaller gun?"

"Yes."

Scanlan asked what Tejeda did with the bag when she got home. "I put all of that up on top in the attic," Tejeda replied.

Scanlan knows the Sheriff's office had visited Tejeda late in the evening. They had gone seeking information about Delmer's car which they took and impounded at their lot. However, there were questions concerning the bags Tejeda had stored in her attic.

"Okay. Now, a few days later, did the police come in your house and start asking you questions about him?"

Not completely grasping the meaning of the question, Tejeda does her best in replying. "I call the police and they would come," Tejeda frowned wondering if she had answered correctly.

"Okay. The first time though, it was at night. Did the police come to your house before you called them?" Scanlan asked.

"Yes."

"On that night, did you say anything to the police about the items that you were hiding for him?"

"No."

"The next morning, did you have another phone conversation with him?"

"Yes." Tejeda nodded.

"And did you talk about the gun again during that phone conversation?"

"Yes."

"And tell me what it is that he told you during that conversation?"

Tejeda licked her lips and a frown crossed her brow as she said quickly, "To throw out the gun. But I would say to him, Did you kill somebody? And he said, 'Just throw it out. I have not killed anybody. That was Michele's and she put it there.'"

Scanlan asked if Tejeda had told Delmer about being visited by the police. "Yes," she said.

"Okay. And what, if anything, did he say about the —" Scanlan paused for a moment "giving the gun to the police?"

Tejeda glanced over at Delmer for just a flash of a second, then back at Scanlan, "He told me not to give it to the police, the gun; to throw it out."

But that is not what she did. She went to work and spoke with her manager trying to get her thoughts in order. She was confused and very frightened. "She told me to go back, to call the police, she gave me the number. And when I was getting home, the police was already there that I had called."

Scanlan asked if it had been Tejeda's intent to turn over Delmer's possessions and that was why she called the police.

"To give them everything."

Scanlan wanted to know if she had, in fact, turned over all that belonged to Delmer that she had been keeping for him.

"Everything."

Scanlan said she had no further questions.

The gun continued to be a focal point when Bender cross-examined Tejeda. There was confusion in the testimony because of a difference in language and in understanding of what was being asked and being answered. This applied to both the attorneys and to Tejeda.

When Delmer had been on the phone to Tejeda he had a fellow prisoner who spoke Spanish helping him communicate to Tejeda. At one point the word "pistola" was used. Bender wanted to know what that meant to Tejeda and she responded that it meant "gun." But there were two guns. The one was "the big one" as described by Tejeda and then there was the "small one."

"When he called me in the morning," Tejeda said, "he told me about the small gun."

During the phone call in which Delmer was giving instructions to Tejeda while she was at American Storage and opening up his locker, he explained that one of the items was a BB gun. She had spotted it and had called it a "rifle."

"It's just a BB gun. I want you to take that out of there."

"Okay," she agreed.

"Okay. Listen," he pressed, "take all the bags out of there."

"Okay."

He went on to talk about the "red bag" and the importance of her getting that bag out of there. Then his voice rose and he said quickly to her "…you got to get that and take it and don't let the other kids go in there because it got that other thing in there. You know what I mean?"

"The kids, I give it to (the recording was unintelligible)."

"Huh?"

Tejeda responded but what she said was not intelligible on the tape.

"No," Delmer said quickly, his voice rising, "I don't want the children to get—I don't—."

"No, no, bye." She needed to get off the phone.

"Huh?" Delmer suddenly found himself being cut off.

"Bye," she said, "call me later."

"All right," his voice dropped in volume. Then, quickly, he said, "Love you, baby. Hey. Okay?"

There was no reply, she had already hungup.

Bender stepped up for her cross-examination and immediately began by questioning if Tejeda had, in fact, given everything that belonged to Delmer to the police. She mentioned a large screen TV that was in Tejeda's master bedroom, and had been photographed by the Sheriff's Office.

Tejeda, probably confused, did not confirm to Bender at that point in her testimony that the TV in her home was owned by her and not by Delmer. There was a second TV that had been in storage. However, Delmer told her that she could pass that item on to one of relatives. And that is exactly what she had done. Tejeda had no knowledge at that point that the TV had been stolen. She thought it had all been bought or bartered for by Delmer. She was completely oblivious of his actions, believing that the numerous problems he was facing was because of Quinones.

In the phone call on September 11th, 2009, Delmer told Tejeda, "Michele stole all my computers and everything."

"What?" Tejeda questioned, her voice sharply rising. She had grown very protective of Delmer, very jealous, and had told him she would kill Quinones if the other woman caused her any grief.

"She stole everything," he lied, voice calm.

"When?" her reply was shrill, angry.

"Yesterday, when they arrested me."

Bender questioned Tejeda about her not informing the Sheriff's Office personnel about Delmer's property being in her home. She pursued Tejeda over why it was that on the first visit by "the police" that she had not told them that she had Delmer's bags in her attic.

"And you lied to the police the first time [they visited her at home]."

"I didn't lie to them." Tejeda vigorously shook her head a pained look on her face. To be referred to as a liar was hard for her to hear.

"You didn't tell them that you had taken his property out of storage."

"Because it was at night." She leaned forward in her chair, her voice rising, body going rigid.

"What does that mean?" Bender asked, frowning.

"Because the police came at night," she tried to explain. "I went to make a statement because they came in a car." She wet her lips. "They didn't ask me if there was anything else. And then the next day they were there and I gave them everything."

"Okay," Bender continued. "So the police never asked you whether you had property of Mr. Smith's at your house?"

"At that time, no. It was ten at night." Tejeda shook her head back and forth not understanding why it was so clear to her and not to Bender. She didn't know how else to explain her actions and it frightened her to not only be called a liar but the continued pressure was taking its toll on her. Her eyes were locked on Bender, brows lowered, hands clenched.

Bender basically asked the same question over again adding, "Were they just interviewing you because you are not a U.S. citizen?"

Tejeda's eyes went wide.

Scanlan immediately objected citing "relevance," but the Court overruled.

Not understanding, Tejeda asked with an uncertain tone, as she shifted in her chair, "What?"

Bender restated the question. Tejeda frowned, cleared her throat, and answered that she didn't think so. Then Bender asked, "Okay. Were they interviewing you about Mr. Smith?"

Scanlan shook her head and objected. Bender glanced back at her and then up to Curly waiting for the Court's response when Scanlan began to walk forward as she requested the right for them to approach the bench. Curly nodded and said, "Okay."

However, as the attorneys approached the Bench, Scanlan began chuckling to herself. The laugh was not overly loud but loud enough that the Court heard the prosecutor.

Curly scowled and sat forward in her chair. She narrowed her eyes and, looking directly at Scanlan, spoke softly but sharply through narrowed lips. "Please —," she paused, "and with all due respect, please do not laugh. Keep your emotions to yourself."

Curly looked over to Bender whose eyes had gone wide. The judge sensed that the defense attorney was not aware of what had just taken place and so she explained, "She is walking up laughing, and I think that is disrespectful to you, Ms. Bender." Bender looked from the Judge, who was clearly displeased with the prosecution, to Scanlan and then again to the Court as Curly sat back in her chair. "But go ahead," she motioned to Scanlan to continue with her objection.

Scanlan stepped up alongside Bender. She felt the need to respond to Curly's remark, "Well, Judge, she keeps asking this question. Ms. Tejeda probably only answered it this way and started talking about all the other things, which is this whole conversation with the police about every other crime that was committed. It is not an objection; this is just a warning."

Curly showed no physical response to Scanlan's comment that she was issuing a "warning." The judge calmly replied that Bender just wanted to know if the police had asked Tejeda about whether or not she had any of Delmer's property. Scanlan replied that she did not think Tejeda would respond by saying that she had not told the police that, meaning that she had withheld the fact from the police intentionally.

Curly sat forward again. She looked from one attorney to the other and then responded keeping her voice low, "If she walks into it, she walks into it. I don't know."

Feeling there was nothing else to say about the issue, she shrugged her shoulders and nodded. She glanced at the Jury and then back to the attorneys in front of her. "All right," she said. "This is a good time to take a break." She called for a ten-minute recess in the proceedings.

When they returned, Bender opened by again asking a question about Tejeda's first meeting with the police. Specifically, she wanted to know if during the first visit Tejeda had told the police that she had Delmer's property in her house.

"No," she replied. The police had not asked her if she had it. They were there for Delmer's car.

Bender next questioned Tejeda closely about her being able to put the bags up in the attic herself or did she require help. "I put all the things in the attic," she said in response.

Bender continued, disregarding Tejeda's reply, not believing her, "Who helped you put all of those heavy items up into the attic? Because it wasn't you by yourself; was it?"

"Yes," Tejeda said, "I did it by myself?"

"Oh. No other man helped you?"

"A cousin of mine who was there came over."

"Right. And your cousin is approximately or was approximately how old in 2009?"

"Around 41 years old."

Bender then wanted to know how tall Tejeda's cousin was and about his build. Tejeda responded that he was small, like her.

"Okay. And he helped you, actually, isn't it true, Ms. Tejeda, not you, by yourself, but your cousin is the one who put the heavy objects up to the attic?"

Bender was seeking an opening hoping to draw in the potential for evidence tampering by introducing the fact that others besides Tejeda had access to the contents of the bags. Tejeda had claimed she was the only one who looked inside the bags prior to law enforcement picking them up as evidence. If Bender could prove that Tejeda had help and/or that others had access to the bags then that could have brought in a reasonable doubt that someone had put the items in question in the bags.

Bender also wanted to cause Tejeda to also stumble in her testimony. She was hoping she would catch the woman in a lie, or at least in a way that it sounded like she had lied. That would then allow her to bring into question anything that Tejeda said and discredit her testimony against Delmer.

However, Tejeda stood her ground and, even though Bender did her best to create a crack in the woman's testimony she was unable to do so. Tejeda had nothing to hide and in her innocence she won out.

"No. He only helped me get the things out of the car." Tejeda frowned and shook her head back and forth.

"So all by yourself, at five-foot-one you moved all those heavy bags and things up to the attic; correct?"

"Yes." The frown deepened.

Bender continued to push. "So your cousin, 41 years old, who sounds rather weak, didn't move anything up into the attic for you; he only moved things out of the car; is that correct?"

"He got them out of the car; correct."

"Okay. And why didn't he help you move them up to the attic, Ms. Tejeda?"

"Because he had to leave."

Bender continued with her line of questioning asking virtually the same questions over again in the hopes that Tejeda would stumble. Finally, Scanlan protested saying "asked and answered" to a repeat question and the Court sustained the objection. Bender then said, "Nothing further." The Court then turned to Scanlan who also said she had no questions and Tejeda was excused.

CHAPTER FORTY THREE
A Question of Size

Bender began a series of questions concerning Delmer's method of storage of the items then being held as evidence in the case. She referred to the recording of a telephone conversation between Martha Tejeda and Delmer that took place while Delmer was in custody for violating his federal parole. That recording disclosed the fact that Delmer had several large bags in a storage facility located in North Port, and that he had instructed her in how to go about retrieving those bags and then placing them in her attic above her garage. She questioned Delmer if he thought it possible that Tejeda could have lifted the 100 and-some-pound bags up into her attic.

Scanlan objected. She believed the question calls for speculation. The court sustained.

Bender attempted to continue but decided to change her path and concentrate on Delmer's ability of handling the bags. "Was it difficult for you to lift those bags? You're pretty strong; right?"

"No, it was kind of easy for me, yes."

"How much do you weigh?"

"Right now?"

"Right now," Bender confirmed.

The attorney's line of questioning would soon become clear as to her intent. Bender had concluded there was a weak spot in the evidence and sought to capitalize on it.

"I'm 281," Delmer responded.

"And in March of 2009, do you recall how much you weighed?"

"I was weighing anywhere from like 295 to 300 pounds."

"Tell us," Bender continued calmly, "what size did you wear back in 2009?"

"My pants size was size 44 or 46. My shirt sizes were 5X to 6X."

Bender paused for a moment to let Delmer's comment standout. She then asked, "How tall are you?"

"I am six-foot," he replied.

"Delmer, you ever try to squeeze yourself into or through a small jalouslie window?"

"No, ma'am."

"Do you have any estimate of what your size of your shoulders were in 2009, in March of 2009?"

"Large, very large."

Bender asking for clarification on what he meant by "large." He only responded that his shoulders had been large and that they were smaller then as he gave testimony.

Bender had previously brought up, in an indirect manner, Delmer's size when speaking to a prior witness, Rhonda DiFranco, on December 6th, and then again on December 7th. During the latter testimony she questioned about the point of entry referencing size and ability of a large person making entry through the jalousie window that was considered by DiFranco and Dumer as being the "point of entry" into Marshall's rented home.

DiFranco, a sergeant in the Sarasota County Sheriff's Office, had been the forensic officer that processed the Carmilfra crime scene in March of 2009. Bender carefully went over DiFranco's work that night reviewing photographs the detective had taken. The focus of her questioning finally settled on the jalousie window and the room into which the window made entry.

"I believe the window was the entry point," DiFranco testified.

Bender did not disagree with DiFranco that the window may have been the entry point for someone. It fact, it was damaged and appeared forcibly pushed open. However, she believed that Delmer's physical size would have prevented him from being responsible for the damage or from gaining entry into the home through it. Curiously, in developing her argument, Bender questioned DiFranco about her physical build resulting in an immediate objection from Scanlan.

DiFranco testified that while photographing both inside and outside the home, she had entered the master bedroom where the damaged window was. She wanted an interior shot of the window. However, once in the room, she discovered a problem. The space in front of the window was small because a table occupied part of the area, and then there was a very large television sitting on top of that. This made obtaining the photograph of the window that Bender was displaying for the Jury extremely problematic. Bender recognized that and wanted to capitalize on it.

The attorney looked from the photo to the detective and asked, "And is that the window that you determine was the point of entry?"

"Yes, it was."

"Okay. All right." Bender paused and then pointed at a shape in the photo while asking, "And this object right here, is that the desk?"

"That was a table."

"In the corner?"

"Yes."

"Okay. And was there a very large television set?"

"Yes, there was. That's why it was difficult to get the angle," DiFranco explained.

"And it was difficult to get the angle so that you can see the screen?" Bender asked.

"That you could see the window in its entirety."

"Okay. Did you take any measurements of that small space?"

"No, I did not."

"Did you take any measurements of the window?"

"No, I did not."

"How much do you weigh or how much did you weigh in 2009, if you don't mind me asking?" Bender asked DiFranco quickly.

Silence.

A stunned DiFranco sat back in her chair and looked to where the prosecution sat taking notes. No one had ever asked her a personal question like that while she was testifying.

Scanlan immediately stood. "Judge, I think the witness wants me to object. If we can ask her size, perhaps, instead of her weight?"

"No," Bender replied shaking her head, looking from DiFranco to Scanlan and then to the Judge Curly. "That won't work."

"Counsel, approach the bench," Curly ordered, a frown on her face as she sat forward in her chair. She looked closely at Bender. "Is it for," she hesitated, thinking the situation thru, "to see about getting in?"

Bender replied, "Uh-huh."

"Okay," Curly said slowly. Her eyes strayed from Bender to Scanlan. The slight frown had not disappeared. She sat back in her chair having made her decision. "I think I have got to let her do it." She glanced from Scanlan back to Bender and then back again to Scanlan. "I got to let her do it. Go ahead." She nodded her assent to Bender.

Bender replied, "I'm sorry."

"That's okay," the Court continued. "Please explain on the record the reasons you want her weight. Go ahead."

"Because I want to find out if she could go through that window, you know, at her age, ability, and size and weight."

Curley sat forward again with a raised eyebrow. "If it's comparable to—?"

Scanlan interrupted, "I'm going to object."

"I understand. Thank you."

The bench conference was concluded and the attorneys return to their prior position. Judge Curley sat back in her chair again. "All right. Objection is overruled."

"Okay." Bender said looking to the witness.

"Answer the question," the Court told DiFranco.

"You can hate me forever," Bender said to a startled DiFranco. "I'm sorry." She glanced at the floor as she paused for a moment thinking of how to word her question and then asked the witness, "In 2009, because you're significantly thinner now, what was your weight two years ago in March?"

DiFranco replied, "I am heavier now than I was in 2009."

"You didn't have to tell us that. What were you in 2009?"

"I was at 160."

"Okay. And how tall are you?"

"Five-six."

"And did you try to get through that window?"

"No. No."

"Did you try to get in between," Bender continued, "I know you said you had difficulty getting your camera into that small space there. Did you physically put your body between a television set and the desk? In other words."

DiFranco thought for a moment, "I was," she hesitated, "yeah, I got in a position that I felt was the best angle that I could get out of there without moving everything out of the way."

"Right. Because you didn't want to move any of the furniture that was actually there; correct?"

"Correct."

"Because you need to, by protocol, [make sure] that everything was in place; right?"

"Yes," DiFranco replied.

"Okay. But am I correct then, that doesn't mean you physically got your size, your weight into that small area; correct?"

"No."

Bender then went on to discuss the damage to the window. She wanted to know if DiFranco had measured any of it. She wanted to know if DiFranco had measured the distance from the floor to the window.

DiFranco had taken no measurements.

Bender asked why.

DiFranco said she had no reason for having not measured.

Bender inquired about fingerprints. DiFranco said there were no fingerprints found. According to the victim, Delmer had worn heavy gloves to conceal his hands, and the gloves had damaged the skin on her face. And so the conversation went riding high and then low across the work DiFranco had completed at Marshall's home until Bender finally looked at Judge Curly and said, "Nothing further Judge.

CHAPTER FORTY FOUR

The Point of Entry Debate

Bender continued to question DiFranco about her findings at the scene and used DiFranco's photographs displaying them on an overhead for the Court and the Jury to see. She told DiFranco that she quickly wanted to show and discuss the photo of the window that DiFranco believed was the entry point into the Carmilfra home "… Defense Exhibit A70. Can you see that? Do you see the jalousie windows in that?"

"Yes, I do."

Referring to the fact that the window in the picture was open, Bender questioned DiFranco. "That's the way you found it; correct?"

"Correct."

"And is that the bottom window that you took other images of that you believe was the entry point?"

"I believe the window was the entry point. Yes."

Bender asked DiFranco if she had changed the position of the window from that as she found it.

DiFranco replied, "The photograph is as I found it."

Bender continued, "The screen wasn't torn any more than what you already indicated?"

"Right."

Scanlan took up the photo on her cross and asked, "The screen was popped out all the way on the bottom all the way across?"

"Yes."

"So a person could either crawl and fit in that space between the bottom of the window and that last window pane; correct?"

"Correct."

Scanlan noted that the window was a jalousie and that the panes could be removed and replaced. DiFranco agreed with her but added that she was not making the suggestion or had evidence that someone had removed any panes or replaced them. She was simply stating that it was her belief that the window in question was the point of entry.

Bender then returned for a redirect. She questioned DiFranco on her knowledge of the window's construction. DiFranco responded that she had grown up in Florida and was familiar with jalousie windows. She stated there were two major types and that she, as a teenager, had snuck out of her house many times at night to visit friends by slipping through the space between the open panes of glass. In some windows, she testified, the glass panes are more easily removed but the one in question did not fit that profile.

Bender asked, "But the glass pane itself, there is no indication from your examination that the glass pane was ever removed; correct?"

"No," DiFranco replied, "not from my determination."

Bender jumped then from the window to showing defense photographs taken by DiFranco of footprints found outside the home and below the window. She peppered DiFranco with questions about the shoe prints. She wanted to know if DiFranco could tell the size of the shoes that had left the prints.

She singled out a photo that had a ruler in it. "Defense Exhibit A45. Is that your ruler?"

"Yes."

"Do you remember the size approximately of that?"

"No, I don't recall."

"Is it large, is it medium, is it small?" Bender inquired watching DiFranco. "Don't know?"

"I can't remember."

DiFranco would testify that there were multiple overlays of prints. She felt that one print had the characteristic of being a tennis shoe. Bender pressed her on the others showing multiple photos asking if DiFranco had made any molds.

Dumer later testified that he had found eight pair of shoes in Delmer's personal belongings.

"And did you," Bender questioned, "when you personally inspected all of these shoes that you don't know were his or not, did you make any notes as to the size of all of those shoes?"

"No," Dumer replied, "they didn't appear to me to have any particular evidentiary value at that time, correct."

Bender pressed on. "Well, I mean, it would certainly be common sense that if one of the pairs of shoes is a size 7 and one of the pairs of shoes as a size 11, it wouldn't be the same— they wouldn't belong to the same person; right?"

"Specifically," Dumer replied, "I was looking at tread patterns because I was not aware what the size of those shoe impressions were around the house."

"Well, you could have found that out, based on her measurements; correct? You could have had that analyzed?"

"I could have."

"But you chose not to?" Bender pressed.

"At that time I didn't feel it was necessary, correct."

"So we don't know what size that shoe was of that impression that she was able to find around the entry point to Ms. Marshall's residence; right?"

"As a lead investigator in conducting this investigation, those tread patterns there did not offer any evidentiary value to me at that time," Dumer calmly replied.

Bender continued pressing, repeating herself, which drew an objection from Scanlan that the question had already been asked and answered, but was overruled by the court.

"Yes or no. Detective? "Bender demanded. "Yes or no?"

"The answer is, the tread patterns were sent to FDLE in Tampa. It's not as if we ignored them."

"So what size are they?"

"I don't know."

"Because I did not examine any report from them and at the time it did not offer any value to me."

"So it never occurred to you that it would be important with all of your law enforcement experience to figure out what size of print they were?"

Scanlan stood, "Objection, argumentative!"

The Court overruled and told Bender to continue.

"Yes or no?"

The duel continued drawing more objections from Scanlan that, as the others had been, were overruled.

In a similar fashion, Bender wanted to know why DiFranco had not looked for fingerprints on the screwdriver and wrench, tools that had been used by Delmer for removing the television from the wall. She rejected DiFranco's reasoning that as Nicole Marshall had said Delmer was wearing gloves and so she felt there would be no fingerprints left on those tools.

Mike Dumer supported DiFranco's reasoning and found himself also being pressured in a round of questioning that brought about multiple objections for being argumentative by the Prosecution.

"So in other words, you didn't think that there would be any possible value of seeing if there were prints on the tools that you knew were used by the perpetrator?" Bender asked.

Dumer calmly replied, "Based on the interview conducted with the victim, she clearly stated that the perpetrator was wearing gloves."

Bender tried to twist the statement. "She stated she *believed* the perpetrator was wearing gloves; correct?"

"That's correct."

"Do you, in your experience as a detective, as a law enforcement officer, base all of your forensic decisions on what to test or what not to test based upon the victim having—the statement of the victim having a heart attack in a hospital, yes or no, sir?"

Scanlan objected, and the Court overruled. But in the end Dumer remained calm and steadfast in his belief that neither he nor DiFranco had made any errors and Bender was unable to create or establish any.

CHAPTER FORTY FIVE
Size Comparison

The next witness called by Bender was a man named Jeremy Scott Young. This was part of an obvious and well-planned, final attempt by Bender to inject the possibility of reasonable doubt into the juror's minds regarding Delmer having been the burglar who broke into the residence located on Carmilfra Drive. She had been methodically building to this point.

"Mr. Young," Bender began, focusing her eyes squarely on the defense witness, "do you know a man by the name as James Cellecz?"

"Yes, ma'am."

"And can you tell the Jury his approximate size, height, and weight?"

Young sat forward, his attention on the woman questioning him. "Proximate size," he paused, thinking and wrinkled his forehead, "probably about 145 pounds."

"And height approximately?"

"5'10", 5'11"." He sat back in his chair.

"How tall are you?"

"6'1"."

"Is he shorter than you?"

"Yes, ma'am."

"How much shorter than you is he?"

"About 3 inches."

"Okay. And you know his approximate age?"

"He's probably about three years older than me. About 31."

"Is he smaller or larger than Mr. Smith?"

"Smaller."

Bender looked away from the witness and turned to face Judge Curley. "No further, Judge."

The Court looked to Scanlan. "Any cross on that?" Curley asked of Scanlan who immediately stood.

Scanlan walked slowly across the courtroom stopping in the middle of the room. She focused on the witness. "If Mr. Cellecz was standing next to a woman who is five foot two and weighs approximately 100 pounds, is there any way she could convince him," she paused, then corrected herself, "confuse him with being more than twice as large as she is?"

"No, ma'am."

"Thank you." Scanlan turned and walked back to the prosecution table.

The Court looked from Scanlan to Bender. "All right. Anything?"

"No."

The Court thanked and then released Mr. Young. However, before he was able to stand and walk from the courtroom, Judge Curly remembered that the Jury might have questions and so she stopped him. "Oh," she said "hold on. I'm sorry. Any questions by the witness—," she caught her error and corrected it, "—by the jurors?" She looked over to them for a response. "Any questions? No?" She looked over at the witness, "Okay. You many step down." She watched as Mr. Young left the courtroom and then said, "Ms. Bender, next witness?"

"Your Honor, at this time the defense rests."

Judge Curley looked to Scanlan. "Rebuttal?"

CHAPTER FORTY SIX
James Cellecz

Scanlan had previously informed the Court that, depending on what Delmer said when called to the stand, she would recall Detective Dumer as a rebuttal witness if needed. And so he became the last witness on December 8th, 2011 before the case was turned over to the Jury.

Scanlan's purpose was to bring to rest any misunderstanding about the relationship between Delmer and Cellecz. She wanted to firmly establish the fact that the two men had more than a casual relationship and that it was known by others in the Venice area.

Dumer testified that late in the afternoon on September 15th, 2009, he met with a man named David Watmough in Venice. Watmough was not regarded as a suspect, but Dumer felt he could provide information vital to his investigation. He could also provide evidence that the relationship between Delmer and Cellecz had been ongoing and more than casual.

Watmough agree to be interviewed and recorded by Dumer at the local sheriff's substation. During that meeting, Watmough told Dumer that Delmer had months before purchased an 18-foot trailer from him and had then left it on Watmough's property. He told the detective he believed Delmer used the trailer to store tools. He went on to say that Delmer had also left a red Hyundai on the property, but it had been recently removed by a woman named "Martha." Watmough did not know where she had taken it.

However, Detective Ortiz would later notify Dumer close to midnight that the car had been located in Martha Tejeda's driveway and that it was being impounded by the Sheriff's Office.

Dumer continued questioning Watmough about James Cellecz. He was aware that Cellecz had been known to associate with Delmer on more than a casual basis. The detective believed Cellecz was someone who regularly carried Delmer's ill won goods to local pawnshops representing himself as being the owner of those items. He hoped Watmough would be able to color in some of the pieces needed to tie the two men together.

Watmough told Dumer that he rented a small apartment to Cellecz there on his property. He further told Dumer that to his knowledge Cellecz made his living as a computer programmer. He was also aware that Cellecz and Delmer were known to each other but could not comment more on their relationship. As it was, Cellecz would not be a major contributor in the current trial, other than for Bender's attempt at drawing the Jury's attention to his being a possible suspect based on his physical stature versus that of Delmer's. However, that would change when Manatee County began prosecuting Delmer for the murder of Kathy Briles.

He then suddenly became a major threat to Delmer following his own arrest for his having received and sold items stolen by Delmer. That relationship would seal the link between Delmer and the crimes he was being prosecuted for. Cellecz would be in a position to ask for a plea bargain with the offer to testify against Delmer.

Delmer was facing a death penalty and Cellecz could easily put a noose around Delmer's throat because of his knowledge of the other man's criminal activities. He soon found himself to be the object of several documented death threats made by Delmer who hoped such threats would make him shut up.

CHAPTER FORTY SEVEN
Closing Arguments

Closing arguments began on December 8th, 2011. The prosecution led off. Ms. Scanlan began by telling the Jury that the state had "...two main things that have to be proved in this case." The first was that a crime had been committed, and the second was that the defendant was the person who had committed the crime. She told them that the testimony of Nicole Marshall was crucial to establishing that a crime had been committed.

She next told the Jury that the defendant had been charged with two crimes. Both the crimes involved a firearm. The first was home invasion. The second was kidnapping. The display or use of a firearm during a felony in the state of Florida is extremely punishable by Florida law. If a firearm is displayed during the commission of a felony, it is an automatic 10 years in prison. If the weapon is fired, the result is a 20-year sentence. If somebody is injured, it results in a life sentence.

Scanlan spoke about the elements of the crimes. She stated that there were four elements that established the crime of home invasion robbery. She went through each element as it pertained to what took place on the night of March 14th, 2009 at the residence located on Carmilfra Drive.

The first element was that the defendant had entered the dwelling. She reminded the Jury that during Nicole Marshall's testimony that she told them she had been sitting on her couch alone at home working on a beading project while watching TV. She told them that Marshall had felt the presence of someone in the room with her and that when she looked up there was a large man standing near her wearing dark clothing. Then the lights went out, and Marshall was suddenly attacked. She was thrown onto the floor. Her face was shoved into the couch cushions.

"That establishes the first element of the crime, that the defendant entered her [Marshall's] dwelling," Scanlan told the Jury. She went on to clarify that her purpose was to address the issue of whether or not a crime had been committed. "The only thing," she said, "for the first element [to be established] is the entering of the dwelling."

Scanlan was aware that one major issue Bender was likely to bring up was the means of entrance. She said, "Ms. Bender may get up here during her closing argument and argue to you that you cannot be sure how, in fact, he entered." Scanlan conceded that fact. She told the Jury that they may not be able to determine how he entered. She went on to say that Sgt. DiFranco had told them, and used photographs, to explain how she believed Delmer had made entry.

"It is most likely that what he did was pop the screen door, walked across the lanai and go in through the window in the bedroom." She paused using the overhead with a photograph pointing at the window. "That's most likely what happened."

She added that Bender would most likely argue that Delmer could not have fit through the window. And, she felt that Bender would also state her belief that Delmer could not have walked across the lanai without being seen. "Believe what you want about the manner in which he entered the house," she said. "The fact is," she continued after a slight pause, "it does not matter for your determination of that element of the crime. It's not an element of the crime, the manner in which he entered the house. The element is that he did enter the house. That is established when Nicole Marshall tells you, 'He was standing next to my couch.'"

The second element of the crime was established by the defendant's actions. He drug the victim room by room through the house looking for things to steal. Scanlan said that Marshall's testimony established the second element that Delmer intended to rob her.

The third element of the crime was established by evidence that force and violence were used that created fear in the victim in order to take her property. "She [Marshall] testified that the defendant repeatedly threatened to kill her, that he treated her roughly, dragging her from room to room by her hair or the back of her robe, causing bruises and terrifying her, and then he tied her up on the floor while he gathered the items that he had decided to steal."

The fourth and final element was that during the "…commission of the crime a firearm was used." When he dragged Marshall into the master bathroom, "…he forced her down and showed her the gun…."

Scanlan paused for a moment, and then brought up the second crime: armed kidnapping. She began by explaining to the Jury that as it had been with the prior crime of home invasion and robbery, there are four elements that she was going to address.

"The elements," she began, "of that crime are that Delmer Smith forcibly, secretly or by threat confined, abducted or imprisoned Nicole Marshall against her will; that he had no lawful authority to do so; and that Delmer Smith acted with the intent to inflict bodily harm or terrorize Nicole Marshall."

And, again, she told the Jury, as it was with the prior crime of home invasion robbery, the fourth element is that he displayed a firearm that Marshall saw and feared that he would use to harm her with.

Scanlan reviewed with the Jury that Nicole had testified how Delmer had told her to get on the floor where he hogtied her. Scanlan said, "Tying someone up for an extended period of time is by its very nature confinement." She then went on to say, "That [act] establishes the first element of the crime of kidnapping."

"Obviously," she continued, "the defendant had no lawful authority [to restrain Nicole Marshall]." She then used the legal right of a police officer to handcuff someone as a juxtaposition against what Delmer had done. The defendant did not have the authority. Therefore, his actions constituted the second element of the crime of kidnapping.

The third element of the crime was established by the physical injuries sustained by Marshall to which she testified. "She had bruises to her hands, bruises to her ankles, the marks on her neck." While hogtied, Marshall managed to wiggle free using her right hand. That action caused bruising of the tissue on her hand and her wrist that became worse over the next few days following the attack that required medical attention. Scanlan recalled that the victim's heart was beating unnaturally hard while tied. This was because she was fearful that her attempts to free herself might result in her accidentally strangling herself and that no one would find her for several days. So she decided to fight for her freedom and in doing so injured her hand and wrist. But the fear was so intense she had a heart attack.

"Through her testimony alone," Scanlan said, "it is clear that the two crimes with which the defendant is charged were committed."

Scanlan then told the Jury that the judge would read to them options of finding for lesser- included crimes. She told the Jury that the Court was required to do that when it's not so clear that the evidence had been committed. However, she felt that should not be the case regarding these crimes. She went on to say, "There is no question that what was done to Nicole Marshall was a home invasion robbery with a firearm and kidnapping with a firearm."

Scanlan paused momentarily, letting what she had just said filter through the minds of the jurors. Next, she told them, the remaining majority of her presentation would then be on reviewing the evidence in the case that proved Delmer Smith was the one person who committed the crimes.

Scanlan begins by talking about the property stolen from the Marshalls. She reminds the Jury that Michele Quinones testified that she had seen the articles taken from the Marshall residence in Delmer's possession prior to her tossing Delmer out of her home in August of 2009. That was after his arrest following the fight at the Tavern on the Island.

The prosecutor tells the Jury that these articles will be placed in the Jury room. She tells him to feel free and turning on the computer and accessing the files. She wants them to do this. She wants them to find and see the emails written by Nicole and responded to by her husband and son. She tells him to look at the music that is on the system. Not only is there music from Canada that Nicole had placed on there, but there is also the music that Quinones placed on there for her job as a DJ. They will find Nicole's iPod, her Cassiopeia, the defendant's identification card, and his credit cards. The prosecutor goes on to tell them that they will also find Nicole's docking station and a medication bottle with Delmer's name on. All these loose items were found in his duffel bag.

She then brings up the BB rifle and the handgun. She replayed the tape of the conversation that took place between Tejeda and Delmer focusing on comments made by the defendant regarding getting rid of the "pistol," and making sure that the "kids" would not go into the duffel bag.

Scanlan reminded them of Delmer's comment on the tape, "Make sure you throw that pistola in the trash or we will all get in trouble."

"Martha wouldn't do it," Scanlan said. "She knew that that was wrong. She did the right thing, and she gave that gun to the police and everything else that she had in her house."

Scanlan told the Jury that the very fact that Delmer was in possession of so many stolen articles so soon after the robbery, "… could by itself be enough to convince you that he's been identified as the robber." However, she went on to say that the prosecution had more evidence.

She next discussed the DNA that he left in droplets of wet sweat found, "... all over her house. He has no explanation for how... [that happened]."

Knowing Bender will attack the droplets as being contaminated because they were "discolored," she offered that there was no evidence to support any contamination of the samples taken. After all, she argues, Delmer simply had been dirty and so the sweat running off his body contained some of the surface dirt which caused the sweat droplets to have some color. However, the color issue in the sweat does not introduce contamination.

The, she added, "The defendant confessed." He confessed to a prison law clerk. He had approached Phillip Casciola for advice while in jail. Casciola told the Court that he expected nothing in return for his testimony and he got nothing for it. He had said he testified because he felt he only had a few chances of doing something good in his life.

Scanlan closed her statement by telling the Jury that they would be given options on the verdict form. They could find him guilty as charged, guilty of a lesser offense, or not guilty. But she wanted them to consider two primary questions. The first question she asked them to think about was: had Delmer been in possession of firearm? Was it a real gun? The second question was if it was not a real gun then what sort of weapon was it. With that, Scanlan closed her statement and returned to her seat at the prosecution table as Bender stood and walked to the lectern.

Judge Curley watched as Scanlan walked back to the table for the prosecution, and then turned her attention to Bender as she rose and started toward the lectern. "Ms. Bender," she nodded toward the defense attorney, technology and granting her the right to present her argument.

Looking toward the Jury members, Bender allowed a momentary friendly smile to cross her face. "Good afternoon, ladies and gentlemen."

She had spent a good amount of time preparing her closing remarks and went right to work. "The confession," she began, as she looked at each Jury member. "Let me start with the confession. Okay?"

"There is no confession," Bender said firmly, but calmly.

During her examination of Phillip Casciola, the attorney had focused on how tight the security was where Delmer and Casciola supposedly had met for the discussion regarding the crime Delmer allegedly had committed. "The state made the comment that it was not done where it could be monitored." She paused for a moment. "Ladies and gentlemen," she slowly shook her head back and forth for emphasis on what she was about to say, "there is no place that is more monitored than the place where Mr. Casciola claimed this alleged statement was even made."

That was the centerpiece of her argument.

She questioned where did the discussion between Casciola and Delmer take place? Where was the evidence that such a discussion had occurred? The argument presented by the state was that Casciola had come forward solely because he wanted to do something good in his life. Casciola had said he knew he would never get out of jail alive, and so this testimony, he said, provided him with an instance of having done something proper as he would likely not get any opportunity for such a deed ever again. At least, not outside the confines of his imprisonment. And yet, at no time were the inmates unmonitored. So how did the discussion take place that was not witnessed?

"Ladies and gentlemen," Bender argued, "there is no place that is more monitored than the place that Mr. Casciola claimed this alleged statement [Delmer's confession] was even made. It was in the confinement part of the jail where there are video monitors and cameras watching every move those inmates make. They are monitored in person with the law enforcement officers there shuffling them back and forth. They don't walk by themselves. They don't work out by themselves. They don't talk among themselves. They don't play cards. They are in confinement.

That means one man to one cell. So let's just dispel that. It certainly wasn't a non-monitored situation. It's as monitored as it gets." She paused to let her words sink in, and then added emphatically, "There's no confession."

"Look at the shoes. Good gravy." She mentioned the pattern on the sole of one of the shoes. "The pattern on that photograph is excellent. Even Detective Dumer said it's pretty good, pretty good." She stopped momentarily and frowned, her forehead wrinkling with the question. "But who followed up on it? No one. Who checked those shoes to see if all of them were indeed size eleven? No one. No one. Why not? Those shoes walk around the house, the way the attacker went, and right underneath the only point of entry in that house."

Then there was the issue of the gloves. "Did he have on gloves? Sure, sure. At some point he had on gloves. But why is a law enforcement officer, would you be so complacent as to not think, well, can you use big fabric— rough fabric gloves, as the victim described it, to tie little knots? Can you use big fabric rough-textured glove's to operate electric trolls and manipulate wrenches in and screw things and pull wires out? Can you do that? Why wouldn't even— why would not they— think, well, maybe he had to take the gloves off at some point? Why not, ladies and gentlemen, why not, why not test those things? Because they were complacent, because they were looking for someone that matches contaminated droplets on the floor."

Bender paused for a moment, then continued, "Are there a million shoes in the world? Yes. But when they had it narrowed down to his property and the only had six or eight, they still did nothing."

Bender's next attack was focused on one word: complacency. She defined it for the Jury quoting from a dictionary. "It is," she said, "'a feeling of quiet pleasure or security, often while unaware of some potential danger, defect or the like.'"

She recalled that Scanlan had used the word "excuses" when referring to Delmer's testimony whenever he attempted to provide a logical response to her questions. "Ladies and gentlemen, explanations, receipts, jobs, certifications, those aren't excuses, and it is not a simple way of putting it off on someone else."

She paused, and then continued. "Think of who has been complacent throughout the course of these past two years. Think of who has told during this trial, well, you didn't ask the right questions. You weren't specific enough in your questions." She took a few steps from the lectern.

"Ladies and gentlemen, this is not the time to hide the ball. We want to show you all of the balls. Okay? We want to show you everything. All right? That's why you have all of those photographs. Take the laptop, take the photographs, take the documents back there, please. Because the simple matter is that law enforcement was complacent when they found the laptop in Delmer's possession. Six months after the attack they find him with a laptop." She shakes her head.

She went on to say, her palms were open and up with her arms spread slightly, "Did he have other equipment? Absolutely. And where did he tell you that he got it? Did he try to hide those? He never tried to hide the laptop." She went on to argue that Delmer had obtained all those items from James Cellecz. She said that Scanlan had attempted to pressure Delmer into saying that Cellecz was the one responsible. But how, she wondered, could Delmer ever testify regarding the activities of Cellecz. "He can't. Why can't he? Because he wasn't there. He didn't see James crawl through the window. You can be darn sure that if he thought James had crawled through the window and sold him some stolen property 62 hours after doing something like that, he sure as heck wasn't going to have it and use it around and giving it to his girlfriend six months after the fact."

She then concentrated on detective Dumer. "Do you remember," she asked the Jury, "what detective Dumer said at the very end? At first he's responsible. He carries that mantle. He's in charge of every decision. And then when you say, well, why didn't you do this or why didn't you do that, then it's someone else's decision. It's not hide the ball time. It's answer the questions and look at every single puzzle piece and examine it with scrutiny, absolute scrutiny."

Next Bender turned to Marshall's inability to properly describe the alleged firearm. She questions why it took two years before Marshall was shown the pistol that allegedly had been used when she had been robbed. The defense attorney offered up as a reason that the prosecution knew Marshall would not be able to identify it. That being the case, how is it that the prosecution can say that gun was the one used during a robbery.

Bender agreed that Marshall had been through a horrible ordeal. "But the primary question is who did it?" Bender said. She draws in the fact that the victim cannot identify her attacker. She reminds the Jury that Marshall said her assailant "had the voice of an African American."

Tapes of Delmer's voice were played for the Jury with Marshall present, and she was asked if the voice on the tapes was the same voice she heard the night of the attack. Marshall replied that she could not say it was the voice of her attacker. Even though she had been in a position to hear him say multiple things to her, horrible things. "'I'm going to kill you,'" Bender reminded them, "'I'm not a nice person. I want crack, I want crack, I want crack." She told them that the attacker had said multiple things and had clearly defined the attacker as having spoken like an African-American might speak.

Next she brought up the question of the entry into the Carmilfra Drive home. The State believes Delmer made entry through a jalousie window without breaking it, or moving any furniture inside the room. "How does a size 5X, 280 pound, 5 foot 11 man squeeze through that little jalousie window?" she asked. Marshall had testified that all the doors and windows were locked. The only window that was open was the alleged point of entry. Upon close examination, the window appeared to have only a slight amount of damage done to it. Bender continue with her argument that it would have been impossible for Delmer to get through that window without causing substantial noise and damage to the window.

Bender then brought up the fact that the attacker had been wearing gloves. The question was how could her assailant have been wearing rough textured fabric gloves, "… as the victim described it …" and yet be able to tie little knots? "Why wouldn't they [the prosecution] think, well, maybe he had to take the gloves off at some point? Why not, ladies and gentlemen why not, why not test those things? Because they were complacent, because they're looking for someone that matches contaminated droplets on the floor."

Bender then suggested that perhaps the house has been rented before the Marshalls had stayed there. Perhaps Delmer, who is a personal trainer, had worked with someone in that house before Nicole moved in. Perhaps he had dropped sweat then. "You know if he's a personal trainer and had been in that house before and he sweated on the floor, which is a true possibility given his profession and given what he testified to, it could have been on the floor. What do we know for sure? We know that those samples were contaminated. And I know they don't want me to use that word, and she [Scanlan] says [about me], she's going to talk to you about contamination. Of course I am. No person in their right mind with any sense of color in their eyes could look at those photographs that they say are damning evidence of Mr. Smith and not say, why did it look like syrup. Why are they brown?" Bender paused for a moment, taking stock of where she was in her presentation before continuing.

She then commented about how the attacker was dressed. Her focus was on the fact that the assailant was wearing gloves, a mask, and some heavy clothing that would have tended to have absorbed any sweat manufactured by the wearer. The inference was that if the attacker was dressed as reported then how did any sweat managed to be left behind.

"You know," she said, "the complacency regarding the DNA comes in because no one tested what else was in that substance. What was it mixed with? When it was dabbed off of the floor, right— remember, only five of the 10 were even bothered to be tested; right?" She wanted to know why it was that tests were not performed to determine what else was in the sweat droplets. "Why be complacent?" she questioned with a shrug of her shoulders.

"Ladies and gentlemen, a reasonable doubt can come from evidence, the lack of evidence or a conflict in the evidence. All we are asking you to do—that's what the judge is going to tell you—all we are asking you to do is examine all those things with scrutiny and then make your decision because you have a lack of evidence. You have a victim that cannot identify the gun they claim belonged to the person they claim attacked her. You have a victim who cannot identify her attacker and, in fact, who says specifically it's not his voice. You have someone that has been identified as the attacker primarily because he has the property that she had six months after the fact, six months after the fact." She stressed the last.

"You know that the crime scene was not preserved," she then said. "We know that. There is no dispute to that." She commented that law enforcement had entered the house, and then moved through it prior to forensics arriving on the scene making the suggestion that the crime scene had been contaminated by the action of the Sheriff's deputies checking out the crime scene.

"Three cops running through the house, walking through the house, being stealthy through the house. I don't care how they go through the house. They go through the house. That's called not preserving the crime scene."

Scanlan stood. "Objection to miss characterization of the evidence."

Judge Curley sat forward in her chair, looked directly at the Jury, and said quickly, "Ladies and gentlemen, this is closing argument. You rely on your memory of the evidence." She then looked to Bender, nodding her approval for the defense to continue with her statement. "Go ahead, Miss Bender."

CHAPTER FORTY EIGHT
Bender versus Scanlan

Bender resumes her attack on the State's position. She continues speaking about what took place when law enforcement arrived at Marshall's home. She specifically wanted to register reasonable doubt in the six-person Jury regarding crime scene preservation.

"They walked all over the house. In fact, you know, Sergeant Tutko doesn't even know what rooms they went into. Presumably, they have to go into every room to make sure there are no other victims and no suspects hiding in closets, behind couches, etc.; right?" She went on to remind the Jury that no crime scene tape had been put up and that Tutko had told Detective Dumer that was all right for him to enter the dwelling even though forensics had not arrived. "The crime scene wasn't analyzed yet."

She tells the Jury that Dumer knows he should not go into the dwelling until forensics arrived. "He knows well enough that that's how you preserve a crime scene," she says. "What happens to sweat when you walk on it? What happens to syrup when you walk on it? Right? What happens to whatever that stuff was on the floor when you walk on it? It's contaminated."

Bender then discussed the fact that it wasn't until later on that hair fibers were seen in the photographs taken by Sergeant DiFranco. "You know, what would lead them not to collect the hair samples?"

She said she wished that DiFranco had collected some. She then made reference to one of the photographs and said, "There's goop on the floor. I don't know what the goop is. Could be evidence of a crime? We don't know because no one knows that. They focused on what they chose to focus on and ignored the other things that were staring them right in the face. And when they found Mr. Smith with that property six months after the fact, boom, that's him, let's assume it."

Bender then brought up the question posed to Delmer by Scanlan during Delmer's testimony regarding the possibility of an alibi on the night of the crime. Delmer had made comment about Quinones' DJ work, about he was always with her at the club. "'Oh, so this is your alibi?'" Bender recalled Scanlan asking. "'You are producing this alibi? Now you are telling us that you were at the club?'"

"Who told us that alibi?" Bender asked. "Who was the first witness to say that Delmer Smith was at that club every Friday and Saturday night? It was Michele Quinones. She testified that Mr. Smith was with her while she worked every night …. And when did she work? From 9 P.M. to 2 A.M. in the morning every Friday and every Saturday. This crime, as the state said, happened on Saturday. The state's own witness provided that alibi for Mr. Smith."

She went on to discuss the fact that it was not unusual for those individuals who barter and trade to have inventory on hand. "You're not going to sell all your inventory," she said. "You're not going get rid of it because that is your savings plan; right?"

She discussed that it was not unusual when it pertained to "used" items that there might be visible wear or some form of personal marking that would identify it as being used. She then used that to promote her argument that Delmer had purchased the computer equipment unaware that it was stolen even though it had existing files that were clearly placed there by someone other than the manufacturers of the machines. She told the Jury that even when the prior owner believes the machine is clear of such personal files, in many cases it is not.

Next, she addressed the phone call recordings regarding a firearm that Delmer wanted Tejeda to remove from his storage unit. At one point, it was referred to as a "rifle" and at another it was referred to as a "pistola." Her position was Delmer was referring to a "BB rifle" and not a handgun. She claimed the confusion was a result of Tejeda not understanding what he was trying to get her to understand because of a language barrier.

However, Delmer was a convicted felon and could not legally own a firearm. Therefore, he was desperately concerned about getting the BB rifle out of his possessions for fear his having possession of it would violate his federal parole. But, Tejeda was having an extremely hard time understanding what Delmer was referring to over the phone. So, Delmer did what he had to do, turn and ask a Hispanic male near him for help talking with Tejeda. That person used the term "pistola." Tejeda instantly knew then that Delmer was asking her to find and remove a firearm. She was not aware of the legal significance, just that Delmer wanted the "pistola" to be located and gotten rid of.

The following morning when the two spoke on the phone, Bender told the Jury, Delmer used the term when speaking with Tejeda because he knew that Tejeda viewed that phrase as meaning any type of firearm which would have included the BB rifle which, according to Bender, was what he was referring to. "He doesn't say 'pequeno pistola' or 'porquito,' whatever the word is, 'pistola.' He says what he knows that now she understands."

With that, she said regardless of how hard the prosecution wanted to put the gun into Delmer's hand, it could not. Bender said there was clearly no evidence to support that assumption and, in fact, she recalled that the victim, Marshall, was also not able to identify the gun.

She then went on to call Martha Tejeda a liar. She questioned how anyone could believe that Tejeda had, by herself, placed Delmer's bags in the attic.

"Remember when Martha Tejeda told you that she put all of that stuff up in the attic? She said it was her." She paused for a moment and then resumed. "Her cousin," she began, "he only helped take the stuff out of the car, and then he left, left her to do all of the hard work." She paused once more, looking down at the floor. Then she took a step forward opening her arms wide, showing the palms of her hand and, looking directly at the jurors one by one she raised an eyebrow. "She is 5 foot one," she spoke slowly and surely while looking at them with disbelief. "Ladies and gentlemen, that is not reasonable for you to believe that at all, at all." She shook her head back and forth looking away from the six-person panel, and then back again.

"Conflict in the evidence? Is it not a conflict in the evidence that Detective Ortiz, the men that were on the scene, had to get that stuff out of the attic?" She shook her head. "That's when you're tearing it down. That's easier. That's not when you're hoisting it up." She stopped momentarily, looking each juror in the eye, and then said slowly and distinctly, while pointing a finger at the floor in a jabbing fashion, "Martha Tejeda had help."

She went on to say that it was in her belief that those actions and statements proved Martha Tejeda lied. "For the second time we know she's lying. And what's the other thing it proves? It proves other people had access to that stuff up in the attic."

She reminds the Jury that Tejeda did not inform the police of the fact that she had Delmer's belongings when they came and took his car. "That's when she first lied to them and said she didn't have anything. The second time she knew they were coming back. So if you're trying to hide something, what better place to do it than to put it in somebody else's stuff?"

She recalled that the technician said there were latent prints on the gun. "Remember?" She asked the Jury. "Latent prints on that little gun, the one in the box over there in evidence." She pointed in the direction where the box was being held for them to examine. "We don't know whose prints they are because they didn't test it. We don't know," she said shaking her head. "Complacency, ladies and gentlemen. That is complacency. Okay? Why wouldn't they? Why wouldn't we here? Because you know darn well it's not Delmer Smith's."

Scanlan immediately stood. "Objection. I need to approach to explain."

"Okay," Judge Curley nodded her assent.

"I was going to let it go," her eyes flashed anger, and she shook her head, "but she kept talking about the testimony was that the latent prints were found on the magazine that was not entered into evidence, not on the gun that's in evidence. So I'd just ask that we stop this argument because that's not what the testimony was."

Curley glanced from Scanlan to Bender and then back again to Scanlan. "Okay. Well, can I just instruct the Jury that they can rely — what was the —," she glanced at Bender, "do you agree with what she's saying?"

"No," Bender replied, "I don't."

Scanlan told the Court that she never followed up on having the latent prints looked into because they were not on items that had been introduced into evidence.

"She [the technician] wasn't even asked about any of those other items."

Scanlan glanced over at Bender who was standing next to her, then up at the Court. "I know", she said dryly. "She was asked about latent fingerprints, and her answer was there were latents that were found on the magazine."

Bender stiffened a bit, and replied quickly, "I don't think she ever said the word 'magazine.'"

Scanlan responded firmly, slightly shaking her head, "She absolutely did."

Bender turned slightly to face in Scanlan's direction. "I made no recollection that she violated the Court's ruling on that. She was talking about the gun, so that's," she paused, "all I can do is go back to my notes. That's what I remember or I wouldn't be arguing that."

Curley leaned forward in her chair. "My notes are silent as to the latent prints I wasn't focusing on that, but did you," she stopped midsentence realizing that Bender wanted to add something. "Go ahead."

"I'm sorry," Bender replied quickly, acknowledging that her actions had interrupted the Court's statement. "All I was going to say is that we know it's not Delmer's print that was on it."

The Court responded, "Well, if there had been — I think the argument can be made without referring to any latent prints that were found."

"But that's what's she's been arguing," Scanlan said.

"That if there had been prints located on the gun you would've heard about it, if there were," Curley clarified.

"Right," Bender said

"But when she's talking about latent prints that were found that were not tested —."

"Okay," Judge Curley interrupted. "Let's just leave it alone then. Okay. Sustained." The Judge sat back in her chair, Scanlan returned to the prosecution table, taking her seat next to Earl Varn, and Bender returned to stand before the Jury.

Bender began again by saying to the Jury that if there had been any fingerprints on the gun that it would have been disclosed. But, there were no prints on the gun. She went on to comment that there was no evidence to prove that the handgun in question had been used in the commission of the crime.

"Did her [Marshall's] attacker have a firearm? We believe yes. But was it that gun? No. She [Marshall] can't say it is. She can't identify it. Trying to say that that gun was the gun that was used based on the evidence that's before us is as ludicrous of an idea as a size 5X guy trying to squeeze his bulk through that little jalousie window with no noise and no disruption of what's on the other side."

Bender concluded by saying that she believed there was no evidence to support a conviction, and expected a not guilty verdict.

CHAPTER FORTY NINE
Scanlan versus Bender

"'If his fingerprints had been found on the gun,'" Scanlan began her rebuttal, slowly quoting a comment made only a few minutes before by Bender, "'you certainly would have heard about that.'"

She paused, glanced at the floor as if thinking over what she wanted to say next, then looked up at the silent but attentive Jury that was waiting patiently for her to continue. "And she's right," she said nodding her head, "you would have heard about that." She paused again, her face taking on a thoughtful appearance.

"And then the defendant would have come up here," she jabbed a finger at the witness chair, "and he would have explained it away by saying, James Cellecz sold me the gun when he sold me the computer, when he sold me the iPod and the speakers and the Cassiopeia and everything else."

Scanlan lowered her arm while her gaze swept over the Jury and then she added, "Sure, I had that gun. Sure, I touched the gun." She leaned forward; arms open wide and continued feigning what might have been the emotional posture of the defendant while arguing his case, if he could have presented it standing before them. "I certainly didn't use it in a crime." Scanlan shook her head slowly from side to side, her eyes wide.

"That's what would have happened. And that's why she finished by saying, 'And fingerprints wouldn't have proved anything anyway.'"

Scanlan proposed that because Nicole Marshall had given a general description of the weapon, even though she wasn't able to identify it specifically, the very fact of the desperation in Delmer's voice as he worked so hard at getting Tejeda to secure and get rid of the pistol was evidence that he had used it to commit a violent crime. "He knew it," Scanlan said. "You can hear it in his voice.

Bender had brought up the possibility of an alibi when Michele Quinones had testified that the defendant accompanied her when she was working as a DJ at a bar on the weekends. Quinones never specifically stated that he was with her on the night of March 14th of 2009. Had she that would have been testimony for an alibi. However, the testimony given was general and not specific and so Bender, according to Scanlan, could not use that to establish an alibi.

Scanlan went on to talk about the fact that Bender had said that the crime scene was not preserved. Scanlan said, "… with all due respect to her, she does not understand law enforcement procedure and terms and what is done to preserve a crime scene because the very first thing that must be done when the crime scene is a person's home is to clear the home of all people, which means that necessarily the first step in preserving a crime scene is that law enforcement officers enter the crime scene."

Scanlan added that making entry into a crime scene, as she described it, was necessary in order to preserve the crime scene. "It has to be done. It has to be done for officer safety. It has to be done for evidence collection." Scanlan told th payment e Jury that saying that because law enforcement officers entered the crime scene to clear it did not establish any fact that they had failed to preserve the crime scene.

Scanlan then took on the defense DNA argument. "Let me see," Scanlan began, "if I understand the argument that you're supposed to believe about the defendant's DNA being inside Ms. Marshall's home"

Delmer had said he could not explain how DNA could have been found in the house. His position was that he had been a personal trainer and that perhaps he had been in the house once before, and that he had left behind sweat containing his DNA. There was no explanation as to how the droplets of sweat could have survived from that point to the night of the home invasion. Scanlan mentioned the number of drops collected, the fact that the drops were in various rooms, the kitchen, the pantry, and the living room. How was it she wondered, that a personal trainer would have been in the pantry. She also established a time line suggesting that Delmer might have been in the house in November 2008.

"Judge, I'm going to object," Bender said. "It's in the statement of the evidence, November 2008."

The Court immediately sat forward. "Okay. Ladies and gentlemen, you— this is an argument. Please, you rely on your memory of the evidence. Go ahead, Ms. Scanlan."

Scanlan immediately picked up from where she had left off. She continued to argue that, based on Bender's statements concerning the DNA that it had to be left four months prior to Marshall moving in. She reminded the Jury that the droplets of sweat were wet at the time of collection. So how, she mused, could the droplets have remained wet for four months. And, she added the fact that one of the wet droplets also contained Ms. Marshall's DNA along with Delmer's. That fact further substantiated her argument that the DNA had been left behind on the night of the attack and not four months prior.

The next point Scanlan addressed was that Delmer had possession of the stolen goods.

She began by reminding the Jury that according to the defense "the defendant was very, very concerned, that he would never ever, ever use stolen property, and that's why he was so sure to get a receipt for all of the things that he bought from James Cellecz." She went on to say that she felt, in a sarcastic way, that Bender's position regarding Delmer's firm commitment to not use any stolen equipment was a "fair interpretation" regarding any persons purchase of 300 iPods for five to $20 apiece as being not really concerned about buying stolen equipment.

Scanlan reminded the Jury that Bender had presented a receipt as evidence that Delmer had purchased the items from James Cellecz. She told the Jury that there was a 100% certainty that the receipt presented was not for the stolen computer. She gave two reasons for that.

The first reason is that she felt that Bender wanted Delmer to be uncertain in his answers concerning the receipt and the computer. Scanlan said she believed, based upon how the questions were formed, that Bender wanted Delmer to respond to her by saying "'I think it was for that computer. Maybe not. It was definitely for a computer that I bought from James Cellecz. I'm not exactly sure." Scanlan said the reason for Bender wanting Delmer to display that uncertainty was due to the date on the receipt being three weeks prior to the commission of a crime, and yet Delmer had insisted in his testimony that the receipt was for the stolen computer. Scanlan did allow that the date may have been entered incorrectly. However, she pointed out that the first item on the list of equipment shown on the receipt had a model number on it that was HPDV9000. That model number did not match with the number reported by Detective Delmer for the stolen computer. Therefore, the receipt presented had nothing to do with the stolen computer.

"Now," Scanlan began, "what does that tell you? That tells you that the defendant lied about everything about how he got all of Ms. Marshall's property because he said specifically, 'I got it from James Cellecz. I can't tell you for sure what date it was. I got it with all the other stolen property … this is a receipt for it.'" But the receipt has a date on it that is three weeks before the theft and the identification number listed for the computer is wrong. Scanlan works on making sure the Jury understands these issues.

"This is absolutely, 100% not the receipt for that computer, which means that it is not how he got that computer. He got that computer when he stole it from Nicole Marshall's house, when he threatened to kill her, when he tied her up like a dog and left her on the floor." She pauses.

"Now," she begins again telling them, "when you go back there and deliberate, there are many different items of evidence that I've gone through that show why the defendant is guilty."

She quickly reviews again each major piece of the prosecution's case, telling the Jury that there may be only one of those issues that will make the determining factor for each individual juror as to the guilt of the accused. She reminds them of the DNA. She recalls the confession made to Philip Casciola. She remembers the gun, and the stolen property. Her point is that the Jury does not have to make a decision based on all the information. One issue, one area of evidence, can be sufficient to bring about a guilty verdict. In addition, she reminds them that the verdict has to be unanimous, but not on any single issue. She cites an example, "It may be that the fact that he had all of the property that was stolen in the robbery in his possession in different places and that the excuse that he gave you for it is a flat out lie."

Bender objects, "It's a misstatement that he had all the property that was alleged to have been stolen."

Judge Curley once again tells the jurors that they need to rely on their memory of the evidence.

In conclusion, Scanlan stresses that the Jury does not need to agree on any one issue. "It does not matter to which degree you believe things, it doesn't matter which weight you put on things. If all of you agreed that for one reason or another the state has proven that he is guilty and the state has proven it beyond a reasonable doubt, then that is a unanimous verdict, and that is the just verdict in this case." She then thanks the jurors and returns to her seat at the prosecution table.

The Court asked the Jury if they would like to take a break before instructions and, upon acknowledgment of that request by one of the jurors, the Judge recesses. It's 2:19 P.M..

CHAPTER FIFTY
The Verdict

When the court reconvened after lunch, Curly read to the Jury an extensive disclosure of definitions and explained to the panel what was required by each element to pass the "without a doubt" issue in order to convict Delmer of the crimes. She advised them that great care needed to be taken in their findings, she then discussed the verdict form and how they were to use it. Soon after that, the Jury was removed to a separate room for their deliberations. The time was 2:55 P.M..

The Jury met for just under an hour before notifying the Bailiff that they had made a decision on both charges.
Curly returned to the courtroom and reseated the Jury at 4 P.M.. She took the verdict form from the Jury foreperson, read it, and then turned it over to the clerk. She called for the Jury to be re-seated. She then recognized the foreperson and asked if the Jury had come to a conclusion. The foreperson stated that they had. The Court then reviewed the document submitted by the foreperson, and then handed the document to the Clerk who read the verdict.
The six-person Jury found Delmer guilty of both counts on December 8th, 2011. At a later date, Delmer was sentenced to life imprisonment.

Following his conviction, Delmer remained in the Sarasota County Jail where he awaited his murder trial in Manatee County for the horrific murder of Kathleen Briles. That trial started August 8th, 2012 and is featured in *Book Two, Predator: The Man Who Didn't Exist, The Woman in a Pink Top*

GORDON KUHN

PREVIEW OF BOOK TWO

THE WOMAN IN A PINK TOP

She lay face down.
At least, that is how *they* found the body—face down.
They being her husband and the hastily-established Manatee County team of sheriff's deputies, forensic personnel, fire department paramedics, and the county coroner's office staff that had been called into service on August 3rd, 2009, in the middle of the night. It was their job to descend on the horrifying scene at a residence in a quiet neighborhood in response to her husband's frantic 911 call.
Manatee County 911, what is the nature of your emergency? [18]
The operator's voice was calm, well-practiced, having responded thousands of times in the same cool manner during stressful telephone calls as this would soon become.
Caller: (Unintelligible) I just got home, my wife is on the floor!
The voice was breathless, filled with shock and terror.

Three years after the Manatee County 911 system recorded the emotion-filled phone call from a distraught man, the prosecution introduced the tape as evidence in Case No. 2010-CF-000479, The State of Florida vs. Delmer Smith, a murder case.
The Court, Jury, and gallery would sit and listen completely absorbed by the conversation being played back for them. While the horror of the night slowly became

---

[18] The 911 call posted here and in subsequent pages was taken directly from the court transcript.

indelibly evident for everyone else in the room, the defendant appeared indifferent. He spent most of his time looking at the highly-polished wooden conference table-top where he sat, or at his handcuffed hands which were kept low behind the table so the Jury could not see them.

He focused on them, turning them over, then right side up. He twisted them one way, then another, carefully examining each hand like a person would checking to see if they might need to wash them. Perhaps, in this case, to remove the invisible stain and erase the scent of his victim's blood that only he was conscious of.

The 911 operator immediately obtained the caller's name, address, and phone number. He then went on to ask questions of the caller concerning the nature of his call and then:

Caller: (unintelligible) she's tied up. It looks like someone hit her on the head with something here. I don't know. It's just....

The man's voice stumbled, falling away, trailing off. His breathing was haggard, short gasps for air recorded and now played for the courtroom.

911: Are you with her now?

Caller: Yeah (unintelligible)—I think she's already dead!

911: How old is she?

Caller: Kathy is in her — 40s. She was — born in — 1960. Holy — shit. Please (unintelligible)....

The painful distress in the caller's voice was clearly palpable as it tumbled into a stumbling pile of meaningless garble.

All who sat in the relative safety and comfort of oak-paneled courtroom 5-A of Florida's Twelfth Circuit that day in Manatee County and listened to the replay of the taped telephone call made that alarming night would never forget what was said; nor would they ever be able to erase from their memories the emotions they felt individually as a result of hearing the heartbreaking descriptions of the scene as addressed in that tragic recording.

It was an alarming conversation between a professionally calm 911 operator, who identified himself as "operator 143," and a distressed husband who had just entered into a nightmare world of epic horror-filled dimensions. When it was finished, the courtroom would be left chilled and silent for several moments before the prosecuting attorney cleared her throat and thanked the bailiff for having turned it off.

But the tape was just beginning to be played then, and the victim's husband sat on the witness stand quietly listening, as did everyone in the room, to his voice telling of the horror he had found upon his arrival home the evening of August 3rd, 2009.

THE END OF BOOK ONE.
THE STORY IS CONTINUED IN BOOK TWO.

www.ingramcontent.com/pod-product-compliance
Lightning Source LLC
Chambersburg PA
CBHW020847090426
42736CB00008B/270